T0123450

ENDORSEMENT

"The truth of this book comes with a capital "T." The essence of the book will nourish and strengthen your soul through the Spirit of Christ, which reveals all truths. If you are serious about your faith and about bringing Satan's kingdom down by standing on the Word of God and by constant prayer, then you will benefit from reading "Hitchhikers, Hijackers, and Faceless Hackers in the Earth Realm." This is a great book and I hope every Christian will get a copy and read it."

—Reverend Dr. Ronald Ward, Sr.
Retired United Methodist Pastor

"Among the many obstacles the church faces today, this book could not have come at a better time. De'Ron Hopkins thoroughly breaks down the old topic of spiritual warfare for all to comprehend with her new voice and engaging analogies of truth. This book is an exceptional must read for the body of Christ."

—Wilton David

HITCHHIKERS, HIJACKERS, *and* FACELESS HACKERS *in the* EARTH REALM

SEEING BEYOND SIGHT THROUGH
THE EYES OF THE KING

DERON HOPKINS

WESTBOW
PRESS®
A DIVISION OF THOMAS NELSON
& ZONDERVAN

Copyright © 2015 De'Ron Hopkins.

All rights reserved. No part of this book may be used or reproduced by any means, graphic, electronic, or mechanical, including photocopying, recording, taping or by any information storage retrieval system without the written permission of the author except in the case of brief quotations embodied in critical articles and reviews.

This book is a work of non-fiction. Unless otherwise noted, the author and the publisher make no explicit guarantees as to the accuracy of the information contained in this book and in some cases, names of people and places have been altered to protect their privacy.

WestBow Press books may be ordered through booksellers or by contacting:

WestBow Press
A Division of Thomas Nelson & Zondervan
1663 Liberty Drive
Bloomington, IN 47403
www.westbowpress.com
1 (866) 928-1240

Because of the dynamic nature of the Internet, any web addresses or links contained in this book may have changed since publication and may no longer be valid. The views expressed in this work are solely those of the author and do not necessarily reflect the views of the publisher, and the publisher hereby disclaims any responsibility for them.

Any people depicted in stock imagery provided by Thinkstock are models, and such images are being used for illustrative purposes only.
Certain stock imagery © Thinkstock.

ISBN: 978-1-5127-1402-9 (sc)
ISBN: 978-1-5127-1403-6 (hc)
ISBN: 978-1-5127-1401-2 (e)

Library of Congress Control Number: 2015915810

Print information available on the last page.

WestBow Press rev. date: 11/19/2015

Scripture taken from the New King James Version. Copyright © 1979, 1980, 1982 by Thomas Nelson, Inc. Used by permission. All rights reserved.

All Scripture quotations in this publications are from The Message. Copyright © by Eugene H. Peterson 1993, 1994, 1995, 1996, 2000, 2001, 2002. Used by permission of NavPress Publishing Group.

Scripture taken from the Holy Bible, NEW INTERNATIONAL VERSION®. Copyright © 1973, 1978, 1984 by Biblica, Inc. All rights reserved worldwide. Used by permission. NEW INTERNATIONAL VERSION® and NIV® are registered trademarks of Biblica, Inc. Use of either trademark for the offering of goods or services requires the prior written consent of Biblica US, Inc.

New Revised Standard Version Bible, copyright © 1989, Division of Christian Education of the National Council of the Churches of Christ in the United States of America. Used by permission. All rights reserved.

Scripture taken from the *Amplified Bible*, copyright © 1954, 1958, 1962, 1964, 1965, 1987 by The Lockman Foundation. Used by permission.

Scripture quotations taken from the New American Standard Bible®, Copyright © 1960, 1962, 1963, 1968, 1971, 1972, 1973, 1975, 1977, 1995 by The Lockman Foundation. Used by permission. (www.Lockman.org)

Scripture taken from the King James Version of the Bible.

CONTENTS

DEDICATION

To my Lord and Savior, Jesus the Christ, thank You Father for entrusting me with such an assignment. You alone are worthy. Thank You for speaking Your heart through me that I may convey Your love and the richness of you mercy to Your people. I pray Father that You are magnified, glorified, and exalted in every word written and spoken in this book. In a high and lofty place, You are God and *all* the glory belongs to You. Thank You.

To my husband Lamont Hopkins, the head of my life under Christ Jesus, thank you for loving me. Thank you for the encouraging words, wisdom, wiping away my tears, soothing my fear when I wanted to quit, and never allowing me to do so. For this I say, thank you. I love you. To my children who were steadfast throughout this entire process, thank you. Thank you for your patience, love, encouragement, support and cheering mommy on to be the best. You are my heartbeat.

To the memory of my late maternal grandparents, James and Annie Mae Ireland, my paternal grandparents, the late Walter E. Howard Sr., and my thriving 95-year-old grandmother Clara Howard, thank you for modeling beyond words what righteousness is and what it is not. Thank you. To the memory of my late great-grandfather, Reverend George White and the memory of my late great-aunt Reverend Lizzy White-Glenn, thank you for the impartation of the Spirit of Christ resting upon my life. The mantle of righteousness has not fallen to the ground and I vow to share the richness of God's grace and the truth of repentance until He calls me home.

FOREWORD

There's an array of Christian books who can tell you a lot about theology but little about how to apply it. This book is not one of them. "Hitchhikers, Hijackers, and Faceless Hackers in the Earth Realm" is insightful and, more importantly, practical for victorious living. It is by far a treat for lovers of historical and Biblical truths.

De'Ron's passion for the Word of God leaps off every page and ignites its readers to desire more of God. The Father is using her prophetic voice and her love for Him to call the body of Christ to the attention of the cross and its completed work through Jesus the Christ.

This book declares theological and Biblical truths of what this world is facing and shall face according to the Word of God. Its foundational message addresses the deceptions of Satan and his wicked devices of evil sent to distract many within the body of Christ from hearing and moving in their god-give position in the Father. Many in the body of Christ are hungry for what is next in God, however, we have not postured ourselves at the foot of the cross repenting, travailing in praying, seeking His face, and thirsting for a new heart fitting for the King.

This heart stirring, thought-provoking, and prophetic teachings of this book provides a more in-depth knowledge of God and supernatural insight into the sacrifice that Jesus made on Calvary's cross for the sins of humanity. Without a doubt, the grace of God resting on her life isn't just for a select few; it's for a people, for a nation, and for a heart thirsting after the true and living God.

—Reverend Dr. Jerome E. Howard, Sr.
Senior Pastor of Hope For the Living Ministries, Inc.

QUOTES

"Faith is taking the first step even when you don't see the whole staircase."
—Dr. Martin Luther King, Jr.

INTRODUCTION

If My people who are called by my name will humble themselves, and
pray and seek my face, and turn from their wicked way, then I will
hear from heaven, and will forgive their sin and heal their land.
—2 Chronicles 7:14, NLT

*I*n the new age occult movement, many seek demonic
fortunetellers and tarot card readers and yield to the powers
of darkness. Unfortunately, many in the church use dark
methods without understanding they are interacting with Satan's demons.
These dark powers seduce and manipulate many in the body of Christ
because they have unknowingly left themselves accessible and uncovered
to these powers. These spies of Satan seek open doors to access the flesh
through unidentified sin, in the lives of many of God's people.

The alluring offer Eve received in the garden is the same that Satan
entices us with today. Satan seeks "whom he many devour" (1 Peter 5:8)
contrary to the skepticism of many. He and his cohorts manipulate our
age just as they did when the prophet Jeremiah foretold of God's judgment
on Israel for forsaking Him and responding to other gods (see Jeremiah
2). The noise of "Nor the pestilence that walks in darkness, *nor* of the
destruction that lays waste at noonday" (see Psalm 91:6, NASB) should not
be foreign to the ears of those who believe in Christ.

Although the enemies of the souls of men are actively sending out
scrambling patterns of deception in the atmosphere, the ear of the believer
ought to *catch* the sound, *address* what is perceived, and take authority

over the *assignment* of the *sound* as the Spirit gives utterance. When Satan attempts to encrypt the sound by displaying it as truth, the Holy Spirit living in us will **arrest** that demon *and* the **sound** *before* it is manifest.

Though Satan attempts to distort his demonic frequencies in the atmosphere as "normal," we can be so in tune with Christ that we can decode Satan's message. Christ Jesus has left His mantle of righteousness on us to live according to God's Word. Even during catastrophic events, pestilence, and devastation, God says to His people that *He is God.*

God told Moses to tell the Israelites that *He was God* and was all they needed (see Exodus 3:14). Today, God announces Himself in like manner to those with open spiritual ears. Where are the ears that will hear God's message of supremacy and overthrow everything opposed to Him? Our hearts must thirst for God and proclaim His holiness even during confusing times. In 2 Chronicles 7:14, we read, "If My people who are called by My name will humble themselves, and pray."

We must turn to God, who will forgive us, whose spirits have become broken. He will return us to our original state if we pray and seek His face. Prayer is the *key.* The church must stand on His Word to become righteous and execute righteousness on earth. His name alone produces godly change, but many have become so preoccupied with conforming to the image of this world that Satan's subtleties have gone undetected, even in the church. Our eyes have become dulled, and we no longer hear the rhythms of heaven and the throne room; we are not clothed in humility and righteousness.

Many of God's people are blind to their position in God, and this allows darkness to rule over the dominion God had handed Adam. Though Adam forfeited his position in the garden, Jesus gave us a new covenant through His shed blood. The second Adam—Jesus requires us to call on Him, humble ourselves, pray, and seek God's face.

Where are those seeking the face of God? Where is the alignment of the church? Kingdom authority is given only to those called by His name, thus it is accessible only when we humble ourselves, pray, and seek His face. He has given believers the authority to thwart demonic forces by His Word, which strengthens the church and believers.

Through His Word and our prayers, Christ has given us the supernatural ability to take nations by storm. Prayer connects our spiritual ears to God's will. Moreover, the power of prayer connects the church to a heavenly language where we are permitted to access by the blood of Jesus the Christ. However, believers must respond to God and His Word just as Christ responded to His assignment on earth—through prayer and fasting. We must comply with the Father's will to change in the midst of disorder, war, and rumors of war.

God still has a plan and a purpose for His people, His church. We must comply with the rule of heaven in order to execute God's will for the church on earth. However, the question is how can the body of Christ change earth when it is misaligned with God's will? God wanted His children to stand in dominion of the earth, not give it up.

Many are standing in the spirit of pride, arrogance, self-centeredness, and religiosity rather than in Jesus, the King. Many within the body of Christ have taken on the spirit of the world rather than the Spirit of Christ; consequently, the righteousness of the King is not present in the hearts of many of God's people. There is a disconnect between the Father and many of His children, who should make up the hedges of protection and sound the alarm about the intruder.

From God's eternal chambers of heaven, He is saying woe to His people—the church (see Revelation 8:13). Woe be to those who were sanctioned by the Father to represent His kingdom on earth and sugarcoat the truth of His Word.

God is speaking, but are we listening? We must incline our ears to His words that call for us to be righteous. Woe be to those who do not listen to God's truth and fall into the trap of Satan's deceptions. The earth is groaning for the manifestations of the sons of God, and the war cry heard is "Woe." Romans 8:22 says, "For we know that the whole creation groans and labors with birth pains together until now." **Woe** is an *anguished cry* in *response* to what is taking place on earth. Creation is groaning because the body of Christ listens to too many sounds, and the voice of the King is hard to decipher.

John 10:27 tells us, "My sheep hear my voice; I know them, and they follow me." It is imperative that the body of Christ listen to His voice alone and be led by the Spirit of Christ. We must position ourselves under the King to hear His Word and to hear what heaven is saying to the church in this hour. In Jude 1:23, we read, "Be *merciful* to those who doubt; *save* others by *snatching* them from the *fire*; to others *show* mercy, mixed with fear—hating even the clothing stained by corrupted flesh." Now is the time to shine heavenly light on Satan's darkness to help those in the church who are distressed, discouraged, faithless, and detached from the King.

The eyes of faith have grown dull, ears have become compromised, and many have lost the sense of urgency of carrying the message of repentance and truth. The mantle of impartation through Christ Jesus will instruct us as believers to be righteous for His namesake. It will instruct us how to tear down the imagination of the mind, which the Enemy aims for at full throttle. This book will help believers see with *new sight* and listen with *new ears*. This is the season of preparation; souls are at stake, and God is calling His sheep to stand in truth. The Father is calling *His* people—the church *back* to kingdom order.

CHAPTER 1

Master of Manipulation

Be sober, (clear-headed) be vigilant; (watchful) because your adversary the
devil walks about like a roaring lion, seeking whom he may devour.
—1 Peter 5:8, KJV

The Devil's demons make up the dark forces and are hosts
of unseen wickedness; they are governed by Satan. They
are on the hunt, roaming like lions, and are brutal in their
pursuit of anyone seeking safety from them outside his corrupt systems
of this world.

The master of manipulation, who wants to destroy the people of God,
wages war on the body of Christ nonstop. These dark forces are after our
souls before they are condemned eternally to the lake of fire (see Revelation
20:7–15). In 1 Peter 5:8, Peter told members of the church of Christ to be
vigilant and watchful, to walk in the spirit of humility before God and
those who labor in the faith of Jesus the Christ. Peter said we must put
humility on every day just as we put on clothes. We must recognize the
spirit connected to pride that maneuvers in Satan's darkness.

Thus, when the spirit of pride is activated, what you and I must
understand is that there are other subordinate spirits wrapped in pride
itself. If pride is not dismantled and destroyed by the power of God, it will

allow other spirits in, those that open gateways to other spirits, and it will be exposed to higher-ranking, demonic powers of darkness.

What are subordinate spirits? Subordinate spirits are lower in rank in demonic activity having less power than other dark spirits, but they nonetheless dominate in darkness under the powers of Satan. Thus, the individual operating in the spirit of pride opens his or herself up to a host of other demonic activities. The prince of the air, which is Satan, and his dark powers of deception methodically operate under the umbrella of evil lies, schemes, and devices of wickedness, attempting to divert us from pursuing and applying the spiritual truths of God's Word to our lives. This is why Peter warned the church to be sober and vigilant at all times and walk with God. Peter says to the church that the believer must earnestly seek to walk circumspectly before a holy God.

Peter told us that you and I are to always be clear headed, watch over our tempers, be godly in character, walk in self-control, and stand in a good conduct before the King. If we do, we will be able to discern Satan's presence through the eyes of the Spirit of Christ and His Word. This can happen only when we are connected to the King.

The blood and power of our Lord Jesus Christ gave us the power of His Word and the authority in His name to resist Satan and his powers of darkness. James 4:7 tells us that when we submit to God, He will give us the ability to resist the Devil, who will flee for a season. James says that when we draw near the Father, He draws near to us. Drawing closer to the Father will allow us to stand under His divine protection. Christ Jesus affords you and me the power to stand tall in our armor, repel those darts of evil, and destroy them because of whom you and I have chosen to draw near. Peter said we should be sober and vigilant as we are the chosen people of God Most High.

Satan's scheming deceptions are not physical because Satan is not of the flesh. His powers of darkness become evident in our physical being, our behavior, and in our language however, the demon itself cannot be seen by the naked eye. The Holy Spirit gives us the power to see evil through spiritual eyes in order to destroy its effects on earth. God will give us revelation to detect the presence of darkness through dreams, the eyes and ears of the spirit, and visions. We must understand that Satan continually seeks to destroy us, to snatch our souls away from the safe protection of

Jesus and the eternal reward due to all who receive Jesus as Lord. Satan's aim is to subject us to a place of eternal damnation along with him and those under his command.

This is the plan of Satan. These attacks are not fleshly, although the evidence of physical manifestations of the attack may stand present in the flesh; its origin of an attack is spiritual. Satan is a celestial being and thus operates his system of darkness as the prince of the powers of the air, which is a domain that operates in the spiritual realm outside heaven. Satan is not a cute, friendly, red devil with a pitchfork we can keep in the closet as a stuffed pet; he and his fellow demons are spirits seeking for that place of open access that they may come in and wreak havoc through the corridors of our flesh. Thus, in an attempt to destroy, he plans and waits.

These spirits of darkness are subtle, well restrained, and crafty in each approach to overtake the mind-set of unguarded, shackled, and defeated individuals. Thus, this polished attack on the unguarded mind-set of men are handcrafted, tailor-made for each individual according to his or her lusts and desires of the flesh (see James 1:4). Each occurrence and every attack is structured and detailed in accuracy according to specific individuals' desires and enticements of the flesh. These powers of darkness wait patiently for their appointed orders handed down through the chain of command to apprehend and arrest the mind-set of the unguarded person inside and outside the will of God Most High.

For instance, the lion, as shown on the *National Geographic* channel, prowls, strategizes, and waits to seize a door that has been left *unguarded* by that which he hunts. Thus, the lion lies low, ears open and eyes sharp, waiting for and anticipating the opportunity to strike and take down its prey.

These spirits are methodical just as any wild beast in the jungle hunting for its next victim. They wait for the *right* opening when we are not on guard in order to slither in and gain an advantage for the purpose of manipulation. Thus, the apostle Peter said that we were to *remain* vigilant so we could identify the devices of Satan.

What Satan does not want the believer in Christ Jesus to fully understand is that the he and his demons are prohibited, restricted, from operating outside of authority, outside of seasons, and outside of the timing of God. Just as Satan had to ask the Father's permission to attack Job, the same rule applies to those called by His name today. Job opened the door for darkness to enter into his life through what he spoke out of his mouth. What Job spoke in his life, contradicted the truth of what God spoke, which Satan used for the bases of his request to ask the Father's permission to attack Job. The attack he faced was on his entire family; nevertheless, what he experienced was not solely about the loss of things.

The attack was on his faith in God, his life, his family, and all that he was assigned to accomplish on earth. Likewise, the attack on today's society is not just about a person, it is about a people. It may not be equivalent in destruction or degree to what Job himself experienced or even the same demonic force as Job was up against, but just as God was with Job, so **shall** He be with His people. The Bible says that at the end of Job's affliction and disappointment, God restored everything Job lost because God's hands of protection never left Job (see Job 42:1–17).

Satan and his minions are subtle, crafty, and wicked in their efforts to overtake unguarded, shackled, and defeated people. Their attacks are always tailor-made; pulling from the corruption that is within each of us, according to our lusts and fleshly desires (see James 1:4). These spirits of darkness are controlled. They lurk and wait on orders from the chain of command to apprehend the minds of the unguarded just as lions waits for an opportune time to pounce on their prey. These spirits are as methodical as any wild beast; they wait for the right time to attack us.

Just as Satan had to ask the Father's permission to attack Job, he needs God's permission to attack you and me. God does permit a time of buffeting, testing, and refining in our lives in order to purify the sinful desires of the flesh; that seek to operate through pride and destruction.

In 2 Corinthians 12:7, Paul said, "But to keep me from being puffed up with pride because of the many wonderful things I saw, I was given a painful physical aliment, which acts as Satan's messenger to beat me (to buffet me) and keep me from being proud." Paul was given an ailment in the flesh and Job was given painful sores over his entire body, that the glory of God would be revealed in each of their lives on earth (see Job 2:1–7). God's divine protection never departed their lives, even in the midst of a fight.

Understand, when facing demonic opposition, we may not experience the attack Job did or the aliment Paul received in his body, but it will be the same demonic forces of Satan at work. When encountering demonic forces, many see the face of an individual but not the manifestation of darkness beneath the flesh; that can be seen only through the revelation of the Holy Spirit. Unless God pulls, back the covers of revelation, that which the natural eye sees is only the flesh, not the spirit.

Unless believers walk in the Spirit of Christ, they will not see or discern the manifestation of darkness ruled by Satan in operation through the individual. According to Genesis 3:1, the serpent was the most cunning of all creatures on earth. Satan wanted Eve to disobey God and her covering—Adam. The plot of the serpent on Eve was to have her begin to operate and live outside His will and exalt herself, and Satan waited until Eve was alone before he seduced her.

Eve was the one who allowed the seducing serpent to rule over her ears, which enticed her to eat that which God had forbidden her and Adam not to partake of. Once Eve yielded to enticements of Satan, granting her flesh satisfaction over the authority of what God spoke, she chose to satisfy the cravings of her flesh, over the authority of the King. Though she knew it was forbidden, she deliberately allowed the devices of Satan to cause her to rebel against God.

I believe she felt the same guilt and remorse all believers experience when they rebel against God. When believers rebels against God, the darkness of sin takes root in our lives and the soul becomes restless because it detects that there is a shift in the relationship between God and His children. When this happens, the heart becomes sorrowful within us and Satan tries to use this toward his advantage. When the heart is sorrowful because of sin, guilt steps in attempting to keep us from confession and repentance. Satan uses guilt as a distraction to keep our ears disconnected and our minds bound by our sin. This distraction keeps us focused on the sin and not our ability to *see Christ* as our way out of sin and back to God.

Believers must understand that Satan operates only by God's divine permission, but contrary to the beliefs of many, our flesh, our senses, cannot identify the deceiver by our eyes or diagnose what category of darkness exists in an individual.

When discerning the powers of darkness on earth, all believers should understand it is not with the five senses of the flesh that darkness is recognized. It is not with the taste, touch, hear, smell, or sight, which are all

God-given to use in the natural realm. Darkness is unrecognizable unless it is exposed by the Spirit of Christ to the spirit of man that has been *born again* through Christ. There must be a connection through *surrender* to the realm of heaven through *Christ,* the *Word of God* wrapped in *prayer* and *fasting*, which will **unlock** our vision into the supernatural realm, all the way to the throne of God. God has to bring revelation to our spirits, not to our flesh.

Demonic spirits are real, and only through the Father, the Son, and the Holy Spirit can believers see beyond sight, hear beyond hearing, and sense beyond sensing what is demonic and thus false. The Holy Spirit awakens our spiritual knowledge of God's will. These evil demonic powers, seek human bodies in which to dwell to cause destruction to the person as well as others in the world.

As a result, darkness attempts to paralyze the mind-set of men and undermine their ability to recognize his schemes and devices, rendering the mentality discombobulated and crippled. Once an unguarded mind has become mentality discombobulated, crippled, and weakened, one's conscious state of being provides minimum results at best of vitality. So then, defeated in its position, it presents itself as a counterfeit, a falsified origin of truth, while fiction rises up and rehearses its position in the mind. If the powers of Satan are able to seduce the mind's eye to remain crippled in the person, the counterfeit spirit of darkness will continue to be undetected unless the Spirit of Christ brings revelation to the spirit man of the presence of darkness.

There has to be a *relationship* with the Father *before* spiritual revelation can take place. There has to be submission to God. His Word, along with prayer, will expose Satan's darkness on earth. Such intimacy with God brings us a level of sensitivity to Satan's devices, tactics, and schemes. The Word of God neutralizes and destroys the plans of Satan every time. The Bible instructs us to submit to God and *resist* the Devil. We must never submit to Satan, his army, his wickedness, or his beliefs; we must submit only to God. Submitting to Satan renders the mind powerless and causes death of the physical and of the spiritual.

"Therefore submit to God, resist the devil and he will flee from you" (James 4:7). Scripture tells us what to do—obey God, not men. How do we bring ourselves into alignment with the will of God? By submitting, which means to give over or yield to the power of authority of another, to defer to another's judgment or opinion. Therefore, submitting to God aligns us with Him, which reveals His person and moves His mighty hand in our lives.

Therefore, in the act of submitting to God, we must position ourselves under the authority of the almighty God, thereby yielding to Him in action, word, posture, and position daily. In this way, we will demolish the gates of the Enemy through the power of Christ. The Word of God, the blood of Christ, and the power of command causes Satan and his powers of darkness to cease their activity in our lives. This is power in the blood of Jesus.

We must learn to **stand** on the *Word of God* and **appropriate** *the blood of Christ,* which has *all authority* and *is* sufficient in what it has been sent to do—*win* the final *victory.* Doors can be open to darkness if Jesus Christ do not reign in us. We must be in total compliance with God's will before we can victoriously stand against Satan's many wiles.

On the Mount of Olives, Jesus prayed in the posture of submission unto God. In Luke 22:41–42, Jesus prayed to the Father during His time of vulnerability and agony as he was facing death on the cross. He showed us how to surrender to the will of the Father.

The eternal part of Jesus was not concerned about His crucifixion; as He knew it would not be His permanent position. Nonetheless, Jesus in His human robe of flesh became weary of the agony of the cross He was about to experience. Nevertheless, King Jesus surrendered to the Father's will. What does it mean to *surrender* to God? It means to agree with Him, to stop fighting or resisting Him. When we stop resisting the will of the Father and relinquish ourselves to Him, change occurs. We will gain clarity, soundness of mind, and the peace of the Lord beyond what we have ever experienced.

Choosing God increases our spiritual insight and *awakes* the kingdom of God in us; we become new vessels of honor for God. The Bible says we live in this world but are not of it (see John 18:36). In Christ Jesus, God the Father shines His light on darkness revealing hidden lies appearing as truth. In John 17:15–17, Jesus said, "My prayer is not that you take them out of the world but that you protect them from the evil one. They are not of the world, even as I am not of it. Sanctify them by the truth; your word is truth."

Therefore, as the Father reveals Himself to us, He covers. As He reveals the mystery of the gospel, His glorious splendor, and the truth of His grace—Jesus, He covers us. Psalm 91:1 says, "He who dwelleth in the secret place of the Most High shall abide under the shadow of the Almighty." In the secret places of God, under the shadows of His wings, He protects those called by His name. He covers our minds and thoughts when we are hidden in the secret place of the King. He protects us from the evil snares of Satan by the shed blood of Christ and power of His Word. Psalm 95:7 says, "For He is our God, and we are the people of His pasture, and the sheep of His hand." He covers us!

He alone grants believers access to His person, understanding of His deity, and knowledge of His truth. The Holy Spirit alerts believers to the presence of darkness. Though we are flesh, we walk in the realm of the Spirit. In sweet communion with the Holy Spirit, fasting and praying before God, our spirits connect with heaven.

When a person is in Christ Jesus, he or she stands under the umbrella of the full embodiment of the Godhead, positioned to represent God's kingdom on earth. It is by faith; it is by the power of the resurrection of Jesus, that the children of God have been given authority to walk in the stead of the righteousness on earth under the Triune Godhead. When a child of the King is walking in **harmony** with the full embodiment of the *Godhead,* the *Holy Spirit* will **unlock** that which is not seen by the naked eye, and will reveal the presence of darkness in our midst. The stench, the aroma of the serpent ought to be recognizable in the atmosphere by those who stand under the power of God, because our eyes and ears are opened in another domain outside of where we are on earth.

We receive access by faith through our connection to Christ Jesus as Lord. *Prayer* brings divine *revelation* and **releases** the *mind* of *God,* which brings awareness of the Enemy. It is in reading His Word and prayer that the Father provides tools to dismantle and destroy the workings of darkness on earth because of the dominion of Christ within us. The dominion God gave to Adam in the garden now rest on those under Christ through an inheritance. Jesus said in Luke 10:19, "I give you authority to trample on snakes and scorpions and over all the powers of the enemy, and nothing shall by any means hurt you." God gave Adam the same authority He gave His disciples in order to "overcome all the power of the enemy" (Luke 10:19).This means Adam could have resisted the temptation to eat from the forbidden tree because of his dominion as king under the Father.

The serpent seduced Eve into disobeying God as well as her king Adam. Satan wanted Eve to abort truth by operating outside the will of God and exalt herself in the process. This cunning serpent waited for an opportune time to approach Eve. He waited until she was alone before he addressed her and seduced her. Satan manipulated Eve, not Adam. Understand that Eve was the one who allowed the seducing serpent to rule over her ears, and as a result of her being uncovered by her husband, she gave the fruit to Adam, resulting in them both walking in this rebellious spirit.

As mentioned previously, demonic hosts work in seasons and timing and seek to apprehend and imprison the mind-sets of the believer from pursuing after the God of truth. Contrary to the beliefs of many, the flesh cannot detect the deceiver—neither Satan nor his agents—with the natural senses. These dark powers of the air are literally spirit beings, which is the reason they attempt to find human bodies to dwell in to work their destruction. As you and I submit to God through His Son, He covers us! The key word is *submit*—submit to God. Return to God.

Do not be seduced by your fleshly wants and desires. Do not submit to Satan, his army, his beliefs, or his devices. Submitting to Satan *renders* the *mind incapacitated* and *powerless,* and this inevitably *produces death* mentally, physically, and spiritually. James 4:7 declares, "Therefore submit to God. Resist the devil and he will flee from you."

What we must understand is the manipulator is not a physical, tangible substance. They are demonic spirits that Satan has given his authority to as powers of the air for the destruction of men, on earth. Moreover, Satan has positioned various demonic forces to operate over cosmological systems, others maneuver within nations, others are set over regions, others are sent to hinder prayers, and others infiltrate bodies to possess men outside of Christ, while others orchestrate tangible attacks, and so on. Nevertheless, it is vital that we understand the spirits behind every attack; and every trace of wickedness in the sphere of evil and chaos are all under the powers of Satan operating from within his kingdom of darkness. The Enemy uses disembodied spirits that infiltrate persons on earth on an unlawful basis seeking to destroy their lives, piece by piece.

These spirits do not have dominion or authority to operate on earth as Adam (man) was given by God (see Genesis 1:26). Spirit is spirit and soul is soul. The soul of a man comprises life—desires, appetites, emotions, conscience, mind, will, and passions. Had God not formed Adam from dust, he would still be a spirit existing only in the mind of God. The law—the legal ability to function on earth—lies within the scope of flesh and blood, predetermined by God's rule for operating this domain. Likewise, flesh and blood do not have legal access to heaven; only the spirit of a born again believer of Christ Jesus, has legal access to the kingdom of God.

According to heavens rule, Jesus came in the earth in a carnal state—flesh and blood to redeem humanity from the fallen position of Adam. God followed His own divine spiritual protocol to access the earth He created. Therefore, for these dark powers of the air to gain access to the land, they need a soul that breaths life in order to gain access and function on earth. "So the demons begged Him, saying, "If You cast us out, permit us to go away into the heard of swine." And he said go them, "*Go*" (Matthew 8:31–32). In order to survive on earth, dark spirits need a body.

In the Garden of Eden, Satan infiltrated a snake to gain access to Eve in order to move beyond the air to entice the appetite of her flesh; as Satan and his minions are locate in the second realm of heaven, outside of the earth. Understand, darkness cannot access earth without a body, neither can any flesh access heaven. 1 Corinthians 15:50 tells us, "Flesh and blood cannot inherit the kingdom of God." This means to access heaven legally in spirit, the blood of the Lamb—Christ must be applied. He is our access to enter into heaven—the place where God is.

The righteousness of God sets the stage for the separation of heaven and earth, as He stood outside of time preparing a place for humanity to dwell (see Genesis 1:1–20). Satan persistently seeks to manipulate the mind-set of humanity into believing that heaven and earth are the same and that all may freely reside in heaven without there being any requirements before entering into an eternal rest with the Father. Satan's desire is to manipulate many into believing that the carnal flesh has the ability access heavens domain on its own merit, outside of Christ.

Satan does not want us to understand that he is restricted from entering into the heavenly realm without the Father's permission. Moreover, Satan and his forces' only access to the earthly realm is through inhabiting flesh and blood, by permission. Principalities, powers, rulers of darkness of this age, spiritual host of wickedness, and so on must *submit* to the authority of Christ as King, in heaven, on earth, and under the earth (see Philippians 2:10).

These spirits are endlessly seeking a body to dwell on earth. In Satan's organization of darkness, he has dispensed his powers of evil onto his demonic cohorts to govern nations of this world before their final day of judgment (see Revelation 20:7–15). Understand, many of these demonic spirits maneuver in the cosmological systems of the air, and for these powers of darkness to enter into a person's life on earth; there must be an open, unoccupied door for them to gain access. Sin, rebellion, and pride are entry points that these powers seek after to gain legal access on earth. These demonic spirit governing the affairs of Satan, are sent on a specific course to "Steal, kill, and destroy" which is their mission (see John 10:10).

In John 10:10, Jesus said, "The thief does not come except to steal, and to kill and to destroy. I have come that they may have life, and that they may have *it* more abundantly." Hence, this is the reason for Jesus entering the earth as *grace* on behalf of the Father's extension of love for His children—to have life.

Jesus the Christ, the God-Man, stood on earth fully God for the benefit of love, for the benefit of redeeming man back to the Father. In order for Jesus to identify with humanity, He had to come to earth in the form of human flesh according to God's law of separation. Understand God will never alter His rule of heaven to appease the flesh of men. God is holy and as such, He will by no means go against His Word. Therefore, God followed His divine spiritual protocol of separation, called forth Jesus out of heaven, and positioned the King on earth to reconcile us back to God. Therefore, in order for the powers of Satan to gain access on earth, they must have a physical body to dwell. They need something living in order to move on earth.

The Scriptures says in Genesis 2:7, "And man became a living soul" positioned to subdue and dwell as the representation—carbon copies of King Jesus on earth. Equally, in order for God's children to enter into the place where God is, their flesh of corruption must be done away with. There must be a transformation by the Spirit of Christ on the inside of us, in order to enter into the place where *God is*. Jesus the Christ is the only way for you and me to access the Father. It is only by and through the shed blood of Christ that the believer has access to enter into the *most holy place,* while standing on earth in posture—*yielding* in our spirit to the King.

Thus, for you and me to *ascend* into the most holy place, the **blood of Christ** *must* be found *on us*. In other words, in order to access God, Jesus the Christ must be present as King. The power of the Word, fasting, and prayer escorts believers into the divine places of God outside of the flesh, into the throne room of the Father. In order to be elevated to this place in spirit where God is, Jesus must be Lord over your life. The Bible says, "The mind governed by the flesh is hostile to God; it does not submit to God's law nor can it do so" (Romans 8:7). This means there must be a separation between the two. Moreover, there has to be a separation of the flesh and of the spirit in order to align spiritually with the Father. A transformed mind *submits* to the lordship of Christ as King.

A mind and a heart that is has not submitted to the Father is hostile and separated from the Father, seeking after its own will to please the flesh, not the will of the Father. There has to be a separation of the carnal flesh and the *circumcised* heart that has been made new, in order to align with the King. Therefore, flesh and blood cannot enter heaven; as it would be unlawful and against God's law of separation. In 1 Corinthians 15:50, Paul said, "Now this I say, brethren, that flesh and blood cannot inherit the kingdom of God; nor does corruption inherit incorruption."

According to God's decree of separation, light is divided from darkness, heaven from earth, life from death, and spirit from flesh. God separated them all one from the other during His creation process (see Genesis 1). Nevertheless, Satan attempts to obscure the eyes, influence the mind, and distract the ears of men with the deception of believing that there is no other power outside of his darkness. Understand, Satan's only doorway and entrance on earth is through the appetite of sin. The dark powers of Satan must come through flesh-and-blood to move on earth. Again, Satan's demons are disembodied spirits seeking homes, trying to find rest in an animal or a human being. Matthew 8:31 says, "The demons begged Jesus, "If you drive us out, send us into the herd of pigs.""

Much like Satan, fallen angels carry immense power, as they were once carriers of light created by the master Craftsmen Himself, yet they chose to follow the darkness of Satan over that which God called forth during creation. These fallen beings had a particular kingdom assignment according to God's original plan for each of them. They too carried specific assignments in the heavenly places where God is. Nonetheless, of their own free will, they followed the enticements of Satan rather than being faithful to God. These fallen forces of evil elected to become rebellious, thereby deciding to turn toward the darkness of Satan.

Understand that spirits are unseen by our natural eyes, and if a person is not connected to the King, rooted and grounded in the Word of God, he or she will not be able to identify these powers of darkness at work. Satan is exposed to the believer only through the Spirit of Christ Jesus, the Word, prayer and fasting. God will then reveal the workings of evil to the spirit, which must be connected to the King. The believer must then arm himself or herself with the Word of truth to guard the heart and mind from hostile takeovers. Understand that it was never God's intention to have a barrier of the heart or the mind between Himself and His people.

Adam communed directly with God in the Garden of Eden; he didn't need to be reconciled with God. He had no need to provide God with a sacrifice for sin at first. The Bible says Adam walked with God, which indicated direct communication between the two. Adam and Eve's fall stopped them from clearly hearing the voice of God.

Even after the connection was disturbed in the garden, our loving Father stood in His own *preeminence* and *predestined* a *sacrifice* of *perfection* to interrupt the manipulation of Satan, and *His name is Jesus*. One must understand Satan's ultimate plan in the garden of Eden was to disrupt God's children from receiving that which was no longer accessible to him except by permission of God: to enter into the eternal realm. Satan's goal for the believer is still to steal, kill, and destroy. He wants to steal our joy and peace, kill our faith and witness, and destroy us as children of God. John 10:10 says, "The thief does not come except to steal, and to kill, and to destroy. I have come that you may have life, and that they may have it more abundantly."

Satan is eternally condemned already; this is why he seeks to destroy God's people on earth because he does not want you or me to have what he cannot—life more abundantly. God sent fourth His Son Jesus, to provide for humanity what the first Adam forfeited in the garden, as an atonement for our sins because of love.

MANIPULATION OF THE SERPENT

In the Garden of Eden, God instructed Adam and Eve as to what was forbidden and permissible under His rule. Genesis 2:17 says, "But of the tree of knowledge of good and evil you shall not eat, for in the day that you eat of it you shall surely die." That was not a suggestion but a command that if not obeyed would alter divine provision, instruction, wisdom, and time. It would disrupt Adam's direct access to God in His most holy place. Adam allowed the cravings of his flesh to remove him from a place of intimacy with the Father, without having his flesh oppose the divine nature of who God.

Our carnal flesh separates us from our Father, so we have to press past the flesh, our situations, our mind-sets, our wills, and our emotions to get into God's presence. Adam and Eve had sweet communion with God until they rebelled against Him! It was when they ate the forbidden that rebellion overrode their sweet communion with God and the deposit of darkness postured itself in full effect. In other words, their eyes were open! The spirit of manipulation stepped into the Garden of Eden, deposited doubt in Eve, and gave her a thirst for something she should not have wanted. The master manipulator seduced her by asking, "Did God really say …?" She succumbed to his mental manipulation. He had come to her at the right place and time, when her covering was not in the vicinity.

This caused Eve to disobey God. As a result, Eve began to cast off instructions as she deliberately walked in the stead of rebellion, refuting the command of God because she became enticed by her own appetite and the cravings of her own flesh by the simple question, "Did God really say …?"

How many in the body of Christ are being fed Satan's simple question and falling into that same attraction of the flesh as Eve? Satan does this even today. Once manipulation enters through an ear not shielded by the Word, the mind starts seeking self-gratification because it is not covered by truth. When we succumb to the tricks of Satan, it disrupts our lives and alters our relationship with God and His perfect will.

This is how the serpent broke Adam and Eve's connection with the Father in the Garden of Eden. When Eve responded to the serpent in the garden, her actions coupled with Adam's *choice* to *respond* unlocked an awareness of good and evil, right and wrong, light and darkness. In *rebellion,* they unknowingly *exchanged* what was familiar for the *unfamiliar.* Adam and Eve's thought patterns shifted, their language shifted, their environment shifted, and their mind-sets shifted due to Satan's manipulation. Adam and Eve entered a space, place, and time so different from what God had originally intended for them.

Their decision to eat the fruit awakened cravings of their flesh, and sin reigned where righteousness once did. Their divine connection with God was interrupted because they chose to yield to the wickedness of Satan and respond to his darkness instead of walking in their dominion.

Nonetheless, God in His loving-kindness provided redemption outside of Eve's action because of love. Had it not been for God's compassion, humanity, as we know it today would not be in existence. God in His love and mercy toward us provided in Himself a permanent place of reconnection beyond the disobedience of Adam and Eve. Romans 5:8 says, "But God demonstrates His own love toward us, in that while we were still sinners, Christ died for us."

Prior to the command God gave Adam pertaining to what was permissible for them to consume, everything Adam and Eve needed, God had readily and willingly provided. God provided every provision for this husband and wife; they needed nothing outside of what God allotted them through dominion.

God did not create a person without providing for that which He had created. Man broke the connection and pattern of provision, not God. For His earth, He spoke. For His firmament, He spoke. For His creatures, He spoke. For His waters, He spoke. For His Mountains, He spoke. For the life of men, He reached down with His hands and fashioned Adam into His image, and then He blew His breath into the nostrils of Adam and called him by name.

Though Adam's decision drove him to hide from God's presence in the garden, the Father did not abandon the only creation He fashioned with

His hands and blew His holy breath into (see Genesis 3:8). God's love has covered us from the beginning of time. Adam and Eve were provided for out of God's love, not obligation. Love created Adam and Eve. God loved Adam so much that He wanted Adam to experience His unconditional love that He felt in His heart every time He looked on Adam. Because of God's love toward Adam, He created Eve out of him so Adam could experience that same love, as God loved him.

Though Adam was created first, Eve was given that same inheritance as Adam; the covering was extended to her and their children through Adam. Eve came under the same convent as Adam and the dominion God gave to him, was upon her through promise. In other words, there was no lack in the garden of plenty for Adam or his wife. There was no need to worry about what to eat, drink, or wear as God had already set provisions for them under grace.

Because of love, God gave Adam full dominion—power—over everything on earth because of His powerful, uninterrupted connection with his Creator. In fact, Adam in all of his understanding knew nothing about worry or struggle before he was driven out of the garden, which resulted in Adam's parallel, divine, one-on-one connection with the Father being broken.

Adam's God-given dominion was over all that the Father created, which is why I believe the serpent addressed Eve rather than Adam. Satan the serpent slithered in the garden illegally in an attempt to regain that, which was stripped away from Satan, and given to Adam because of love. That place is called *divine covenant*. The ears of Adam's wife were open and easily influenced because she was not guarded by Adam, her husband. Thus, the divine connection with God was hastily broken because Adam's response to Eve's action was misguided and misplaced, causing Adam to move out of alignment in his position with God. When Adam responded to Eve, there was a break in his one-on-one position with the Father. Adam forfeited his place of alignment with God as well as his assignment to cover his wife in the process. Adam forfeited his position in the garden even though Eve ate of the tree first. God had told Adam before Eve was created that defying God would mean death (see Genesis 2:16–17). Adam was the head, not Eve; he was given the authority by God to cover that which God had entrusted to him. Nonetheless, he chose to yield in his authority as the head for what his wife was offering, over the command of the Father.

Everything in the garden designed according to God's plan was misaligned, causing a disruption due to the manipulation of the serpent. Adam *rebelled* against *God*, and that **realigned** his *focus, purpose,* and *posture*. Genesis 3:6 says, "So when the woman saw that the tree was good for food, that it was pleasant to the eyes, and a tree desirable to make one wise, she took of its fruit and ate." The Bible also says, "She also gave to her husband with her, and he ate" (Genesis 3:6–7). Their connection with God underwent a major change. Eve had listened to the serpent rather than to her husband, who was being led by the Father.

Eve allowed the serpent to place a question mark where God had placed a period (see Genesis 3:1). God specifically gave them a command not to eat of the tree of the knowledge of good and evil, however, Satan crept into the garden and manipulated the mind-set of Eve with doubt. His first deception was telling Eve, "You shall not surely die." The moment the Enemy whispered into the ear gate of Eve and dared her to walk in disobedience to God, he knew there was something in her that would allow him to draw her further toward his deception of evil.

He deposited a thirst in her belly, and a craving in her mind-set to think there was something else she required that God Himself had not completely satisfied. His manipulating implications was for her to think that there was more outside of God; and that she needed more because he manipulated her into thinking that she stood incomplete; she thought she was insufficient in her posture as Adam's wife.

Satan's deception was an attempt to have Eve place God on the back burner of her thought process and him on the front. The Bible says in Isaiah 55:11, "So shall my word be that goes forth from My mouth; it shall not return to Me void, but it *shall accomplish* what I please, and it *shall prosper* in the thing for which I sent it." The command God gave to Adam was to not eat of the tree of knowledge of good and evil or they shall surely die (see Genesis 2:17). His Word did not return to Him void.

Satan's second deception with Eve was to suggest that she stood mentally incompetent in her understating of what God wanted. He put doubt in her mind to deceive her into thinking God had not sufficiently supplied her and Adam's needs.

The sneaky serpent's third deception was to imply to Eve that her level of intimacy with God was not complete, that she did not have a spiritual connection with God. Understand, a *divine* connection with *God* **surpasses** the superficial *ear* and *bypasses* the *flesh*. *Intimacy* with *God* is a soft, sweet, divine relationship beyond what we can give another individual. This soft, sweet, divine relationship with God bypasses the old heart, mind, will, and emotions and connects our spirits to *God's heart* through the *Holy Spirit*. That is worship, something the human mind cannot fully comprehend and the new heart can experience only through grace.

Pure worship comes from the heart in reaction to whom God is, not for what He does. Pure worship flows through love. Pure worship allows the believer to pass beyond the outer court by permission of the blood of Christ, to access the most holy place—God's throne. People of God, this is the hour of true worship, for the Father is seeking such to worship Him.

> Jesus said to her, Woman, believe Me, the hour is coming when you will neither on this mountain, nor in Jerusalem, worship the Father. You worship what you do not know; we know what we worship, for salvation is of the Jews. But the hour is coming, when the true worshippers will worship the Father in spirit and truth; for the Father is seeking such to worship Him. God is Spirit, and those who worship Him must worship in spirit and truth.
>
> —John 4:21–24, NKJV

The intimacy Adam and Eve shared with the Father in the garden went well beyond the fabric of their fleshly beings. The intimacy they shared with the Father carried them before His presence to such a degree that when Eve interrupted their sweet communion, she knew instantly that something was different.

Once Eve ate of the tree, she was crippled in her thinking to such an extent that she enticed her husband to disobey God just as she had. Their minds shifted from their original state of being God had originally given them. Eve's desire to become wise intensified to a measure of self-satisfaction as she overrode truth; unlocking an appetite for lust that caused her to shift from one posture to the next.

Why was this? Because of the open door of the mind, the ears and eyes of Eve were unguarded by her own volition. She allow the manipulation of the serpent to ignite her appetite for what she could not have, causing the gate of her flesh to crave more. The enticement of her flesh conquered her rather than being obedient to her husband and her King. She became careless in her actions by disobeying the one command God had given Adam, which she was to follow under the covering of her husband (see Genesis 2:16–17).

Once she tapped into the spirit of rebellion, she instantaneously stood unguarded and uncovered, which awakened her awareness of good and evil and of the cravings of the flesh. Eve was exposed to darkness and accessible to the tricks of the devil, which caused her to be neglectful over being a doorkeeper of God's creation, even in the Garden of Eden.

Eve unknowingly broke her posture of position in God and neglected to guard the Father's Word within her heart. She allowed the outside influence of the serpent to breach her position and authority in God, and when Adam ate of the tree, he in turn broke his covenantal position with the Father because of what Eve offered him.

Because Adam had been created first in the order of authority, his position of spiritual covenant was with God long before Eve was created. Adam was to cover Eve just as God had covered him. Once Adam disobeyed God and ate the fruit, he no longer stood *in* the *accuracy* of *truth* as his eyes and spirit became open to something foreign, something he had never known. His vertical relationship and spiritual position through covenant realigned him because he chose to follow instead of lead.

In other words, God called Adam to be the head over his wife, but instead of him keeping watch in the garden, he left Eve exposed, manipulated, and subject to death in a fertile place of plenty. As a result, Adam's place in time was altered; he thus required God's highest expression of grace to leave His throne and position Himself on earth that humanity might be redeemed from the surrendered position of the first Adam.

In Genesis 1:26 when God announced the creation of Adam, He said, "Let Us make man in Our image, according to Our likeness." He was speaking as a member of the Trinity. Adam was given headship, so

God's plan was for husbands to lead wives, not the other way around. God gave Adam authority and dominion over all the earth. Eve stood under a covenant agreement between God and Adam, as Adam being her covering on earth. The order of marriage will not alter in spite of Satan's wiles to deceive the minds of men of God's original design of holy matrimony and "two becoming one flesh" (see Genesis 2:24). *God will not modify His Word* of a husband and wife becoming one flesh, to satisfy the appetite of lust and sin, to appease the hearts of men (see Mark 10:6–9).

Satan is desperately scheming to abolish God's holy law of marriage on earth. Understand the powers of darkness are manipulating through the worlds systems permitting on earth what heaven has ruled as an abomination to God. The powers of darkness have made legal on earth what heaven has forbidden and labeled it as marriage, when God demonstrated through Adam that His plan for holy marriage is a man and a woman.

The deceptive powers of Satan seek to destroy the divine union of marriage, permitting men to marry men and women to marry women defiling the holiness of God's Word. This spirit of perversion is seeking to alter the process of reproduction given to Adam (see Genesis 1:28). The bed of a same-sex union is tainted by the darkness of Satan, its fruits are evil, and the power of Christ shall cut it and its fruit off to be thrown into the fire, unless true repentance takes place. Matthew 7:19 says, "Every tree that does not bear good fruit is cut down and thrown into the fire."

Now the fourth deception Satan skillfully practiced on Eve was to challenge her place and position under the submission of her husband as well as her God. This is the place Satan often seeks to destroy in the lives of many, and that is the marriage of a husband and wife. That which a woman—Eve—was born out of is now broken because of the manipulation of the serpent; she had allowed darkness to challenge her position under submission to her God and her husband, from whom God created her.

One of Satan's deceptive moves on earth is to reverse the position and authority of a husband over his wife. In his attempt to reverse the position of divine order, Satan uses the prideful independences of the ego connected to the flesh that was unleashed through the fall of Adam that says, "I am married but I do not need to submit to the authority of my husband." This woman is corrupt in her thinking because she is still connected to the fallen state of her past while being made new in Christ Jesus. Her prideful ego causes her to become domineering and arrogant, opening the doors of darkness to enter into the marriage.

Satan attempts to blind the eyes of this woman by manipulating her into thinking that she is superior to her husband. Having this superior approach causes her to be dismissive in her attitude and demeaning with her tongue toward her husbands positioned as being the representation of Christ over her life. What she does not realize, is in her dismissive posture toward her husband, she is disobedient to the Father and the order of marriage sent to cover her, as He covers the union. The wisdom of God flows from the head down, not from the bottom up. Which means, the hand of God is resting on the head and the wife is to submit to her husband as he submits to the Father. Understand a godly man is wise under the counsel of the Father and led by the Holy Spirit in all things. He submits to the rule of the Father and positions himself to lead, as the Father is leading him.

The body of Christ must understand that God has a standard in which marriage has been ordained to function while on earth. The sacredness of marriage on earth symbolically represents the marriage of the Lamb of God—Jesus and His bride the—church (see Revelation 19:7). The bride of Christ is called to be holy, separated, and reverent to the Father. Likewise, the husband and wife are to become one flesh, holy, and reverent to each other (see Genesis 2:24).

This is the reason Eve was called to submit to Adam. God gave Adam dominion in the earth to posture and position himself as God's righteous representation of Himself on earth. In other words, to see Adam was to see the likeness, the essence, the love of God in the land. As God led Adam, Adam was to lead.

When God spoke Adam into existence, He was bringing Adam into alignment with the essence, the very fabric of the fullness of the Godhead. The heart of our loving Creator wrapped up in the Trinity called forth Adam and breathed His own breath into the nostrils of man; Adam became a living soul. It was out of the Father's mouth that Adam rose from the dust, and God gave him dominion to cultivate the earth as king.

Once Adam was in the heart of God, he was also in the mind of the Trinity. The heart of God loved Adam, the mind of God conceived Adam, the hand of God formed Adam, and the breath of God gave Adam life (see

Genesis1:7). That which was dust was still dust until God *touched* it, *spoke into* it, *certified* it, and called Adam *out* of what *He spoke* to and certified to be. God poured Himself into something, and out of that something, someone who housed the *express image* of God's brilliance and the majesty of His splendor in the midst of the garden was created.

Once God said, "Be," Adam was! Adam was in the heart of God first, which brought forth the physical manifestation of His presence on earth. Moreover, for this, Satan was envious of Adam's connection to the Father as well as his position of dominion on earth. Adam had a place in God's heart that Satan had no more; this caused Satan to hunt all humanity and devour their souls that were created to worship the Father. Worship formerly belonged to Lucifer in heaven according to Ezekiel 28:13–18 that says, "You were in Eden, the garden of God; every precious stone was your covering: The sardius, topaz, and diamond, beryl, onyx, and jasper, sapphire, turquoise, and emerald with gold. The workmanship of your tumbrels and pipes was prepared for you on the day you were created."

This tells us that Lucifer was worship and was created to worship. The Bible says that precious stones adorned him and pipes symphonically covered him. He was created to worship the King! Nonetheless, because Lucifer became evil God said, "I will put an end to the sound of our songs, and the sound of our harps shall be heard no more" (Ezekiel 26:13).

The pure worship Lucifer once had become tainted and unacceptable before God's holy throne. This is the reason Satan is after pure and authentic worship within the body of Christ. The position Lucifer once had in worship now belongs to the children of God.

This is one of the dark motives of Satan, who manipulated Eve in the garden. The snake tried to destroy the first Adam in the garden by attempting to destroy his intimacy with the Father and the dominion he had over creation. Adam's dominion was not only to rule over animals; God also gave Adam the power to call a thing a thing, and whatsoever he called it, that's what it was. Adam certified the thing to become whatsoever he declared it to become. Whatever Adam declared by heaven's rule, the thing had to conform to and become that which dominion spoke of it to be on earth.

The authority of Adam superseded all living things created by God. Therefore, the serpent set out to destroy Adam's power—his rule and reign on earth. Satan sought Eve in an attempt to have Eve terminate Adam's posture in the Father, but grace showed up in the garden. Grace was on the scene when both Adam and Eve sewed fig leaves together, covering themselves for the sin, they committed. The covering of the fig leaves was symbolic of grace—Jesus's shed blood covering the sins of humanity and restoring a broken people.

There was a ram in the bush—Jesus the Christ! The serpent could not have foreseen that Jesus the Christ would be sent to bruise the head of Satan, disarm his powers, and dismantle and destroy the works of demonic powers of darkness for the sake of love. Colossians 2:15 says, "Having disarmed principalities and powers, He made a public spectacle of them, triumphing over them in it." This means, Christ won the victory over darkness.

Adam and Eve communed in the garden with the Word Himself—God—through a convent of love. At that time, neither Adam nor Eve needed a mediator to access the God of heaven and earth; their access was not restricted. No ark of the covenant was required by them to access God; no sacrificial burnt offerings were required, no priest had to be sent in to atone for the sins of many. Adam had a spiritual, one-on-one connection with God by himself. However, Adam did not recognize that the defiance of Eve was a setup by Satan the serpent in the midst of their having it all.

Satan thought he had won, but Jesus was **already** in place to stand where Adam had fallen. Satan did not recognize that what he thought was victory was only temporary; there was a ram in the bush called Jesus the Christ! The serpent could not have foreseen the prophecy of Isaiah 53:12 of Jesus pouring His soul out unto death; but on the third day He would rise in total victory (see Matthew 16:21).

There was a ram in the bush! The covenant agreement was still in place, and heaven's rule was and still is final. No devil in hell can overturn God's eternal plan. There may have been a pause in the story, but, my God, there *was a ram in the bush!* At the beginning of the story, God met with Adam in sweet communion and free-flowing fellowship as God poured Himself into the vessel He created to worship and love Him. Out of the Father's love, He called Adam forth and created for him a wife to live under his umbrella, for him to pour into her what the Father poured into him.

FORFEIT POSITIONAL RIGHT

The Bible says that Adam and Eve did eat of the tree, that caused sin to enter into the Garden of Eden, and when they were confronted with their sin, they hid themselves. Genesis 3:8 says, "And they heard the sound of the Lord God walking in the garden in the cool of the day." Adam forfeited his position as king of the garden, and as a result, he was no longer walking in accordance with God's perfect will for him and Eve. They had both been deceived.

As a result, Adam became detached as he negated his responsibility of headship, his positional authority. Understand that it was not surprising for Adam and Eve to communicate with God directly. Had it been an uncommon event, this question would have arisen: "Who is that?" Adam did not need to ask the question of God as they communed one on one. Thus, Adam did not need to ask if it was God. Adam and Eve knew it was God they heard walking in the garden in verse 8: "And they heard the sound of the Lord God walking in the garden in the cool of the day, and Adam and his wife hid themselves from the presence of the Lord God among the trees of the garden."

Their reaction to their rebellion was that they hid themselves from the presence of the almighty God. Thus, if the question "Who?" was asked, Adam was afraid to respond to God. He and Eve were ashamed. They hid from the all-knowing God. Sin consciousness manifested itself in them; they perceived the darkness that was not God. They knew it was God who had asked, "Where are you?" Adam was held accountable for neglecting his God-given responsibilities. It was Adam He called forth, not Eve! God called Adam to the carpet for not having covered his wife from the serpent.

Vertical alignment with no horizontal interruption produced Adam's power with God until the serpent tempted Eve. The body of Christ must **stop** allowing outside interference to choke the life out of that which God has **already** given us authority on earth to represent Him as King. Adam was no longer aligned with God as he had been, and he had to face the consequences of his disobedience.

Adam forfeited his position of promise. His covenant relationship had been broken, leaving humanity in need of a Savior—Jesus to bring it back to its state before the cunning serpent deceived Eve. Both Adam and Eve realized something was broken with their relationship with God causing them to experience something in their natural bodies they had never experienced before. Once they ate, they recognized their disobedience to God and were afraid of the consequences (see Genesis 3:9–10). Rebellion produces sin, which causes us to try to hide from God. When our connection with God is broken by sin, our doors swing open and let darkness into our lives.

Our inner spirits tell us when our connection to Christ Jesus as Lord suffers disconnection. We experience an inner shaking of the spirit, which signals the soul that something has been broken. How we respond is up to us individually. Without the knowledge of God, and His truth, we cannot see ourselves as sinful creatures; God enlightens our understanding through the Holy Spirit and allows us to see beyond sight and spot the Enemy.

Eve allowed her ears to deceive her and unlock the spirit of rebellion. It was through her unguarded ear gate that she had been deceived. Understand, beloved, that the ear is the keeper of the soul of men. In other words, it guards the body, and Eve's ears were not protected. What entered into Eve's ear ended up in her mind and because she did not dismiss Satan's deceptions, those thoughts took root and led her into the act of rebellion and sin.

The fabric of whom you and I are, as living souls, was defiled by the seductive words of serpent. When Eve responded, she violated the place of purity; she violated the holiness of God. She and Adam had to be removed for the Garden of Eden. Understand, Adam and his wife stood in close proximity of the Tree of Life. The Scriptures said that Adam could have reached his hand out and touched this tree. "Lest he put out his hand and take also of the tree of life, and eat, and live forever" (Genesis 3:22).

> And the Lord God said, Behold, the man has become like one of Us [the Father, Son, and Holy Spirit], to know [how to distinguish between] good and evil and blessing and calamity; and now, lest he put forth his hand and take also

from the tree of life and eat, and live forever. Therefore, the Lord God sent him forth from the Garden of Eden to till the ground from which he was taken. So [God] drove out the man; and He placed at the east of the Garden of Eden the cherubim and a flaming sword which turned every way, to keep and guard the way to the Tree of Life.

—Genesis 3:22–24, AMP

The tree of life was right in the midst of where Adam and Eve were in the garden. This was before their eyes were opened to sin; the tree had no bearing on them because they were already living holy unto God without sin. It was when their eyes became aware of good and evil that they had to leave the garden. Satan caused Eve to eat from the tree she was forbidden to eat from; that made her realize the difference between right and wrong. Satan had made her lust for eternal life on her own.

When God drove Adam out of the garden, "He placed a cherubim at the east of the Garden of Eden and a flaming sword which turned every way, to guard the way to the tree of life" (Genesis 3:24). Adam and Eve had to leave; the law of heaven does not allow sin to dwell in the presence of the King. Flesh cannot dwell where righteousness is!

There had to be a penalty for the sin Adam committed before God. Christ our King had not completed the cross at this time; nonetheless, a sacrifice had to be offered for the forgiveness of sin outside of the garden. In Genesis 3:21, we read, "The Lord God made garments of skin for Adam and his wife and clothed them." The skin that covered Adam and Eve was indicative to the sacrificial atonement on the mercy seat called Christ. God demonstrated how the blood of Christ would cover humanity and repair what Adam forfeited. Adam and Eve cover themselves with the skin of a sacrificial offering that would ultimately take the place of what our King would do. He is the eternal sacrifice that allowed Adam and Eve to continue to commune with God's holiness even after the fall!

God held Adam responsible for the actions of his wife because Adam had received dominion and thus responsibility for Eve. The rebellious Adam was no longer a reliable person in God's eyes. Adam had followed rather than lead Eve and she led him into rebellion, which released seducing spirits of darkness. Adam allowed Satan to rob him of his divine place of order, potential, pleasure, and position in the garden, where God had intended humanity to live permanently. The desires of the flesh overtook Eve. If Adam's guard had been up and his eyes had been open, would the darkness have been able to manipulate Eve? The Enemy circled Eve, sized her up, and penetrated her heart and mind. He tempted her desires, and through her actions, she reversed her God-give role as being under her husband. She overrode God and Adam's authority. Consequently, she and Adam had to leave the garden, and Adam forfeited his position under the Father when he followed his wife.

SEDUCING SPIRITS

When Eve *entertained* the manipulation of the Serpent, she became *unguarded* and was therefore accessible to the seducing spirit of the serpent—Satan—in the garden. According to *Webster's*, to *seduce* is to "persuade" or "lead astray." Eve was so captivated by the enticement of what the serpent was offering that she deliberately disobeyed the Word God commanded Adam not touch. The serpent was so deceptive that he tricked Eve to follow his tricks over her husband. Satan seduces people by his subtle, sly charm. He tempts them with things of the flesh and corrupts their minds to crave what God prohibits. Satan attempts to persuade people of faith to walk away from the truth of God. Demonic forces will creep in through unguarded gateways of the flesh through doors of lies, lust, pride, and so much worse.

Believers must seek God continually through reading the Word, prayer, and fasting. When the mind's eye is not connected to the King, it wanders and is seduced by the lusts of the flesh. James 1:4 says, "But each one is tempted when he is carried away and enticed by his own lust. Thus, when lust has conceived, it gives birth to sin, and when sin is accomplished, it brings forth death." Seducing spirits attempt to seize the mind of individuals, using deposits of deceit and deception as gateways to a more deadly plot of corruption that produces death in the end. Eve's encounter with the serpent left behind in her a deposit unbeknownst to her.

According to *Webster's*, a *deposit* is something that is "stored" or "hoarded" or "left," or "inserted."

Seducing spirits, the powers of darkness, operate through fantasy, the imaginary realm of darkness, but the Spirit of the Living God reveals this darkness and deception that attempts to deposit evil in our minds. Satan and his cohorts seek to plant disruptive thoughts—those of rebellion, sin, and pride in an attempt to have you and me to abort the truth of God. Once the darkness enters through a small opening, it attempts to leave behind an unfamiliar spirits of its own kind. If the spirit of darkness is not identified through the Holy Spirit, it and its deceptions go undetected producing death from the inside out.

The Spirit of Christ will unveil the powers of darkness beyond human eyesight, beyond the recess of our mind-sets, and beyond the senses of the flesh. God Himself will unlock the depth of demonic affairs and the deceptive methods of Satan seeking to "Steal, kill and destroy" the body of Christ (see John 10:10). What am I saying? Satan and his demonic forces represent death either in the physical, emotional, or spiritual death; Satan is death. Nothing he does, is, or even stands for produces life.

The dark crevasses and the dimensions of Satan produce something the souls of men were not meant to experience, but because of the lies of the serpent, the eyes of men have been opened to life and death. Nothing of Satan or his forces of darkness is produced by light, which gives life. Moreover, because Satan produces death in the lives of men, the Spirit of the living God has to release revelation of whom Satan and his workers of darkness are into the spirit of man connected to His Spirit for the believer to have the *power* and the *authority* to *address, dismantle,* and *destroy* the powers of *darkness.*

We are responsible for elevating ourselves in the realm of eternity where God is, and to seek His face through His Word, prayer, fasting, and communion to receive kingdom instructions (see Ephesians 2:6). Through His Word, prayer, fasting, and communion the Father will download warfare instructions to the body of Christ to fight the Enemy of darkness.

We must learn to fight the powers of darkness through the *Word of God* for a people, for a nation, and for the land, God gave His children dominion over. We cannot fight Satan without God's Word. Satan seeks to destroy the heads of families to overthrow God's plan for kingdom men.

He looks for openings in the family unit from one generation to the next just as he did in the beginning of time. Because Adam and Eve did not identify and destroy the dark serpent in the garden, it infected their off spring and is still lingering in the air, seeking more bodies to invade and deposit their seeds of darkness on earth.

The source of the evil of this world, the prince of the air, is Satan. God exposed the rebellion of Adam while conversing with the other members of the Trinity in Genesis 3:22 about the broken connection between God and man.

Satan did not stop at his deception in the Garden of Eden. That same seducing spirit of the serpent that followed Eve around in the garden followed her and Adam when they were removed from the garden. This influencing, seducing spirit was on standby at the place of their conception of their son Cain.

As clever and as crafty as Satan was in the Garden of Eden, he is the same outside of the garden. Satan's methodical movements of cleverness are often seen as the same methods of darkness, but looks can be deceiving, as he himself is the king of deception. The darkness of Satan can often be likened to that of a skilled chess player eager to win over his opponent during the competition of a game.

Thus, in the game of chess, each of the six types of pieces move differently and have different amounts of authority over the other pieces. In other words, each piece has its own position, but the queen can win the game. Chess pieces attack and capture other chess pieces with the objective of checkmating the opponent's king by placing it under an inescapable threat of capture.

This is the dialog of Satan when he approaches God to try to "shift" the saints of God. His attempt is to apprehend and state publicly before the throne of God "Checkmate!" as he attempts to win the game.

What you and I must understand is that, as it is with the game of chess, the king—Satan—is restricted in movement as it pertains to the "game" on the board. The same is said in this life. Satan is **restricted** in movement, and the queen—*the body of Christ*—has authority over him by the power of the Word. The queen has the ability to move in places on the board that Satan does not have. The queen—the body of Christ—has the power to win the game because it has the fortitude to do so. The queen stands on the thrust of the King of Kings, who has already won in final victory.

Satan needs the Father's permission to attempt his plot of checkmate on us. In Genesis 4:3, we read, "Cain brought an offering of the fruit of the ground to the Lord," while Abel "brought of the firstborn of his flock and of their fat." Cain's offering was only of the fruit, not the firstfruit, not the best he could have given God. He chose himself over God; he wanted his flesh over God, thinking God would provide more. Abel, on the other hand, gave God his firstfruit, his best for the best.

Abel walked in faith and offered his best sacrifice to God out of the abundance of His heart. God requires the first, the best of everything from His children. In Genesis 4, we read of the cleverness of the Serpent. Over time, the curse of sin multiplied through that one corruptible seed in Cain due to his lesser sacrifice and his rebellion against God. Genesis 4:4 says, "And the Lord respected Abel and his offering, but He did not respect Cain and his offering. And Cain was very angry, and his countenance fell." Satan had gained ground through Cain's rebellion and Satan's scheming move of checkmate.

Although the king on the board figuratively represents Satan through this metaphor, his tactics are limited much like the king in the game of chess. Under the authority of God Most High, Satan remains powerless in position and must *always submit* to the divine system of heaven. Thus, much like the lower-case king in the game, Satan's ability to move is not equivalent to that of the queen, which has the capacity to move in diverse patterns like the queen.

Allegorically, the queen (the body of Christ) connected to the King of Kings functions within a freedom Satan is no longer permitted to operate within or out of. Much like the order of the kingdom of God, there is a pyramid order of rank much like the game of chess. In the game, the bishop has no restrictions in distance for each move but is limited to diagonal movement. Bishops in their position are like all other pieces except the knight; they cannot jump over other pieces. The queen can be moved any number of unoccupied squares in a straight line vertically, horizontally, or diagonally, thus combining the moves of the rook and bishop. The queen captures by occupying the square on which an enemy piece sits. Thus, the queen connected to the King of Kings stands in the position of power because of with whom it is associated. Which means the body of Christ stands under the umbrella connection of Jesus the Christ, our King.

Satan figuratively plugged Cain's ear with the spirit of jealousy and declared "checkmate" over Cain, who had received a deposit of darkness from his mother and father because the curse of deception had never been attacked at the root. The fraudulent spirit rose up in Cain and caused him to rebel against the Father just as his parents had done.

Satan planted the thought that lingered in Cain's mind-set, causing him to go against the Father just as his parents had done in the Garden of Eden. Satan made Cain question why his sacrifice was not good enough for the Father. The Bible says that God had not respected Cain's offering. It did not say God did not love Cain; it said that God did not respect him or his offering as his actions had displeased God (see Genesis 4:5). This seducing spirit made Cain think Abel had received preferential treatment because of his sacrifice. This manipulating spirit of darkness caused Cain to overlook his own rebellion, his own sin against God.

So Cain became very angry. His countenance had fell. God asked Cain, "Why are you angry? And why has your countenance fallen?" His countenance had changed because of sin, an inner matter that manifests itself on the outside, on the countenance (see Genesis 4:6). Sin causes the body's language to shift, alters the minds, and changes attitudes. Darkness will manifest outward in the flesh when it is entertained. Over time, that one encounter of manipulation with the powers of darkness was never dismantled and destroyed by the power of God's Word. As a result, the deposit of darkness left behind was the seed of rebellion he had inherited and passed down to the next generation. Every lingering spirit of darkness—greed, self-centeredness, anger, jealousy, bitterness, selfishness, and so on—*attached itself* to Cain through his *disobedience* because it had not been destroyed in the garden.

RECYCLED REBELLION

The spirit of manipulation was on the offering Cain presented before the Father, which God saw beforehand, unbeknownst to Cain, whose offering was not been pleasing to God. This counterfeit spirit showed up to hinder Cain from believing in and complying with the truth—God. The powers of darkness caused Cain to doubt his belief in the provisions of God over his life and it dried up his faith in the process. Cain rebelled against God just as his mother had allowed the serpent to entice her flesh.

The voice of the serpent was not familiar to Eve, who had previously heard only God's voice. However, Satan's voice became familiar to her once she responded to him and his cleverness, which caused her to eat of the fruit. When she did, she walked into sin, which is rebellion against God.

Did not Cain yield more of the same? The seed of rebellion that was on Adam transferred into another generation with one purpose in mind—death. Cain's act of rebellion made him think he had power over life and death and had more value, more importance than did Abel. That thinking led him to take his brother's life. His anger had been smoldering in him due to the actions of his parents in the garden.

Did not Eve, Cain's mother, do the same by placing her desire above her love for God? Thus, the deception of Cain unfolded here through the operation of the serpent and the curse left behind. Just as his mother did not fully acknowledge and accept God's faithful provisions, Cain did not accept God as the ultimate provider of everything. He stood outside of faith and walked into a broken state of being, the curse his parents had caused to come upon themselves. These calculating agents of darkness had influenced Cain's thoughts and actions into deception. The controlling thoughts infused in Cain were those of selfishness, bitterness, anger, pride, resentment, and much worse. These thoughts of darkness made Cain think that he did not need God, that he was able to produce harvests on his own.

Are we not the same? Many of us do not recognize the provisions God has given us; we choose to hold onto what actually belongs to God and call that a sacrifice! When we *sacrifice* something, we *give up something* of **value** in **exchange** for somebody or something considered *more valuable*. How can we sacrifice something to God that is acceptable to Him as Abel had? God already holds possession of everything: "The earth is the Lord's and the fullness thereof, the world and those who dwell therein" (Psalm 24:1). God created the entire world, but he wants us! He wants the firstfruits of our beings, love, minds, hearts, finances, sexuality, and so on.

> I beseech you therefore, brethren, by the mercies of God, that you present your bodies a living sacrifice, holy, acceptable to God, with is your reasonable service. And do not be conformed to this world, but be transformed by the renewing of your mind, that you may prove what is that good and acceptable and perfect will of God.
>
> —Romans 12:1–2, NKJV

The apostle Paul says, that we are to present our bodies to God as *living sacrifices*. God desires all of us, and in surrendering to Him, we come into alignment with Him; this makes us realize we should not esteem ourselves higher than Him. Satan attempts to overthrow this mind-set of being holy unto God and replace it with lust, pride, greed, sexual perversions, and all forms of dishonesty, so he can destroy the people of God.

Satan is strategic and does send his agents out beforehand and systematically, according to that which our flesh is craving, that which we believe we "need." Thus, Satan plans and strategizes to reduce the influence the Father can have on our hearts. He attempts to plant seeds of resistance, lust, pride, and rebellion in us, and this makes us place God second in everything, just as Satan did with Cain. Humanity has surrendered to such foolish thinking, and the world is in shambles as a result. Many offer God what comes second in their lives, not their firstfruits.

The second spirit on the scene with the fall of Cain was a manipulating spirit of anger, and the third spirit was that of darkness. The last spirit (certainly not the last) on the scene was jealousy. In Genesis 4:7, God informed Cain that sin was knocking at his door. The spirits his father and mother had *failed* to *crush* stood at the doorpost of Cain and sought entrance. God wanted to bring Cain back into alignment with Himself, but he chose sin over truth; he chose to allow his fleshly desires to creep through his bloodline.

Much like Cain, we give precedence to our flesh and allow lust to wreak havoc in our lives, thinking, and actions. Those spirits of darkness will rule us instead of our ruling them if they are not dismantled and destroyed by the power of the Word. Nevertheless, Cain chose to walk in rebellion, and as a result, sin held dominion over his life. 1 Samuel

15:23 says, "For rebellion is as the sin of witchcraft, and stubbornness is as iniquity and idolatry..." Cain allowed the darkness of Satan to penetrate his heart through the avenue of greed.

Nonetheless, Cain did not keep to God's commandments. Cain left his mind and heart unguarded; that let seducing spirits in. Once again, humanity had forfeited dominion over everything on earth. Genesis 4:7 would have reinstated Cain's ability to rule over his mind when he heard God ask the question why in Genesis 4:6. The why was a twofold question that gave Cain time to pause, reflect, respond, and shift. There was a question mark after the why. Cain could have shifted into God's divine plan in Genesis 4:7, but he chose to respond to the wrong king. Cain, the son of Adam, stood in the presence of an omnipotent God, unguarded and openly accessible to the wiles of Satan by choice all because he did not heed the warning of God the Father even after he had heard God ask a question, not make a statement.

The reason the manipulative powers of darkness caused Adam, Eve, and Cain to fall is the same reason many of us stand in rebellion to God today. Instead of shaking off the stench of sin, many of God's people choose to wallow in it as a pig does in mud. The pig enjoys the coolness and the comfort that mud provides. Are not the rebellious people of God the same? Even in the church, many choose the coolness and comfort of sin—that which is familiar, attractive, and comfortable to our fleshly appetite for sin. Cain responded to the wrong king and allowed the spirit of rebellion to rise up in his heart and be passed down through generations. Cain did not destroy these seducing, manipulating spirits he had inherited.

The spirit of rebellion that ruled Cain caused him to kill his brother: "Cain raised up against Abel his brother and killed him" (Genesis 4:8). Our sovereign God is omniscient and infinitely wise, but in Cain's fallen state, this was unknown to him. God destined a more suitable and acceptable sacrifice to cover humanity in its fallen state. Jesus, the complete sacrifice, proceeded beyond the wickedness of humanity and stretched beyond the scope of the first Adam. God has provided out of, for, and through Himself an excellent sacrifice to atone for the sin of humanity for the sake of His love for us.

Christ came to repair that which had been broken in the garden. Christ, the bread of heaven, came to tear down the curtain of separation that had **arisen** in the garden. Christ *is* the fulfillment of heaven in time but stood outside of time in His eternal place of reign to realign a people from the clutches of death through His own body on the cross. Agape love did that!

God knows what Cain did and what humanity is doing and still, God took on Himself every sin through the death, burial, and resurrection of His Son. Nevertheless, this spirit of resistance is still lurking in the atmosphere today. Because this spirit of darkness had not been destroyed, Cain killed his brother Abel. When God asked Cain where Abel was, Cain evaded God's question with a question of his own to downplay his having chosen darkness over truth.

God told Cain, "The voice of your brother's blood cries out to Me from the ground" (v. 10). The ground is indicative of the grave, the place from which humanity came and to which it shall return. Cain did not understand that blood carries its own sound in the atmosphere. It travels on its own frequency heard by God. Blood brings life!

You and I may not hear the sound of blood just as Cain hadn't heard Abel's, but God can. The Bible says in Genesis 4:10 that God said to Cain, "The voice of your brother's blood cries out to Me from the ground." Cain did not understand the importance of blood and sacrifices to God. Did Cain did not know the story of the redemptive blood on Calvary the second Adam would shed as payment for our sins?

When we allow dark forces into our lives and choose ourselves, the Father will allow those things to rule over us. Deliberate sin drives us *away* from God. It is not God's will to have us separated from Him; nonetheless, He will allow it to be our choice. We can choose good or evil, right or wrong, His kingdom or the kingdom of darkness. "Since they did not think it worthwhile to retain the knowledge of God, He gave them over to a depraved mind; to do what ought not to be done" (Romans 1:28). *Rebellion* against *God* **leads** to *destruction*, which weakens our ability to decipher a holy and righteous way of living.

Once Satan discovers our weak spots, we become susceptible to his parasitic contamination. Cain left the gateway open, allowing invasive parasites of recycled rebellion—sin, and demonic activity, to enter. He left open doors for additional seducing spirits to linger in the atmosphere, preying on all his offspring.

CHAPTER 2

Satan's Fall Like Lightning

> I saw Satan fall like lightning from heaven. Behold, I give you the
> authority to trample on serpents and scorpions, and over all the
> powers of the enemy, and nothing shall by any means hurt you.
> —Luke 10:18–19, NKJV

*J*esus said He saw Satan fall from heaven like a lightning bolt.
Satan was lurking in the atmosphere when God formed Adam.
The serpent began scheming and plotting from the beginning.
This cunning, crafty, manipulating, deceptive serpent slithered up to the
unguarded Eve.

Understand, Adam does not give Eve a name until God commanded
her and Adam to leave the garden due to their rebellion (see Genesis 3:20).
The Bible does not say why the serpent went to Eve and not Adam, but I
think the serpent addressed the wife because she was the covered, not the
covering. In other words, Eve stood in the position under her husband
according the plan of God, whereby Adam stood in dominion as being the
covering under God's divine will on earth. Could it also be possible that if a
serpent had addressed Adam first that Adam's connection to heaven would
have allowed him to immediately see beyond sight and hearing beyond
words Satan in the serpent?

Satan bypassed Adam and lured Eve away from her divine covering—Adam. I wonder if she knew it was Satan disguising himself as a friend of truth. You know the kind of "friendly" dialogue, such as, "I got your back."

In other words, the voice of the serpent could not have been harmonious with the voice of God, which she and Adam had heard only while in the garden. Because Adam was created in God's image, the God on the inside of Adam before the fall was unequivocally synchronized with the sound of his Creator. Anything else Adam heard or saw was all in Adam's dominion.

I believe this is another reason the serpent went to Eve and not Adam first. Adam had such intimacy with the Father that he knew the sound of God's voice outside of any other sound. The *distinction* between the *sound of heaven* and the sound of the serpent *is vital to* the *survival* of every believer. Adam knew the sound of the Father's voice, which means before the fall, everything else was foreign. If Satan had spoken to Adam, Adam would have dismissed his manipulation because what Adam would have heard would have been external, not internal.

God gave Adam dominion *over* the serpent, which means, what the serpent spoke, Adam had the authority to rule over it. Therefore, what the serpent communicated to Eve would not have been able to penetrate beyond Adam's external ears because of his dominion and divine connection with God. Genesis 3:10 says, "I heard Your voice in the garden, and I was afraid"; Adam and Eve knew God's voice. Nevertheless, Eve yielded to the counterfeit words of the serpent whom Jesus had seen fall from heaven like lightning and responded to them. Thus, shame was automatically present in her flesh; and the lust in her heart had been exposed.

After they had eaten, their eyes immediately opened to sin and the imbalance it causes. They were exposed to satanic powers in the atmosphere; that uncovered something they had never experienced that caused them to hide themselves from God. The manipulation of the powers of darkness has not changed; Satan uses this same mechanism to confuse many of God's people today. He slithers in as a "friend," but his intentions are evil. What may appear to the eyes as real may be harmful.

The Enemy roams about as the prince of the air and seeks to entice us through the lies he presents as truth so he can dominate us. Because Satan had been thrown from a high-ranking place because of his rebellion, he seeks to overthrow the dominion God gave his children.

Luke recorded that Jesus saw Satan's fall from heaven as being seen with the natural eye as lightning (see Luke 10:28). Jesus saw the heavens split and God call for the formation of all creation from nothing into something (see Genesis 1).

> And war broke out in heaven: Michael and his angels fought with the dragon; and the dragon and his angels fought, but they did not prevail, nor was a place found for them in heaven any longer. So the great dragon was cast out, that serpent of old, called the Devil and Satan, who deceives the whole world; he was cast to the earth, and his angels were cast out with him.
>
> —Revelation 12:7–12, NKJV

Thus, Jesus stood in the realm of heaven as an eyewitness and in full view of Satan when he plummeted out of heaven in his set location in the atmosphere. So now, the question is, how did Jesus see Satan fall from heaven? Had Jesus been there? Yes. John 1:1 says, "In the beginning was the Word, and the Word was with God, and the Word was God." The Word was there from the beginning, inside God, and He became flesh to dwell among us. Thus, Jesus, the Word, is the One to whom John the revelator sent two of his disciples to ask, "Are You the Coming One, or do we look for another?" (Luke 7:19).

Jesus is the Word who became flesh for the ultimate sacrifice for the sins of humanity. This is why Jesus had a front-row seat when Satan tempted Eve. Jesus was there when Satan fell like lightning.

John declared in the gospel, "In the beginning," which voices preconditions before Jesus's tangible manifestation was seen or His voice heard on earth. It is here that the announcement of Jesus's physical person was being called out of the Godhead into the flesh on earth from the very beginning created to dwell with humanity.

The distinctiveness of John's gospel speaks of Jesus's divinity—completely wrapped in the Father, the Son, and the Holy Spirit as One. For this cause, the Word—Jesus—was *already* in heaven from the beginning, eternally in plain view of Satan thrown from heaven.

Moreover, when Satan was flung from heaven, Jesus was not manifest in bodily form or positioned to dwell on earth. Which means, He was present in the fullness of the Godhead and stood in eternity when Satan was flung out of heaven.

Who is the Godhead of eternity? The Father, Son, and the Holy Spirit, which is the core faith of Christianity. Colossians 1:19 conveys the Godhead of heaven and on earth; there is no distinction between the three. For that reason, no one can add to the person of the Trinity, nor can anyone subtract from the fullness of the three wrapped in one. They are One!

Jesus was with God from the very beginning according to His Word of truth in John 1:1. John 1:14 says, "And the Word became flesh and dwelt among us, and we beheld His glory, the glory as the only begotten of the Father, full of grace and truth."

Jesus became flesh for humanity's sake; humanity needed redemption. Jesus stepped out of eternity, positioned Himself in time, on earth to carry the fullness of grace and truth within the fullness of the Godhead to bring *life* to what was dead because of sin. The King came to earth to *recover* Israel's position that Adam had forfeited in the garden. Jesus the Christ was born of a virgin and without sin; positioned to dwell among us. Infidelity and rebellion ruled Satan, while love stepped out of eternity to realign you and me from the fallen state of Adam, to extend His grace to us on earth.

The darkness of Satan caused rebellion to rise up within him because he considered his Creator to be insignificant compared to himself. After God removed him from heaven, and confined him and minions to the atmosphere, his jealousy raged, and he began plotting Adam and Eve's downfall. Satan manipulated Eve by giving her reason to doubt God's commands. He pretended to be Eve's friend who was concerned about her wellbeing.

His forked tongue spoke one thing while his actions displayed something different as he planted seeds of doubt through his words to disarm, interrupt, and alter things on earth. The garden was a divine place of connection as Satan introduced himself as a friendly snake of wisdom. He *misrepresented* himself, causing Eve to respond to his forked tongue that *spoke words of deception*. Satan had disguised himself as an object of truth, causing Eve to eat what was forbidden and her husband to follow suit.

Satan and his minions of darkness masquerade as friendly agents passing off their falsehood as truth. Behind the disguise, behind the smile, behind the laughter lies the culprit of deception that yearns to steal, kill, and destroy. Peter 5:8 tells us, "Be sober, be vigilant; because your adversary the devil walks about like a roaring lion, seeking whom he may devour," and he does so even now.

Satan has released a vast amount of seducing, evil spirits of darkness at his command, and these demonic spirits are on a mission to create a dysfunctional appetite in the carnality of the flesh, of men, even in the church of the Lord Jesus Christ. In his thirst, his attempt to win, Satan allocates demonic systems to operate through the *wicked,* human *appetites* of the flesh, which now has an acquired taste for *sin* that produces *dysfunction, disorder,* and *death* to the *souls* of men and cravings from birth for the forbidden, much like the tree Eve ate from in Genesis 3:6.

Satan subtly uses the impulses of the flesh of men that are connected to Adam's fall to ignite that place of forfeit that came through Adam. The dark, deposited seed of influence ignites the thirst for the forbidden places where God has irrevocably commanded His people **not** to go.

When humanity is unresponsive to God, Satan takes that opportunity to enter hearts. When the *flesh* has not surrendered to God, it will be *pulled toward deception* and *away* from *God* and what He commands. *Lust* and *sin* will overwhelm hearts and make them respond to the wrong god.

Eve opened the gateway of her senses and allowed the serpent to make her to question the authenticity of God. The serpent confused Eve, which led her to eat the forbidden. Because Eve did not reject the serpent's seducing powers, her environment shifted. She *responded* to an *unfamiliar voice* and carried Adam into sin with her. That made them subject to the wiles of a stranger in the garden. In spite of God's specific instructions, Eve allowed her flesh to overtake her spiritual connection with God and her relationship with truth. Eve catapulted Adam and herself into a "fight" where there was no fight. She disregarded the truth and regarded the lies of Satan. Her mind became impaired because there was a breach in the hedge Adam was supposed to protect. Because of the hedge being breached, the serpent slithered into the ear gate of Eve and planted a deep-seated infection that spread in her body, her husband, and his seed, causing rebellion to take over in their offspring yet to come.

Jesus came to the world complete in the fullness of the Godhead; the throne of heaven rested on His heart and the sword of the Spirit flowed from His mouth. He, who came from eternity, positioned Himself in time to restore the seed of Abraham to the arms of a loving King. The restorative process came out of the heart of God because of His agape love for His people.

According to John 1:1, Jesus, the Word, stood in the completeness of the Godhead when God called Himself out of Himself to be present on earth. God the Father split himself into three persons of equal sovereignty, supremacy, and authority to redeem His children from a state of brokenness.

The Godhead was in the beginning. In Genesis 1:26, God said, "Let us make man in our image." Genesis is the first book of the Bible; it describes God creating man in His image. God created day and night, land and water, and creatures of the sea, and He placed them in set locations. Then he created Adam. Here is the grand entrance of man—Adam—on the sixth day of creation. That day, God breathed life into Adam and certified his presence. God declared, "Let us make man in Our image, according to Our likeness." This indicated a specific conversation within the Godhead, which makes Jesus inclusive in this discussion of creation in time—the earth realm.

This conversation is further proof that Jesus stood in eternity when Satan was flung out of heaven like lighting. Thus, Jesus was and is in His eternal position of the Godhead and had witnessed Satan being cast out of heaven.

INTERRUPTED BY GRACE

The fall cast Satan into another realm, where his power is restricted. While Satan was roaming the atmosphere, Jesus showed up to empathize with the struggles of humanity. The seed of grace called Christ came to realign, reestablish, and harvest that which Christ made to be in right standing with the Father. Jesus imputed His righteousness onto the seed of Abraham because of love. The Greek word *Theanthropos*, God-Man, describes Jesus, who came to earth to realign humanity for the second time.

The word *theós,* comes from the Greek word which, literally translated, means *God.* The word *ánthrōpos,* comes from the Greek word which, literally translated, means *man.*

Jesus—the God-Man, stepped outside of eternity because of His love for humankind. He came to dwell with us to retain His rights of ownership to what already belonged to Him but had been destroyed by Adam's fall. King Jesus came to make all things new!

The God-Man stepped out of eternity, came through the same birthing process in time, yet the King of Kings in His sovereign state of being was already God in three persons. Jesus was deposited as God's seed in Mary's womb because of love. Jesus moved from one rule of domain to rule in another complete as One. Luke 1:27–31 says Mary was a virgin, highly favored of God, carrying the righteous redemption for humanity in her womb. Her part in the story conveys the heart of God's love for us. Eternity came to earth and was made manifest in humanity's eyes. Jesus the Christ, the seed of David is fully God and fully Man, which the Bible declares, He is full of grace and truth whose kingdom will never end (see Isaiah 9:7). The reconciliation He offered destroyed the works of Satan.

Christ's shed blood cancelled out all of our sins. Hebrews 9:22 says, "Without shedding of blood there is no remission." *The blood of Jesus passed through the chambers of time, grabbed hold of death, proceeded beyond the veil, and redeemed humanity.* Jesus's death tore down the barrier between God and humanity. His blood alone grants believers full immunity and full access to eternal rest with the Father. Only Jesus's blood could do that! "This is the blood of the new covenant, which is shed for many for the remission of sins" (Matthew 26:28). Jesus came to apprehend false doctrines of demons, to heal the sick, heal the brokenhearted, and raise the dead. The fulfilment of redemption had to come through flesh and blood to satisfy the requirements of the law, His name if Jesus the Christ.

> [In fact] under the Law almost everything is purified by means
> of blood, and without the shedding of blood there is neither
> release from sin *and* its guilt *nor* the remission of the due *and*
> merited punishment for sins. By such means, therefore, it
> was necessary for the [earthly] copies of the heavenly things
> to be purified, but the actual heavenly things themselves

[required far] better *and* nobler sacrifices than these. For Christ (the Messiah) has not entered into a sanctuary made with [human] hands, only a copy *and* pattern *and* type of the true one but [He has entered] into heaven itself, now to appear in the [very] presence of God on our behalf.

—Hebrews 9:22–24, AMP

Jesus came to interrupt the patterns of time and Satan's plan to elevate his kingdom of this world for his gain. Isaiah the prophet wrote that Jesus "grew up like a tender shoot, like a root out of dry ground" metaphorically and was planted in time to make right what humanity had corrupted (see Isaiah 53:2). Through our covenant agreement, Christ made His children incorruptible seeds (see 1 Peter 1:23). The carrier of grace summoned out of heaven and prophesied through forty-two generations provided for us what we could not have provided for ourselves—life. Grace sought us!

Theologians describe grace as the unmerited, undeserved favor of God; we cannot earn it ourselves. Grace is the action of God lavishly applied to us as His love. Jesus positions Himself as King and advocates for God's people beyond what we deserve. The blood of the Jesus carries the believer before the throne of God and pleads for His forgiveness on our behalf. He covers us with His blood! Jesus's blood speaks a language we cannot utter before the Father. Nevertheless, He still wants to hear our voices! When you and I approach the throne of God, He sees the blood of His Son applied to our lives, which permits the believer access to enter His throne room.

Because of love, we understand in part the governing blueprint of heaven, the law of establishment that was firm in heaven first. Its manifestation is complete and made right within the hearts of every believer in Christ Jesus. The body of Christ has been positioned to call down what God has established in heaven on earth.

The Trinity spoke creation into existence from the realm of eternity, and the responsibility of believers is to grab hold of what is spoken through the study of His Word, prayer, fasting, and listening to learn His will. The "us" was the voice of heaven that summoned the spirit of a man to be present from the realm of heaven. The "us" confirmed that Jesus was in the entire plan of creativity. The "us" established a spoken decree sent to authorize and to complete the appearance of Adam on earth made in the image of the Trinity.

Nothing is established, permitted, or authorized on earth unless the Godhead sanctions it. Jesus established kingdom principles on earth: "Thy Kingdom come, Thy will be done, on earth as it is in heaven" (Matthew 6:10). Jesus provided understanding of the realm of heaven and the authority by which earth is governed and made complete by God's will in heaven. Jesus determined what was authorized on earth; God's rules come first.

"Thy will be done" signifies completion in heaven, which reigns over earth. "And the Word became flesh and dwelt among us, and we beheld His glory, the glory as of the only begotten of the Father, full of grace and truth" (John 1:14). Although Jesus had not arrived on earth, victory remained secure in heaven according to the principle of establishment (see Matthew 6:10). The assignment of Jesus at Calvary had not been completed, but the *same* grace called Christ is the *same* grace smeared on Adam, Abraham, Moses, Joshua, and the high priest presenting the offering to God. This same grace was smeared on Noah and his family before the flood, and it's the *same* grace poured on us. God has not changed. The grace of God is Jesus the Christ! When God saw Noah, he saw Jesus!

Satan's corruption has been and forevermore shall be interrupted by grace—*Jesus*. In the fullness of time, God sent forth Jesus, from the line of David, from the tribe of Judah to dwell in the midst of sinners to bring salvation to men. This interrupted earth, time, and Satan's plan.

THE DRAGON AND HIS TAIL

Then another sign appeared in heaven: and enormous red dragon with seven heads and ten horns and seven crowns on his heads, his tail swept a third of the stars out of the sky and flung them to the earth. The birth, so that he might devour her child the moment it was born.

—Revelation 12:3, NKJV

John was transported into another domain by an angel so he might testify to the things he heard with his spiritual ears and saw with his spiritual eyes. John described an "enormous red dragon having seven heads and ten horns," which represented Satan; the seven crowns on his heads indicated his controlling being. This red of the dragon represented the violence of Satan, and the seven heads spoke of Satan's cleverness. One head was bruised. Who had done that? Jesus! (See Genesis 3:15.)

John said the dragon's tail swept a third of stars out of heaven and flung them to the earth during his plummet. Satan's domain is outside heaven in a set chamber for a set time as the prince of the powers of the air. Revelation 12:4 says the dragon used his tail to lay hold of those stars, fallen angels, because of an agreeable pledge between him and those of like mind.

Satan showed ownership of those under his authority. These stars were in agreement with the dragon. They aligned themselves with the powers of darkness depicted as the red dragon. They left willingly; they had not been apprehensive about disobeying God, their Creator.

The stars that fell from heaven were fallen angels who were hurled to earth as followers of Lucifer. They were no longer under the covering of the King. In Revelation 21:1, John wrote of Satan's attempt to destroy the King planted in time who originated out of eternity. Satan wants to destroy every follower of God before Christ returns to receive His bride. Christ was sent to interrupt and apprehend Satan's plans; time had a date with destiny!

> And war broke out in heaven: Michael and his angels fought with the dragon; and the dragon and his angels fought, but they did not prevail, nor was a place found for them in heaven any longer. So the great dragon was cast out, that serpent of old, called the Devil and Satan, who deceives the whole world; he was cast to the earth, and his angels were cast out with him.
>
> —Revelation 12:7–9, NKJV

Daniel the prophet foretold what was to come while John declared what has already taken place as well as what was to come. John spoke from a place of *"was"* and *"is"* and *"is* to *come."* This is the revelation for which John was carried away to convey to us the *"is"* and *"is* to *come"* through the *"was,"*—Jesus. These men received revelation from God that is relevant to us.

The angel carried John to heaven that he might convey the mystery of the unspoken never-seen mystery of Jesus the Christ to every believer of God and announce that *Christ's blood* had already *won* the victory and had overthrown evil's dominion and doctrines of darkness. He had destroyed all wickedness by His sacrifice on the cross. When Christ announced, "It is finished," He meant *all* things had been *completed* in *Him*, thereby commanding all places, people, and things to be subject to His authority (see John 19:30).

Jesus, who rules with an iron scepter, defeated Satan, dismantled his fallen angels, and destroyed every demonic host of wickedness (see Revelation 2:27). For this reason, His bride, the church, must remain steadfast in the faith of our Lord Jesus the Christ. We hold victory, in Christ Jesus! The serpent has been defeated; the red dragon has been thrown from his former position; predestined for the burning lake of fire (see Revelation 20:14). John foresaw Satan being cast into the lake of fire and brimstone with his beast and false prophet (see Revelation 20:10–14). The Bible says heaven rejoices at the fact Satan no longer resides in a place of purity and peace but is roaming for a short time. "Therefore rejoice O heavens, and you who dwell in them! Woe to the inhabitants of the earth and the sea! For the devil has come down to you having great wrath, because he know that he has a short time" (Revelation 12:12). The definition of *woe* is serious misfortune, distress or misery, wretchedness, or calamity.

"Now when the dragon saw that he had been cast to the earth, he persecuted the woman who gave birth to the male child" (Revelation 12:13). The woman here is earth, the bride who brought forth Jesus. The Greek word for woman is *guné*. Because Satan knows his time is short, his mission is to persecute the woman, the bride, before his time of completeness arrives.

The question one might ask is how Satan maneuvers on earth. Satan causes distress, misery, grief, misfortune, calamity, sorrow, oppression, and much worse. He takes action to block believers in God in many ways. He maneuvers through our senses and time, while God does not move through time or maneuver through our senses. The Father moves through *kairos*— right timing of God, not man's timing. This is the reason Satan tempts us through our flesh, attempting to throw us off God's perfect will of timing and release for our lives. James 1:14 says, "But each one is tempted when he is drawn away by his own desires and enticed."

Before Satan rebelled, his name was Lucifer, "son of the morning" (Isaiah 14:12). Ezekiel 25:14 says, "You were anointed as a guardian cherub, for so I ordained you. You were on the holy mount of God; you walked among the fiery stones." Revelation 12 depicts the removal of his name, rank, and position in heaven. The darkness of his core being caused the removal of his name and place in God. The position Satan once had is no longer valid, so he cannot move without the permission of the King. As a result, Satan's authority is beneath that of believers through Jesus's reign. However, we must be saved, as Satan does not respond to those persons outside of the King (Acts 19:13–15). Satan is known as the deceiver, Beelzebub, the serpent, the Devil, the adversary, Baal, the red dragon, the beast, and many more names, but whatever his name, **he has been defeated!**

Daniel spoke of the end times while John declared both. I believe these are the kingdoms, which Satan offered Jesus in the wilderness if He would bow down, and worship him (see Luke 4:5). Daniel 7 and Revelation 13 parallel each other, so we must understand that the beast John saw coming out of the sea was Daniel's vision of a "dreadful and terrible, exceedingly strong beast." Scripture often refers to the "sea" as sinful humanity or nations that rebel against God (see Isaiah 17:12–13, Revelation 13:1, Revelation 17:15). John's vision of the beast coming out of the sea represents the antichrist (see Revelation 13:1). Many scholars believe the antichrist will bear the resemblance in power of the fourth beast in Daniel's vision of Babylon, Persia, Greece, and Rome (see Daniel 7). The symbolism of this beast is also indicative of the world powers of the Roman Empire.

Satan uses the world's governments and religions to deceive the earth into believing his lies rather than God's truth. Daniel's vision in chapter 7 of "the four winds of heaven stirring up the Great Sea" refers to the war and strife of the world's political systems. Therefore, Daniel and John saw through revelation glimpses through heaven's eye of supernatural events.

Through these events, both men exposed demonic systems at work under the powers of Satan. Revelation 11:7 says the first beast coming from out of the abyss was indicative of the second beast. This beast in Revelation 13 is the antichrist believed to arise out of the Roman Empire, who will war against the saints. This beast has two horns like a lamb, but it is like a dragon speaking and is a false prophet. The beast John saw "Having seven heads, ten horns, and on his horns, ten crowns and on his heads a blasphemous name" is the first (see Revelation 12:3–13:1).

The first and second beast will stand in the dragon's authority and prepare for Armageddon. Both beasts align themselves with a red dragon, Satan, and position themselves as enemies of God. The second beast promotes the power, rule, and authority of the first beast as he walks in Satan's authority.

The darkness residing within this world clutched by the prince of the air walks under the canopy of Satan's darkness, many see faces but not the darkness behind the faces. The beast under Satan's powers will cause the hearts of many to turn away from the truth of God and yield to the darkness of his lord, his deceptions, and their lies, through the eyes of lust. Pride parades around in its suit of corruption, craving what is fleshly rather than the eternal God. The flesh is pulled toward the beast and its appearance of power and will be consumed by the beast, whose unchecked lust demands more and more. This produces death beyond the grave. The beast with the two horns is in representation of the Lamb of God, comparing himself to the death, burial, and resurrection of Jesus the Christ.

COUNTERFEIT KING

Satan—the red dragon—the first and second beast, and every demonic force seek to persuade humanity to have an appetite that produces death of the soul and of the spirit. There is a counterfeit among us. Counterfeit is by definition something not real or legal. Satan, the counterfeit king, ignites the flames of the flesh to make his victims yield to that which they lust after. Satan infuses the lustful appetite for more in the mind of the unprotected. He increases the fire of lust until the degree of "want" is ripe for the taking.

Understand that Satan's only access to an individual is by permission. This permission can be granted by the person who leaves a door open and unprotected, or for a time of testing as permitted by the Father's will. Thus, Satan hammers at someone's situation or circumstances with intense pressure to separate him or her from the faith.

Nevertheless, I have great news! Fire produces the oil of God in a person's life. Satan does not hammer only for the present situation in a person's life; he hammers on past experiences, the present, and the future. He hammers for future generations although in the present. He hammers in the present from past generations, situations, or curses. He also hammers from the present situation for the purpose of it venturing into the future.

Satan is methodical and does not stop hammering until someone stands on the Word of God and allows it to destroy past, present, and future hammering. This does not mean Satan will not try hammering on other areas in our lives, but the area destroyed by the power of God's Word will have no effect because it has been nailed to the cross by faith and confession.

Know that these dark forces seek to cause our appetites to yield to their desires and surrender to the world's enticements. Once we do, Satan's toxicity permeates the atmosphere and us alike, causing irreparable damage. The appetite of the flesh is like a lion on the hunt for prey, and it can be ferocious and deadly in its quest for the forbidden.

Do not believe me? Check out Eve's story in Genesis! It was never God's intention for Adam to experience destructive cravings of the flesh. Provisions were set, and everything was inclusive! The flesh, like the lion on the hunt for its next meal, sets out to satisfy a need and targets its prey to satisfy its hunger. *Sin*—the cravings of the flesh—does the exact same thing. This vicious creature lurks inconspicuously and waits for the best opportunity to capture its prey.

The same can be said of Satan and his attempts to pounce on his prey. Satan is ferocious and devious. He maneuvers through the appetites of the flesh through the mind-set, wants, and desires of humanity by setting up counterfeits that pull his victims just as gravity pulls us. Society— counterfeit kings, agents of Satan—are driving the world. These agents move through false religions, idolatry, worship of men, and fleshly craving for ultimate power to rule over something or someone.

They lure men and women, boys and girls by presenting lies disguised as truth. The flesh gives in to its unsatisfied, unquenchable curiosity and pursues something or someone to fulfill the thirst only God can fulfill. Satan and his rulers of darkness offer what looks good but is in reality wrapped in the sentence of death. He wants us to function in a place foreign to our spirits but familiar to our flesh. We must stay connected to the King!

Understand, Satan is trapped in time, but time is his domain of evil; in it, he seeks to blind the eyes of men to eternity and the eternal King. The flesh pursues pleasure and therefore yields to sin and death now and in the eternal. The appetite of the senses provokes the flesh toward corruptibility, whereby deceit burns even more.

Many today refute the truth of the Word and take on the falsehood of Satan. His spirit of deception corrupts the hearts of many, even in the household of faith. This spirit of darkness will cause many to lust after the forbidden and rebel against the King. What emanates from the counterfeit king's mouth, what he regurgitates from his belly, summons the presence of evil because evil responds to evil. Satan, the beast, the antichrist, false kings, fallen angels, and demonic forces are destroyed through the completion of the cross and the resurrection of the King.

Every believer in Christ Jesus already has the same ruling power Jesus had when He arose on the third day after Satan thought it was the end. Because it was not the end of Jesus's reign, Satan seeks to kill the body of Christ; he has loosed his demonic forces to stop believers from releasing the gospel message to all nations. Therefore, Satan hammers until people's ears turn toward his deception. When they do, they focus on the manipulating sound of darkness, rather than the King. If a person responds to the foreign sound proceeding from the counterfeit king on earth, what comes next is a piece of cake. When the sound of the antichrist is loosed by the prince of the powers of the air, those person responding to the hammering or enticing words will turn their unguarded ears and fall under the seduction of Satan—the dragon, the beast. Their unprotected ears and lust of the flesh will draw many to the unfamiliar sound and deceptive signs of the beast, who will then gain complete control over many (see Revelation 13:14).

The second beast coming from the earth is the false prophet, and its sound will cause unprotected men to worship it (see Revelation 13:12). The Bible says great words of blasphemy shall proceed from the mouth of the counterfeit king; the beast will curse God, His name, His tabernacle—heaven, His throne, and His people (see Revelation 13:6). Daniel's beast depicts an oppressive government—political and social agitation—the four winds stirring up the great sea nations of the world. Daniel's beasts represents the four kingdoms—Babylonian, Medo-Persian, Grecian, and Roman. Daniel described each beast, the lion, the bear, the leopard, and a terrifying fourth beast, the kingdom of the antichrist.

Again, both Daniel's and John's revelations parallel each other. Revelation 13:1 describes the first beast that resembles Daniel's vision of four kingdoms is a direct correlation of Daniel 7:7. Now, Daniel 7:17 says that "These four huge beast are four empires with will arise out of the earth" to make war with the saints of God. Thus, the first beast in Revelation 13 is a depiction of the fourth beast in Daniel 7, the antichrist is described as a "huge beast" (Daniel 7:17) that has conquered the other three world powers during a set period of influence. I believe Revelation 13 describes the antichrist in his reign after he has conquered the other world powers during the second half of his ruling in on earth.

Many scholars believe the seven kings in Revelation 17:10-12 are perhaps Roman emperors: Augustus, Tiberius, Caligula, Claudius, Nero, Vespasian (the father as the one who is), and Titus (the son) as the one to come. Others suggest they are nations past (v. 10): old Babylon, new Babylon, Assyria, Medo-Persia, and so on. One should understand these might perhaps originate through an enemy of God—any world organization aggressively seeking to oppress the Christian faith.

In Revelation 12, John received revelation of the precise timing, control, schemes, and manipulations of the first beast and the power of its host, Satan. For one hour in time, these kings will rule in equal power and present a united front under the guidance of Satan (see Revelation 17:12). Thereafter, these kings will relinquish all authority to the beast, the antichrist, to war against the saints of God.

John pointed out that the beast was "like a leopard [Grecian Empire], his feet were as a bear's [Medo-Persian Empire], and his mouth like the mouth of a lion [Babylonian Empire]." This revelation of the beast according to John is the same as the beast the prophet Daniel described in 7:3–8. These kings are believed to stand in political power and social power and rule on earth before the antichrist arrives (see Revelation 17–18).

Likewise, the ten kings John described in Revelation 17:12 who have no kingdom will receive authority for one hour as kings to operate in the political and social arenas governed by Satan. These kings' powers will differ in their respective arenas, but they will be equal in stature to one another and under the control of Satan.

Revelation 17:14 says the ten kings will give the beast of Satan, the antichrist, their power to make war with the Lamb; however, the Lamb will overcome them all. These spirits will be sent to train for Armageddon (see Revelation 16:16). Nevertheless, the beast and his false prophets and every dark spirit will be captured (see Revelation 19:20–22).

John described future events, but today, and that which is to come, Christ, the Lamb, has already overcome Satan, the dragon and every demonic force under him. Daniel gave an account of the fourth beast as being "dreadful and terrible, exceedingly strong" (see Daniel 7:7). Again, this beast is the antichrist which John the Revelator had seen in Revelation 13. This beast will hold immense authority on earth as given him by the dragon as well as the kings in their hour of reign, which is to come.

About the beast with seven heads, John wrote, "I saw one of his heads as if it had been mortally wounded, and his deadly wound was healed" (Revelation 13:3). This beast was able to heal himself, causing the follows of lust of the flesh, lust of the eye, and the pride of life to marvel and follow his works (see 1 John 2:16). He stood as an *imitation* of truth and thus attempted, in John's vision, to deceive the world to surrender to his presence as "truth," though his actions were *counterfeit* and *manipulative*. Men worship the dragon because of the authority he gives the beast.

As a result, many will worship the beast because of what it demonstrates as power and his talk that will be soothing to *itchy* ears. In the ears of many, this may sound right, but what proceeds from his lips is the language of lies that leads to the portal of death.

LANGUAGE OF LIES

Proverbs 14:12 reads, "There is a way that seems right to a man, but its end is the way to death." Those who align themselves with the beast will follow him to the lake of fire and brimstone. Revelation 13:5 says this beast will have a mouth to utter proud words and blasphemies and to exercise his authority for forty-two months. Even so, the language heard by those under Christ should be heard as an amplified sound of darkness spewing from the clutches of death.

Remember that the beast originated from Satan; it has the serpentine spirit of Satan and travels in the serpentine *S* shape, which is not straight, indicating brokenness from within. Its curving path differs from that of humanity. The alignment of the *S* has a curvature within its structure of movement that causes an interruption of form when compared to the structure of man. The snake presses its belly against the ground to gain momentum in travel through the curvature. Its spirit is just as crafty as it was in the garden. It also has a forked tongue that makes its language different from God's. This *S* curve has a separate language from that of the King; a single tongue following the powers of darkness housing a separation of two parts proceeding out of one mouth.

This serpentine spirit carries the same patterns of the snake that manipulated Eve in the garden; its forked tongue slithers in and out in a rapid motion. This forked tongue identifies smells in the environment. Chemical sampling allows snakes to sense chemicals that oftentimes are not distinguishable by our noses. For air-breathing animals, the main olfactory system detects volatile chemicals, and the accessory olfactory system detects fluid-based chemicals.

The tongue of a snake is always moving in and out, back and forth to sample the chemicals in the air. This allows the snake to identify its prey and to determine in which direction the scent of its prey is coming from. Genesis 3:1 speaks of Satan as the serpent who manipulated Eve as he spoke split words into an unguarded ear to control her.

The Serpent who beguiled Eve is the same methodical serpent that seeks to seduce the people of God today. The Bible says the Serpent was craftier than any beast of the field, which the Lord had made (see Genesis 3:1). Satan, the deceiver, has not changed. He still equips his minions to wreak havoc on us solely by God's permission, according to His divine plan for the lives of His children. When God covers us with the blood of His Son, He connects us to a realm beyond where we are. The prince of the air equips his minions with the capacity to retain data from places and individuals they have once visited (see Matthew 12:43). In the dark places and in dark crevasses, the familiar spirits of darkness retain data; they are well equipped to visit and revisit locations, regions, persons, and so on. "When and unclean spirit goes out of a man, he goes through dry places, seeking rest, and finds none. Then he says 'I will return to my house from with I came.' And when he comes he finds *it* empty, swept, and put in order" (Matthew 12:43–44).

Demons cannot possess our bodies, because we belong to the King. Once we accept Christ as our Savior, our old persons are done away with. Asking Christ to be Lord over our lives provides us with the new covenant through His completed work of the cross. Through Christ, our sins are *forgiven,* and we once *again* are alive in God through Christ (see Ephesians 2:5). In the King, our old selves are done away with (see 2 Corinthians 5:17). Hence, because Christ has paid for our sins on the cross, Satan tries to oppress and depress us if we are unguarded.

These unclean spirits believe that once visited—occupied—a body belongs to them. Why is this? These demonic forces believe they can control us once they have crossed our thresholds. The darkness that spews out of the belly of Satan does not relinquish its prey without a fight. Just as Satan was after the seed of David, he sends dark forces to pursue the seed of Christ whereby those who call Him Abba, Father, have received the spirit adaption as belonging to Him.

Satan is after us as God's chosen people, but we have the authority through Christ, according to Psalm 91:13, to "trample upon lions and cobras [and] crush fierce lions and serpents under [our] feet." We have authority over the serpent and every witch and warlock. Jesus gave His seed dominion over Satan's kingdom by the power of God's Word.

Satan, the snake, is a vulture, a scavenger who feeds on the dead. When and where there is no life, the body is vulnerable to things seeking to eat it, and it will have no ability to fight the scavengers. Satan does the same; he lurks, anticipating when his prey will show no signs of life and no presence of the King. Then he rips into the carcass, one piece at a time, until the tissue is exposed and infection sets in. The powers of darkness are scavengers!

When the Word of God and the blood of Christ do not cover us, the scavengers of darkness will swoop down on those, who will be totally exposed to Satan's devices. The dead seek the dead; both are rotten to the core. Satan and his powers will strip the dead all the way down to their bones, leaving nothing behind. This is the way of the antichrist. Only those covered by the King of Kings will be able to decipher his slithery words. We must learn to recognize that Satan is seductive and his words are devious. They are not soothing even though they sound so.

We must never perceive his words as "moral" words and allow ourselves to be drawn to his seductive sounds. The flesh craves pleasure rather than truth, and Satan's lies can sound pleasurable to the ear but produces death beyond the grave. The Spirit of Christ will reveal all truth (see John 16:13). Although the serpentine spirit works overtime to disguise the source of his deceptive words, the Spirit of Christ will run ahead of the sound, decrypt it, and expose its lies and deception.

The counterfeit manipulators on earth posture themselves as bearers of truth. Revelation 13:1 says the beast with ten crowns on its horns, which represent falsified power, legitimacy, immortality, righteousness, and so on, is the antichrist. Each crown is perceived to the blinded eyes as victorious, but they are all the counterfeit presence of Satan presenting himself as holy to an unholy people.

The second crown is the likeness of a legitimate monarchy, but it is a counterfeit of Christ. This antichrist attempts to establish his legitimacy through lies spoken to unguarded ears. The beast misrepresents himself as one having equal power and authority as Christ. However, the Word of God declares that when he opened his mouth, "great things and blasphemous words" fell out (see Revelation 13:5). Its false words attached themselves to empty receptacles and said Satan was the lord.

The beast blasphemed God's name, vilified the saints in heaven, and waged war with the saints of God on earth. Through sweet, smoothing, deceitful words, the Enemy tries to make us worship him, not the King.

No one knows the identity of the antichrist; 1 and 2 John are certain that the antichrist will oppose Christ.

Though many scholars speculate as to where the spirit of the antichrist will arise, many believe this spirit will come out of the Roman Empire. The believer must believe that whoever this demonic spirit is and whenever it rears its ugly head, it has already been defeated by Jesus's sacrifice on the cross and its completion. We, the body of Christ, must stand on guard and keep our eyes fixed on the King, not on other kingdoms. Moses said in Exodus 14:13, "Do not be afraid! Be strong, and see how the Lord will save you today. For the Egyptians you have seen today, you will never see again." The Egyptians, the bondage, we are experiencing or will experience, have been put under our feet through the power of our resurrected King.

Satan holds no power over God's people because he has already been defeated. The mission of Satan is to replicate Babylon's systems of darkness that God has *already* delivered His people from. The Israelites were in bondage, enslaved by dark, oppressive powers day in and day out, but the King of glory brought them out. How many in the body of Christ are allowing this dark, seducing power to drag them back into captivity after Christ has already set us free of it?

A mind bound by Satan succumbs to the spirits of fear and doubt, which produces the spirits of control, manipulation, rage, resentment, and all forms of evil. If we yield to its seduction, we will die spiritually. Satan's plan is for a listening ear to refute the truth of the gospel and its message of repentance. The Bible calls those who give into this darkness the Devil's children (see John 8:44).

Jesus said to them in John 8:42–43,

> If God were your Father, you would love me, for I have come here from God. I have not come on my own; God sent me. Why is my language not clear to you? Because you are unable to hear what I say. You belong to your father, the devil, and you want to carry out your father's desires. He was a murderer from the beginning, not holding to the truth, for there is no truth in him. When he lies, he

speaks his native language, for he is a liar and the father
of lies. Yet because I tell the truth, you do not believe me!

Satan produces voices of lies to disguise his words as love and truth,
but they lead only to death. If the doors of our minds and ears remain
unguarded, we will hear the language of Satan and accept it as truth. Satan
sends his agents to obscure the mind's eyes and ears to the falsity of his
words, and when the language of misrepresentation enters, the voice of
truth falls to the ground because it is perceived as foreign, thus not having
the ability to penetrate.

When Satan opens his mouth, his words connect to the emotions, but
the souls of men should thirst for something beyond temporary satisfaction.
If we listen carefully to the Holy Spirit, He will awaken our spiritual ears,
and we will hear the wickedness spoken against God (see Revelation 13:6).

Satan and his minions are in hot pursuit of God's people and endeavor
to incapacitate them. The Bible says the second beast will perform magical
signs, dazzle our eyes with false images, and seduce many into worshipping
the antichrist, who moves in Satan's power on earth.

> He performs great signs, so that he even makes fire come
> down from heaven on earth in the sight of me. And he
> deceives those who dwell on the earth by those signs which
> he was granted to do in the sight of the beast, tell those
> who dwell on the earth to make an image to the beast who
> was wondered by the sword and lived. He was granted
> power to give breath to the image of the beast, that image
> of the beast should both speak and cause as many as would
> not worship the image of the beast to be killed.
>
> —Revelation 13:13–15, NKJV

In the last days before the return of Christ, the antichrist shall infuse
evil, pervert hearts, and bind the revenue in the land for the purpose of
control. The darkness of Satan wants to put his mark of ownership on those
who lust after the wrong things outside of God. As a result, the antichrist's
enticements will cause people to lust after evil. Because of the lustful

hearts of men, increased evil, war, and famine on earth, many will think there is no other way to live, which will cause them to pursue the beast of death. Out of desperation, many will choose to submit to the wrong king. The church will be removed and those who yield to the darkness of the antichrist will be marked with a seal of ownership on their right hand or foreheads in order to "buy." Satan will brand individuals with the number of the beast, the antichrist—666.

CHAPTER 3

Territorial Power of Darkness

> For we do not wrestle against flesh and blood, but against
> principalities, against powers, against the rulers of darkness of this
> age, against spiritual host of wickedness in the heavenly places.
> —Ephesians 6:12, NKJV

*A*gain, Daniel and John record identical revelations of kingdom language that unlock the strategy of Satan and his demonic forces maneuvering in governmental entities. In Ephesians 6:12, the apostle Paul provided the believer with detailed information about the hierarchy of Satan's army and his influence over governmental systems to establish and infuse his will on earth.

Paul confirmed through the eyes of heaven the pyramid of demonic ranks—principalities, powers, dominions, and so on. Paul began with principalities; Satan's chain of command begins with the prince first. The word *principality* derives for the Greek word *arche*, which means, "to denote rule." The root word *archó* in *archomai* means first in rank and order, to be the first to do something, to begin, to be chief, leader, ruler.

Principalities receive direct orders from Satan because they are superior in rank to other powers of darkness. Principalities, or territories ruled by a prince, rule over nations, cities, and governments. He has set and equipped principalities as commanding generals over his army of darkness to influence kings, presidents, political figures, and so on. Satan has set himself up as a shadow of royalty, a ruler on earth. Satan is a copycat of the Father, who rules heaven and earth. Satan is king of his kingdom of darkness, thus forging himself and his cohorts into something they are not.

Before an earthly kingdom is established, according to the laws that govern the earth, the king of the earth must be present in body before any earthly kingdom can be established. The Word identifies Satan as the "god of this age" (see 2 Corinthians 4:4), the king of this world who leads a vast army of fellow demons. Remember when Satan was thrown from heaven, he already had a following. Because of those evil spirits "following" him, they fell beneath him, and because he is a copycat of God, he has established a pyramid in the air like God's kingdom. Therefore, principalities are in command under Satan.

The second in command are the powers. The word *power* derives from the Greek word *exousia*, which means, "speak or delegate authority." Powers have delegating and jurisdictional authority from their commanding officers, the principalities. They have an effect on structures, the five pillars of society, and systems of the earth (see Ezekiel 28:1–10). Satan is the authoritative driving force of wickedness in every act of demonic activity. He wants to build his kingdom of the air and portray himself as king over the King of Kings. Religion does not look for a relationship; neither does any person walking therein strive to obtain it. The religion of Satan is a system of rebellion. Satan selected and organized his forces of darkness according to rank, authority, region, location, et cetera, for his works of wickedness on earth.

The third in command are rulers of the darkness of this world. The word *rulers of darkness* in the Greek is transliterated as *kosmokratór,* and *skotos,* which means, "lord of this word." Theses spirits have jurisdictional authority over cosmological systems of the universe. They are ruling spirits of darkness who blind the minds and eyes of men on earth from receiving truth. Rulers of darkness are facilitators of wickedness within nations. This category of spirits affect thoughts, perceptions, music, entertainment, religious ideologies, and so much more (see Jude 6, 13).

Again, remember that demons are disembodied spirits seeking to find rest in physical, human bodies (see Matthew 12:43). They have no human form, which means they have no human body like you and me; demons are spirit beings. Just as these spirits begged Jesus to remain in the region during their encounter with the King, they are still requesting permission today. Matthew 8:31 says, "So the demons begged Him, saying, 'If You cast us out, permit us to go away into the herd of swine.'" Matthew 8:31 and 12:43 show the demons' desire to own human bodies. In Matthew 12:43, they were looking for a place to "dwell" or find "rest" on earth.

Satan is the master of darkness—principalities, powers, demons, devils, subordinate spirits, familiar spirits, witches, prognosticators, psychics, and every spirit of darkness under heaven—but even he has to submit to the rule of God. Jesus the Christ has *complete* authority over all the hosts of wickedness under Satan's rule. Satan is the transmitter of many of humanity's offenses.

Paul exposed which ranking satanic officials are commanders and those subject to the commander. Paul also provides insight into darkness, which falls beneath and does the bidding for the office in which they reside. For instance, a particular demonic principality moving in the authority as a general of an army over government world leaders has a general's power beneath him. Likewise, a lieutenant general would rank in the order as a ruler of darkness but beneath the general in rank.

Please understand that spirits operate collectively and cohesively in groupings and maneuver under different umbrellas—familiar spirits, astrologers, black magic, white magic, charmers, warlocks, yoga, horoscopes, the occult, psychics, and many more. These umbrella spirits remain interlocked under a more superior spirit, but these spirits serve different functions according to their assignments from whichever power of darkness rules over them. Nevertheless, they are one and are of the same spirit.

Many people in the body of Christ solicit spirits of wickedness through mediums, or familiars, or "family" spirits. These spirits function by familiarizing themselves with a person's emotions, sexual attractions, addictions, and other personal characteristics; it effects an unwanted infiltration of a person, place, or thing through its surveillance!

Its job is to become one with your being, your attitude, your likes and dislikes, your daily activities, and your habits. In Deuteronomy 18:9–14, God said to His children, not "to take on the abominable ways of life of the nation," which he was calling them from. God told His children,

"Don't practice divination, sorcery, fortunetelling, witchery, casting spells, holding séances, or channeling with the dead" (Deuteronomy 18:9–12); God knew this would corrupt our hearts and subject them to bondage. God says conjuring up dead spirits through witchcraft is an abomination.

> When you come into the land that the Lord your God is giving you, don't follow the disgusting practices of the nations that are there. Don't sacrifice your children in the fires on our altars; and don't let your people practice divination or look for omens or use spells or charms, and don't let them consult the spirits of the dead. The Lord your God hats people who do these disgusting things, and that is why he is driving those nations out of the land as you advance. Be completely faithful to the Lord.
>
> —Deuteronomy 18:9–13, GNB

The familiars form coalitions with demonic spirits to maintain dysfunction in a person's life. Satan attempt to blind the mind's eye by discreetly mingling the realm of satanic fantasy with reality and mingling the meanings of the words he uses to his advantage. If the powers of darkness can keep us from discerning the hidden meanings of words, they have deceived us. Focusing on one word does not connect us to the root of the word, which carries its deeper, true meaning. When this happens, we stand in ignorance of what is beyond our physical sight due to satanic manipulation. Subsequently, many are oblivious to Satan's manipulation of even simple words.

Satan hides his agents in other agents to conceal his systems at work. Focusing on one matter can blind our eyes to other, more-important matters securely obscured so we do not see them sneaking up in our blind spots.

Satan uses blind spots you will not see in your time of transition unless you take the time to turn to see what is coming from behind, "in the cut." Could this have been the case of Saul in his transition out of a position because Satan had manipulated him too? In 1 Samuel 28:3–35, Saul sought a woman operating under the influence of familiar spirits. The

Bible says that Saul requested a woman to conduct a séance to conjure up purposefully for his own gain. "Seek me a woman that hath a familiar spirit that I may go to her, and enquire of her.' And his servants said to him, 'Behold, there is a woman that hath a familiar spirit at Endor.'" This was a familiar spirit, not Samuel. When the spirit of a man or woman leaves the earth in Christ, he or she is present with the Lord (see 2 Corinthians 5:8), not in the underworld of Satan. However, there may be a demonic spirit of deception who has surveilled the person! The familiar spirit assigned to Saul had aligned itself with the familiar spirit assigned to surveil Samuel, thus, Saul responded to both imitating spirits of deception.

Spirits of darkness work with one another to achieve the mission under the counsel of a higher rank of darkness. A witch is a female magician, a sorcerer who practices witchcraft. They form unholy coalitions with other evil powers of darkness under the rule of Satan. With this one word, *witch*, you will find the umbrella of the word covers sorcerer, wizard, witchcraft, and magic, which all maneuver through one host. These distinct groupings of darkness hide themselves in their names, yet they are all under one authority, Satan. For example, Wikipedia defines *familiar spirits* as "supernatural entities believed to assist witches and cunning folk in their practice of magic."

Each word is indicative of the other and represents the counterfeit of their territory, Satan. Hence, when we hear the word *magic*, we do not automatically associate it with demons but with a form of entertainment. Many even in the body of Christ do not recognize magic as a literal form of sorcery and are therefore exposed and unprotected vessels desensitized to the manipulations of Satan. Consequently, Satan can blind and bind, and many are so, even in the body of Christ; many saints are standing in a posture of defeatism.

In 2 Corinthians 10:5, the apostle Paul warned us that one of the weapons Satan uses was our imaginations; the reasoning process of the mind. Satan seeks to distort our thought process of understanding the difference between fantasy and truth. Many consider magic shows a form of entertainment without perceiving that Satan uses them to release demonic spirits. Through the realm of fantasy, these spirits are released into the atmosphere through an open, unguarded gateway of the mind-set of those sitting in the arena seeking to be entertained. Satan's timing and influence are released through the tunnel of obscurity, and many are unaware of this truth. By using these methods, Satan conceals his darkness to the veiled eyes of men. Every demonic activity is transmitted through channels of darkness under the structures of evil.

For something to transfer power or energy, it must be connected to the source of that power; power cannot move by itself! All forces of darkness must be connected to the main source, Satan. He delegates his authority and power to his hosts as well as the beast, the antichrist (see Revelation 13:2). He infects them with his powers just as a virus can infect a computer, just as a parasite can infect an organism and draw sustenance from it. A host is an organism that harbors a parasite. A parasite is "an organism that lives on or in another organism of another species, known as the host, from the body of which it obtains nutriment."

An organism is a contagious living system. "In biology, an organism is any contiguous living system (such as animal, fungus, micro-organism, or plant)." In at least some form, all types of organisms are capable of responding to stimuli, reproduction, growth, development, and maintenance of homeostasis as a stable whole. An organism is defined as "a form of life composed of mutually interdependent parts that maintain various vital processes" or "a form of life considered as an entity."

An organism is a living system that responds to stimuli. Therefore, demonic systems are unable to function outside their attachment to Satan.

Vitality of life is dependent upon the source! Without a source, there is no viability of life. Accordingly, parasites of wickedness attempt to attach themselves to living things, the mind-set of humanity, to survive. They take up residency in their hosts if those hosts are not protected by the Word of God. Once parasites gain access, the nesting process begins. Just as a mother nourishes her child, the mind can nourish this evil, allowing it to grow and advance in Satan's wicked ways.

When a mother gives birth to her child, she suckles it to foster that which is born. After the birthing process, the process of childrearing is the next step in the developmental phase. Hence, there are different levels, different groupings within Satan's camp and the process of advancement. If the parasites are not destroyed prior to the birthing process (in the mind-set), the greater are the chances evil will reproduce after its own kind; evil will give birth to evil! Evil must be destroyed in our minds immediately lest the multiplied effects of darkness become exceedingly superior in our lives and spiritually incapacitate us. We must rise up in authority against Satan and his agents of darkens by the authority of Christ and the power of His name.

The pecking order in Satan's territory differ, as many will have similar functions but not equal influence or rule. In his hierarchy, Satan has thrones, dominions, principalities, powers, rulers of darkness, and spiritual wickedness in high places, devils and demons, spirits of the underworld, and so on, and underneath are groupings. The definitions of *groupings* is "a set or arrangement of persons or things in a group" or "a number of persons or things ranged or considered together as being related in some way."

REGIONAL TURBULENCE

When a region is stronger in the area of healing but lacks economic strength, Satan drives specific powers into that region to apprehend, hinder, and prevent or attempt to destroy the manifestation of healing that governs that region.

For this reason, Satan assigns a high-ranking demonic official over that region to contend with the release of healing just as he did in Daniel 10:12–13. The Bible says Daniel humbled himself before the Father to receive divine revelation. Gabriel said God had sent him to answer them, but the prince of Persia sent by Satan to apprehend him held him. Nevertheless, God sent Michael, one of the chief warring angels on *His* behalf to *release* what the prince of Persia—Satan—had tried to destroy. Daniel had been fasting and praying for three weeks; the Scripture says the Lord sent an angel to contend with and arrest that demonic system, that demonic prince set over that region on the behalf of Daniel.

The prince of darkness penetrated the wicked heart of the king of Persia, attempting to hinder the prayers of Daniel for twenty-one days, but the prince of darkness must not have known God had a kingdom ambassador in the land who set his face toward the King.

Satan assigns lower-ranking subordinates, powers, and rulers of darkness to facilitate the intended demise of the secondary need of the land or an individual. An unguarded mind focuses on its primary needs rather than the Word, causing the Word to take a backseat, thus negating the secondary need. It is during this time of need that many in the body of Christ become preoccupied and allow the Word of truth to take a backseat, passively dropping out of the race instead of affirming the Scriptures over themselves and the situation. Philippians 4:19 declares, "And my God shall supply all your need according to His riches in glory by Christ Jesus," which we must stand on even in the midst of adversity.

Moreover, when an individual's attention is fixated on the primary need at hand, the secondary attack may gain ground and be undetected in its position. This means that when you and I are smack dab in the middle of the primary need, bit by bit, the progression of the secondary need may suddenly increase without notice. We are sideswiped and are abandoned by that which has positioned itself as fact yet is deceptive and causes us to be left in a state of confusion because our focus was on the primary while the secondary was gaining momentum. Why is this? Because we stood excessively focused on one thing and never saw the second attack creeping up because our focus was off. As a result, the Enemy slithers in on the need with a counterfeit (person, place, or thing) to confuse our mind-set and disrupt our focus.

Counterfeit! Are we not any different today? Satan attempted to bring temptation before Jesus in His humanness during His time of need. The book of Matthew gives the reader an account of Jesus being tempted and tested in the wilderness during His time of prayer and fasting, forty days and forty nights (see Matthew 4:2). Why and what was Jesus in His human state in need of? Food. Satan used the distractions of food and power to try to throw Jesus off the focus of His assignment. Had Jesus yielded to the offers of Satan, perhaps His earthly assignment would have been altered. However, Jesus stayed the course set before Him by the Father.

> Then Jesus was led by the Spirit into the wilderness to be *tempted by the devil*. After fasting forty days and forty nights, he was *hungry*. The tempter came to him and said, "If you are the Son of God, tell these stones to become bread." Jesus answered, "It is written: 'Man shall not live on bread alone, but on every word that comes from the mouth

of God.'" Then the devil took him to the holy city and had
him stand on the highest point of the temple. "If you are
the Son of God," he said, "throw yourself down. For it is
written: "'He will command his angels concerning you,
and they will lift you up in their hands, so that you will not
strike your foot against a stone.'" Jesus answered him, "It is
also written: 'Do not put the Lord your God to the test.'"

—Matthew 4:1–7, NIV

Satan tries the same with us; he appeals to our needs, but we must
understand we have no needs God has not already met. Philippians 4:19
says, "God shall supply all of our needs according to his riches in glory by
Christ Jesus." Just as Jesus stood on the Word, so shall those called by His
name. Jesus was *secure* in the *Word* because He was the Word made flesh
and therefore remained focused on His assignment. Matthew 4:4 is proof
that *Jesus is* the *fullness* of *truth*, not a counterfeit.

Because Satan could not successfully pass himself off as the King,
he counterfeits himself as the King, offering something he cannot fulfill.
The counterfeit presents itself as an appealing object through fraudulent
means and appealing illusions and false appearances of attraction designed
to fulfill our "needs."

If the door of the body is open and unguarded, the powers of darkness
enter and convince the body to fulfill the appetites of the flesh immediately;
we say, "I need what I need right now" and override our connection to
God to satisfy the need. To the flesh, "later" is too late; this causes the
flesh to push back any warning signals of "wait" from the Father. The
flesh becomes distracted and is unaware of the existence and deception
the counterfeiters pose as truth. We stand oblivious to the fact that this
agent serves as a hindrance to thwart our spiritual eyes from the primary
agent sent by Satan. This demonic counterfeit position is to stop us from
accessing the truth of whom Jesus the Christ is.

When a person in Christ becomes subject to a permissible turbulence
by God, this serves to *refine the accuracy of faith* and proclamation of who
that person says God is in his or her life. When a person speaks through
confession and declares, "'God will heal my body,'" the heat is turned on.

The instant that announcement is made, demonic agents hear it and immediately prepare to apprehend the demise of that word before its appointed time of approval. Thus, in between the announcement and its fulfillment, an agent of Satan attempts to catch the word released in the atmosphere before the visible manifestation of the promise occurs. In other words, the agent of Satan seeks to *apprehend* our words of *faith* before they take root in our bellies, thus producing the revealed facts of God's truth powered by our faith in Him.

Satan attempts to catch spoken words of faith because they are Spirit, and he understands the authority; Christ has given to believers as heirs to activate the Word of God. Words can produce whatever is spoken, be it life or death, blessing or curse. Words conform, transform, and perform. As children of God, we have authority over every word spoken to produce the will of the Father on earth. Therefore, demons attempt to catch our words before they conforms, transforms, or performs to what it was sent to do and become.

Moreover, if the powers of darkness can slow the process of performance down before the appearance of our words manifest, these dark powers consider this favorable for the completion of our demise. For example, in between stages of promise and performance, many become weary in the waiting process and attempt to do the work for God. This causes believers to move outside of God's timing; shifting the focus away from the Father, which demonic powers await in an attempt to put an end to the believer's faith.

Therefore, the powers of darkness attempt to catch our words of faith. What do I mean by the word *catch*? It is a word given from the Father and received through faith such as a word of deliverance; one must *grab* hold of the word by *faith*, *harness* the word, and *apply* its *truths* by faith.

The mind must now *believe* that word *by faith* before it is seen. In other words, we have to recognize that the promise has *already* happened according to His Word by faith even though we cannot see it. The powers of darkness seek to destroy our faith through the receptacles of our thinking before it manifests itself. The thief comes to steal, kill, and destroy (see John 10:10).

Powers of darkness arise to apprehend the spoken word of faith that declares, "It is already done." These dark, deceptive spirits seek to snatch the seed before it takes root in our bosoms. These spirits also seek to destroy the faith of believers, causing them to resist the Father if the request of faith has not manifest itself in what is considered an appropriate time.

Satan does not want us to declare we received anything by His Word, so he seeks to stop the believer from accessing the truth. Psalm 23:1 says, "The Lord *is* my shepherd; I shall not want." Satan believes that if our need becomes severe enough in our "now," we will crumble and reject the truth of God.

Based on the degree of the need, darkness chisels away at our endurance and applies as much pressure as it can on us. Thus, the place we stand in during our time of need becomes bombarded with darkness, uninterrupted patterns of anguish are sent to excel in its strength to expand and burst uncontrollably, attempting to move us into rebellion and sin. The assigned agents now propose, "Let's see if these persons actually believe what they've professed. More important, do they really believe in the God they say they serve?" Therefore, they work on the mind-set, seeking to apprehend the thought process; bit by bit, evil is in motion to destroy the person and the process.

The agents' goal is to promote our need for instant gratification, keeping us distracted from their primary attack. These agents are precise, inconspicuous, calculating, and deceptive. The person under pressure will not see the secondary attack until it becomes greater unless the Holy Spirit reveals this to the person.

Satan has trained his powers of darkness to be combative, disciplined, and ready to attack upon command over regions and nation. Make no mistake: he and his cohorts are hostile and aggressive. Nonetheless, God says, "At the name of Jesus every knee should bow, of those in heaven, and of those on earth, and of those under the earth, and *that* every tongue should confess that Jesus Christ *is* Lord, to the glory of God the Father" (Philippians 2:10–11). The King positions believers to become ambassadors of God armed and well equipped for battle.

The apostle Paul tells us children of God that our weapon of defense is standing on the Word of God and prayer. These weapons are the foundation on which all believers stand and become mouthpieces of God on earth. Through the authority and dominion Christ has given us, we can "pull down strongholds, cast down arguments [imagination] and every high thing that exalts itself against the knowledge of God" (2 Corinthians 10:4).

We cannot fight Satan or his minions without the Word of God, our armor that produces the authority of God to take dominion of the atmosphere and earth. Satan, the prince of the air, maneuvers through the universe, creation itself. He strategically assigns demonic activity geographically, politically, economically, culturally, personally, educationally, and so on.

There are 196 countries and 7.2 billion people today. There are close to 600,000 cities, towns, villages, hamlets, et cetera, in the world. Envision the countless number of principalities, powers, rulers of darkness, and spiritual hosts of wickedness unlawfully infiltrating victims to aid Satan. The agents of Satan's army are on active duty, engaging in active combat, set on a course of destruction before the Day of Judgment. In Mark 5:8, Jesus told the demon, "Come out of the man, unclean spirit!" Then Jesus asked, "What is your name?" The demon said, "My name is Legion; for we are many" (Mark 5:9). These demons were under Satan, the chief mischief-maker. Mark indicated this man had been tormented and controlled by a legion of demons for many years. These demons recognized Jesus and knew their time of torture was over because Jesus's name and authority banished darkness!

This legion of demons recognized Jesus's supremacy; they had no choice but to fall down at the King's feet! Mark 5:6 says they worshipped Him. Satan and his demonic forces have no authority over or outside Jesus the Christ: "That at the name of Jesus every knee will bow, of those who are in heaven and on earth and under the earth, and that every tongue will confess that Jesus Christ is Lord, to the glory of God the Father" (Philippians 2:10–11). They addressed Him by His name, Jesus, Son of the most high God. They recognized His divinity and supremacy.

> When Jesus was still some distance away, the man saw him, ran to meet him, and bowed low before him. With a shriek, he screamed, "Why are you interfering with me, Jesus, Son of the Most High God? In the name of God, I beg you, don't torture me!" For Jesus had already said to the spirit, "Come out of the man, you evil spirit."

Then Jesus demanded, "What is your name?" And he replied, "My name is Legion, because there are many of us inside this man." Then the evil spirits begged him again and again not to send them to some distant place. There happened to be a large herd of pigs feeding on the hillside nearby. "Send us into those pigs," the spirits begged. "Let us enter them." So Jesus gave them permission. The evil spirits came out of the man and entered the pigs, and the entire herd of about 2,000 pigs plunged down the steep hillside into the lake and drowned in the water

—Mark 5:6–13, NLT

Because Jesus is omnipotent, He already knew He was speaking to many spirits of darkness. What was important to Jesus was the man's deliverance. The demons had to submit to Jesus's authority. Even after Jesus commanded these spirits to leave the man, the legion still desired to remain in the region, hence their request to go into the pigs (v. 12). This was because the demons, disembodied spirits, needed earthly bodies to infect. "When the unclean spirit goes out of a man, it passes through dry places seeking rest and does not find it" (Matthew 12:43).

These demons were so violent that when they entered the swine, the pigs drowned themselves. If the swine could not handle the violence and torment of the demons, how can we expect to without the aid of God? What do you think this man had to endure *until* the Word—Jesus—command his release?

Satan orchestrates his harassment and torment by precisely positioning himself and his agents. Just because a region is stronger in healing does not mean the intensified pressure and persistence will not occur in other areas of our lives. The three Hebrew boys experience this firsthand: Nebuchadnezzar "gave orders to heat the furnace seven times hotter than it was usually heated" (Daniel 3:19); he had been selected by the power of darkness to kill Hananiah, Mishael, and Azariah because they would not acknowledge a foreign god. They knew the truth and stood on it! Because these men did not serve a man-made, golden image, the king wanted them put to death; the King stood under the powers of darkness.

Then Nebuchadnezzar in rage and fury commanded to bring Shadrach, Meshach, and Abednego; and these men were brought before the king. [Then] Nebuchadnezzar said to them, Is it true, O Shadrach, Meshach, and Abednego, that you do not serve my gods or worship the golden image, which I have set up? Now if you are ready when you hear the sound of the horn, pipe, lyre, trigon, harp, dulcimer or bagpipe, and every kind of music to fall down and worship the image, which I have made, very good. But if you do not worship, you shall be cast at once into the midst of a burning fiery furnace, and who is that god who can deliver you out of my hands? Shadrach, Meshach, and Abednego answered the king, O Nebuchadnezzar, it is not necessary for us to answer you on this point. If our God Whom we serve is able to deliver us from the burning fiery furnace, He will deliver us out of your hand, O king. But if not, let it be known to you, O king, that we will not serve your gods or worship the golden image which you have set up!

—Daniel 3:13–18, AMP

Thus, Satan is strategic in his operating methods as his darkness maneuvered through the King of Babylon calling for the influence of seducing music to persuade the call of demonic worship to entice their mood to fall under the spell of idol worship. The king order the music was to be released in the atmosphere during the dedication of a golden image. The magic spell of Satan's charming "music" subliminally entered the unguarded ears of those who yielded themselves to darkness. In Daniel 3, the king summoned music and warned that anyone who did not submit to the sounds or obey the king's command would receive death.

Demonic music summons witches, warlocks, channelers, and others possessing demonic, seducing powers. These charmers are under the umbrella of familiar spirits. What are charmer spirits? Charmer are whisperers of darkness who infuse evil intentions through deceptive music. Understand Satan's demonic assassins disguise themselves through music and other forms of entertainment today just as in times past. When the king created a golden image to worship, this unlocked other pagan practices and allowed the infiltration of demonic powers while keeping the truth outside. It was impossible for Nebuchadnezzar to close his mind to other powers of darkness, once the first demon, the first charmer, had gotten in. Other demonic spirits attached themselves to him through his open portals.

The king's spellbinding music drew others to Satan so they would fall under his influence. Satan used Nebuchadnezzar as a tool of regional turbulence to advance his demonic system. His primary scheme was to hold the Hebrew boys captive in Babylon; his secondary scheme was to make the king command the worship of an image (see Daniel 3:1). Nevertheless, the boys knew the power of God. They guarded their minds and stayed the righteous course even under fire.

WARRIOR WEAPONRY

Satan desires to dismantle countries, communities, churches, and individuals to establish his kingdom before Christ's return. He wants to detach our souls from the King. Even in the church, many do not recognize demonic activity and its devices of manipulation. Many in the body of Christ do not know how to fight the Enemy.

In 2 Corinthians 10:4, we learn that the fight is not carnal but spiritual; it will be waged by the Word of God, prayer, and fasting, principles of the kingdom of heaven by which all believers are guaranteed supernatural benefits. God's Word releases that which is in the mind of the Father. When believers connect to God through prayer, that connects their spirits to Him, and God's Spirit downloads God's essence into them.

Jesus always utilized prayer and the Word of God to rebuke the powers of darkness. He rebuked Satan on the mountain with the Word of God (see Matthew 4:1–11). When He returned from praying in the garden of Gethsemane and found His disciples asleep, He declared the Word. Jesus said to them, "*Watch* and *pray* so that you will not fall into temptation. The spirit is willing, but the flesh is weak" (Matthew 26:36–41). Jesus also refers to the *Word* and *prayer* in Matthew 4:4. These Scriptures show the connection between the kingdom and the earth—the Word of God.

Likewise, prayer connects our spiritual ears to God's realm, which is beyond the flesh. Scripture explicitly offers believers godly principles for fighting the prince of the air and dismantling his schemes on earth. "The weapons of our warfare are not carnal, but mighty in God" (2 Corinthians 10:4). Thus, when fighting the Enemy, we must use the defense of the Word as our weapon to overthrow the armies of Satan. Paul says to "Put on the whole armor of God, that ye may be able to stand against the wiles of the devil" (see Ephesians 6:11–18). God gives believers the ability to pull down all the Enemy's strongholds, arguments, and everything he uses to capture and subdue the hearts, and minds. Paul expounded on the hierarchy of Satan's kingdom and the order of battle for the believer to stand in God by employing God's warrior weaponry—the Word.

> For though we walk (live) in the flesh, we are not carrying on our warfare according to the flesh and using mere human weapons. For the weapons of our warfare are not physical [weapons of flesh and blood], but they are mighty before God for the overthrow and destruction of strongholds. [Inasmuch as we] refute arguments and theories and reasoning's and every proud and lofty thing that sets itself up against the [true] knowledge of God; and we lead every thought and purpose away captive into the obedience of Christ (the Messiah, the Anointed One). Being in readiness to punish every [insubordinate for his] disobedience, when your own submission and obedience [as a church] are fully secured and complete.
>
> —2 Corinthians 10:3–6, AMP

Many in the body of Christ are oblivious to the deception of darkness assigned by Satan to oppose the believer. Equally, many of believers solely think in terms of Satan, the Devil, or the Enemy, failing to realize he employs his agents to do his bidding.

Now there are many reasons why many do not fully walk in their position and posture according to the Word of God and Satan tries to stop us from walking in the Word and learning why we were created. This is to keep us from taking up our warrior weaponry of the Word. Many church leaders do not provide insight into the manipulating ways of the rulers of darkness; many have no idea of their subtle, handcrafted, schemes of darkness advancing right in our midst. The body of Christ must position itself to release the transforming power of heaven on earth. Only the Father can release the authority of heaven onto His seed, but His children *transfer* the *release* of *heaven* to earth. This is the hour of release! The church must position itself to *catch* the *release* of oil of heaven to make the forces of evil *submit* to it.

The darkness of Satan is blinding the eyes of many, and the church of Christ must rise up and release the power of God on earth as it is in heaven. The powers of Satan are aligning with the Scriptures prophetic demand; influencing the hearts of world leaders, authorizing laws on earth that the Father has prohibited in heaven. Thus, under the influence of darkness, political powers have legalized same-sex unions and cannabis pharmacies, while the transgender population has escalated and homicides are rapidly increasing, worldwide. The world is in turmoil and the prophets of God are weeping with sorrow for a nation, a people, who has turned its back on the true and living God (see Jeremiah 5:1–37). Where is the voice of the church?

> I brought them into a fertile land, to enjoy its harvests and its other good things. But instead, they *ruined* My land; they *defiled* the country I had given them. The priests did not ask 'Where is the Lord?' *My* own priest did not know Me. The [rulers rebelled] against *Me;* the prophets spoke in the name of Baal and worshiped useless idols. And so I, the Lord, will state My case against My people. I will bring charges against their descendants. Go west to the island of Cyprus, and send someone eastward to the land of Kedar, You will *see* that nothing like this [has ever happened before]. *No* other nation has ever changed its gods; even through they were not real. But **My** *people* have

> *exchanged* **Me,** the God who has brought them honor, for
> gods that can do nothing for them.

—Jeremiah 2:7–13, GNT

The heart of the Father is grieving because His own people have exchanged gods. Where is the *cry* of the church *travailing* in *prayer* for a people who has forsaken the true and living God? Please understand the Spirit of God will not move in certain situations until the body of Christ positions itself in the posture of *pray* and *lament* (weep) before a Holy God in repentance. The Holy Spirit will not violate His position of authority and move on hearts that are not seeking after Him. In order for the Spirit of God to move where there is no desire or room for His presence, would be a violation of the freewill that God has given to His people. There must be a heart thirsting for His presence in this hour. The Bible says, "Blessed are those who hunger and thirst for righteousness, for they shall be filled" (Matthew 5:6).

We in the body of Christ have to be aligned with the *Father* lest Satan gain an advantage through our ignorance. The Bible says there must be a teacher to teach the Word of God to them that are perishing. Romans 10:14–15 says, "How then shall they call on Him in whom they have not believed? And how shall they believe in Him of whom they have not heard? And how shall they hear without a preacher? And how shall they preach unless they are sent?" If God is not teaching the teacher, who is being taught? We all fall into a ditch because of being blind to the truth of His Word. This is the hour the body of Christ must rise up in dominion, take authority, and prepare for battle under the banner of the King. The body of Christ is the called out of God; it is in position to rule by the plan and purpose of God.

Many bodies sitting in the pews do not comprehend Satan's works because of lack of knowledge of the Word, which would tell them how to disarm the works of darkness in their lives. Matthew provided explicit instructions for the believer through Jesus's rebuking Satan: "Away from me, Satan! For it is written ..." (Matthew 4:10–11).

The key to *destroying* the powers of darkness, "Casting down arguments and every high thing that exalts itself against the knowledge of God" (2

Corinthians 10:5), is in the Word and through Jesus's name. Jesus always used the Word of God when disarming the works of Satan. Zechariah 3:2 says, "The Lord said to Satan, "The Lord rebuke you, Satan! The Lord, who has chosen Jerusalem, rebuke you! Is not this man a burning stick snatched from the fire?" How many of us say, "Satan, I rebuke you," and think Satan submits to our commands because we told him to outside of the covering of the King? Even the archangel Michael did not dispute Satan while contending with the body of Moses (see Jude 1:9). He did not stand on his own merit; rather, he stood on the power and the authority of the Lord. He used the Lord's name, which alone has the power to rebuke Satan. Jude 1:9 declares, "Yet Michael the archangel, in contending with the Devil, when he disputed about the body of Moses, dared not bring against him a reviling accusation, but said, "The Lord rebuke you!'"

Therefore, Jude warned the church with a *woe* to them who defiled the Word of God, which is unknown to the carnal mind. Michael understood he had no authority **outside of God**, and neither does the body of Christ. The authority rest on His name alone! The believer can rebuke Satan only by using the Lord's name, the omnipotent King.

Countless believers do not understand Satan works through the imagination, so they do not know how to cast down imagination using the weapon of the Word. The book of Jude is essential for the body of Christ in this hour. Many are oblivious to Satan's tactics and strategies to attack unguarded minds and use them as a conduit for his powers on earth. Blinded eyes do not identify the spirits of darkness. Those who are spiritually blind cannot cast something down if they are unaware of it. Matthew 12:26 declares, "If Satan cast out Satan, he is divided against himself. How then will his kingdom stand?" If Satan went against his own commands, he would be divided, but this is one of his strategic ploys he uses to twist the truth and attack unguarded minds. As a result, many are ushered into the spirit of division, which operates under the spirit of Ahab attached to the spirit of Jezebel in the church.

The spirit of Jezebel brings seducing division to ease our consciences into rejecting the truth of God's Word. In 1 Kings 21:25, Ahab's wife manipulated him into abandoning Yahweh for Baal—Satan. Thus, Ahab's house perished. The spirit of Ahab is a spirit of manipulation; it fosters demonic control over our behaviors, emotions, and perceptions. Ahab's detachment from God caused his downfall.

It is only through Jehovah God and His Word that demonic powers are exposed and *snatched* out of the atmosphere. God is not to be mocked by anyone or anything. His Word *shall forever* stand. If I rejected the Word, who would I be? If I rebuked His Word by my own my name, that would mean I have the power to also ignore that which I cast out of myself by myself. Satan, the Lord rebuke you!

> Do not be fooled: You cannot cheat God. People harvest only what they plant. If they plant to satisfy their sinful selves, their sinful selves will bring them ruin. But if they plant to please the Spirit, they will receive eternal life from the Spirit.
>
> —Galatians 6:7–8, NCV

We cannot befriend darkness and expect it to adhere to our commands of departure; that will not happen! We must recognize Satan **before** we can drive him out using the weapons of the **Word** and **prayer**. We cannot pretend Satan and his army do not exist. The church stands called to take dominion of earth and produce the environment of the kingdom on earth now. "Thy Kingdom come, thy will be done, on earth" (Matthew 6:10).

The body of Christ should never stand in ignorance of what God has redeemed through Jesus. Now is the season to declare the authority of God and the mandate of heaven through Jesus the Christ. Satan is planting destructive thoughts in unguarded minds, causing an appetite for dysfunction to rise in the body of Christ. Our spiritual eyes have become calloused, and this disrupts our spiritual vision of Satan and the sin he represents.

Fear, lack of knowledge, and unbelief keep us from seeing Satan's manipulations and the works of his agents. Believers must access that mandate of truth in the Word of God and release it on earth; they can no longer entertain uncertain, passive attitudes concerning the things of God. They can no longer walk in pessimism and self-interest; these attitudes will not allow them to destroy the powers of Satan. They must walk in understanding of how to use the weapons of God granted us through Jesus's sacrifice on the cross.

Possession is now, authority is now, and promise is now. Paul said, "For the weapons of our warfare are not carnal but are mighty in God for the pulling down strongholds" (2 Corinthians 10:4). We cannot fight Satan with man-made, temporal, worldly swords; we must use the Word of God as our weapon; this alone will grant us the ability to destroy Satan's works.

Once the Word of God is in operation, the angel's assignment is to take the Word of God to the place of release of what the Word of God declares of itself, that it shall become. We alone do not have the power to make Satan retreat from us without the protection of the Godhead. Satan is a powerful entity and without the covering of the Godhead, we are powerless. Even Michael could not rebuke Satan by himself; he needed the authority of God's name. Lucifer was an archangel created by God, who named him the "anointed cherub who covers" (Ezekiel 28:14). When Lucifer allowed iniquity to rise up in him, he was cast from heaven, the third dimension, and he now resides in the second dimension, the atmosphere outside God. He became a profane thing in the heart of God.

The Scriptures tell us why Satan attacks believers of the cross and the Christ in them who triumphantly defeated death and its sting. Satan and his dark powers reside in the second realm, outside of heavens domain. Job says, "Is not God in the height of heaven? And see the highest stars, how lofty they are" (Job 22:12), while Paul said in 2 Corinthians 12:2, "He was caught up to paradise." In Scripture, heaven is a lofty paradise, and because it is God's abode, darkness cannot be in the place where God is. Satan cannot operate in the same space, place, and time as God.

Colossians 1:16 says, "For by Him all things were created that are in heaven and that are on earth, visible and invisible, whether thrones or dominions or principalities or powers." Because Satan cannot operate in heaven, he operates in the air and on earth in his attempt to enter our minds. He seeks to make us drop truth and pick up his lies, even in church.

Take for instance the lonely child growing up without a father, mother, or even a sibling. Oftentimes, when there is the presence of absenteeism, the child or adult may create pretend friends. Many medical professionals believe this coping mechanism is harmless, but this could open a door to the powers of darkness—Satan, allowing children to blame their imaginary friends for their own transgressions. This can cause a psychological break, a disconnect between fantasy and truth caused by the powers of darkness. This can allow even more demons in.

Believers must spiritually discern through the Holy Spirit that which is *truth* versus that which is counterfeit. Satan searches for open doors to penetrate and infest the mind when there is no presence of God. Once the infestation shows itself, it **must** be demolished by the power of the *Word* before it sets up a stronghold in the mind. Unguarded minds will not spot the intruders and serve eviction notices, but properly guarded minds will be connected to God and reject the intruder.

The body of Christ must learn *when* and *whom* to fight, and this means not fighting each other. Oftentimes, the body of Christ struggles to recognize what the Enemy has seized; many stand outside of kingdom alignment, which will not yield kingdom authority because of an absence of agreement.

Christ has given us the authority to take back the things of God by force (see Matthew 11:12). The *first* step to such recovery is to understand the promises of God; the *second* step is declaring that the Enemy has illegally searched and seized, and we do this with the Word of God, prayer, and fasting. We cannot destroy the works of Satan except by the blood of Jesus and the power of God's Word. Christ gives His seed the authority to destroy the effects of demonic activity at work in our lives. Therefore, the body of Christ must understand, we represent Christ and are kingdom ambassadors on earth and soldiers wielding the Word: "Until now the kingdom of heaven suffers violent, and the violent take it by force" (Matthew 11:12).

Paul says we are ambassadors for Christ (see 2 Corinthians 5:20). We represent Christ on earth; we are His soldiers, and now is the time to fight the forces that seek to control our minds and those of our children and their children. These evil forces attempt to stop us from accessing the truth of God by appealing to our carnal natures of lust, pride, rebellion, appetite, and so on. "The lust of the eyes, lust of the flesh and the pride of life" (1 John 2:16) are the channels by which the powers of darkness attempt to destroy us.

CASUALTY OF WAR

These forces try to disassemble our belief in God with false accusations. If we do not destroy such thinking, it can become deeply rooted and destroy our connection to the King. Satan's wiles are nooses around our thinking that disrupt our ability to recognize truth and spread decay in our minds. We will be powerless, crippled, and decapitated, and more demons will enter us because the entryway of the soul was unguarded.

For centuries, the U.S. military has fought continuously for freedom in the land called America. Tragically, many soldiers are wounded in battle. Some have premature scars, and some have permanent scars. Consequently, there are physically wounded soldiers as well as those who carry emotional wounds during and after battle.

Moreover, many soldiers unfortunately become fatalities during the war itself. With any of these injuries, men and woman of the U.S. military are called causalities of war. Soldiers are currently fighting in battle daily defending several causes in the name of freedom.

There are several components involved in engaging in war, one of which is establishing and assembling a defensive team. A defense team is set in place to prevent an unwarranted act of terrorism in the land of the free. What is terrorism? Terrorism is a systematic act of inflicting unlawful terror or pain on others by opposing systems. Actions of illegal, threatening violence are produced out of a rebellious mind-set to invade territories that differ in many belief systems.

A single threat of terrorism whether directed at international or domestic targets most often transports with it the threat of fear, which produces panic and a host of other emotions brought on by the threat. The U.S. military sets up parameters within its perimeter of soldiers in set locations to securely defend the world from unseen threats against the nation and its people. Terrorists who hide in political parties, nationalistic groups, and religious groups are inconspicuous to the natural eye. These terrorists are willing to die to complete their missions.

Causalities by definition are members of the armed forces lost to service through death, wounds, sickness, capture, or because their whereabouts or conditions cannot be determined.

Terrorists entertain violent minds that are under the control of the darkness of Satan. Mark 9:14–29, a story of a boy who was a victim, a casualty of war against demonic spirits, tells us that when the demon saw Jesus, he threw the boy into convulsions. The demon reacted when he saw Jesus; thinking his day of judgment, his day of sentencing, his day of reckoning and eternal damnation to a bottomless pit had arrived. The boy was tormented by a demon assigned to kill him, and the boy's torment grew worse when the demon saw Jesus. The father ran to Jesus for help in releasing the demon from his son.

Recognizing the demonic spirit in his son was the *first* step toward his recovery. You **cannot** *recover* what is covered! This boy was a casualty of war; the demon caused foam to come out of his mouth and made him convulse and gnash his teeth. At the same time, his father's faith was incomplete, as was the disciples' faith. Jesus called his disciples an "unbelieving generation" because of their lack of faith in the authority that rested upon each of them as distributed by Jesus. The disciples walked with the Master and studied under His lordship but still lacked faith. The father was standing right in front of the Word but doubted Jesus's authority to heal.

There was questionable doubt of "if" in Mark 9:22 that stood in the back of the father's mind. The instant of "if" was pondered in his mind and his heart showed the uncertainty of the father's faith in Jesus's capability. I believe it was through the association of Jesus's disciples, who walked in little faith much like the father. The condition of the father's heart caused doubt to silently take root and rise above the fact of Jesus standing before him. The Enemy uses this same tactic on believers today. Many in the church read the Scriptures yet doubt God's healing, miraculous powers, and His authority to deliver. Many ponder the "if" factor much as this boy's father did in Mark 9:23.

The Scripture does not indicate if the man had heard of Jesus's other healings, signs, and wonders, but Jesus's disciples had. He knew those who went up with Him during His time of the transfiguration on the mountain inside and out. He knew each of His disciples stood in their own deficiency, which prevented them from delivering this man and his son. The father concluded the same of Jesus because of mere association. You know the saying: "'Jesus's boys. Well, you know if Jesus's boys could not heal my son then how could He?'" Guilt by association.

The disciples saw only the situation they faced, what stood before them, not beyond. Although they walked with the King, they had not completely *responded* to His teachings. Therefore, when the father approached the disciples for healing, he did not know of their imperfect faith. The deliverance Jesus effected was not only for the deliverance of the father's son but also for the liberation of the father and the disciples. The same men who had just come off a high mountain and had seen the King dimensionally transform ("He was transfigured before them. His face shone like the sun, and His clothes became as white as the light," Matthew 17:2) did not believe they could heal the boy. Their faith needed to be stirred.

Jesus Himself requested the three to go with Him to the mountain; thus, they bore witness to something incomprehensible. They needed their faith stirred again! Apart from the others on a high mountain, a place of significance to which the visible manifests signs that heaven was on earth, they became evident of the God-Man called the Christ. He was on earth, and the Bible says Jesus's clothing became exceedingly white like snow. They had seen Jesus standing outside of time, but it was beyond what their minds could fathom. King Jesus supernaturally shifted from one realm to the next before their very eyes.

This defining moment for the three disciples was the beginning of their preparation for ministry as disciples of Christ. Exodus 33:18 says Moses asked God "Now show me Your glory." and God said to Moses, "I will make all my goodness pass before you, and I will call out my name, *Yahweh*, before you." God granted Moses's request and *cradled* Moses in the cleft of the rock while He passed by! In Exodus 33:22, God said, "While My glory is passing by that I will put you in the cleft of the rock and cover you with My hand until I have passed by. Then I will take My hand away and you shall see My back, but My face shall not be seen." All Moses saw was God's backside; even Moses could not gaze directly into His face; that would have been looking directly into the sun.

Jesus the Christ, the Theanthropos—God-Man on the high mountain—was transfigured right before them, but their faith needed stimulating again. The Bible says Jesus's face shone like the sun (see Matthew 17:2)! The *highest* form of *God's glory* stood *present* on earth. If you or I were standing on the ground, neither of us could directly stare at the sun when it is shining because the eyes cannot behold the splendor of its rays beaming from it. The Bible says the presence of the King was as the sun so much so that it was radiant. You cannot tell me a more exceedingly heavier weight of God's glory was made manifest to the disciples; heaven touched earth and radiated on Christ, the King of Kings, outside space and time. Still, they had no clue about the transfiguration or the process of what was happening on earth. Jesus was starting to dispense His authority; this preceded the descending of His Spirit during Passover. Jesus had *already* activated what they needed, and all they had to do was *respond.* "Now faith cometh by hearing and *hearing* by the Word of God" (Romans 10:17). The deposit flowed from Jesus, which summoned them to operate in faith.

They could have healed the boy themselves if they had believed Jesus had *already* positioned them to be a *conduit* for the *power of God.* However, faith **cannot** flow through unbelief then or now; we *must* **respond** to *faith* by *prayer, fasting,* reading the *Word,* and responding to *God's voice.* That *will* stir our faith sufficiently. To stand saturated in unseen faith, we must abide in the Trinity, which reveals what is unseen. This is why Jesus responded to their lack of faith, "O faithless generation, how long shall I be with you?" (Matthew 9:19), and this was after they saw Jesus transform. Transfiguration is defined as "the supernatural and glorified change in appearance of Jesus on the mountain" or "to change in outward form or appearance; transform."

Right before the very eyes of the three, Peter, James, and John, Jesus began the process of metamorphosis or transformation for the preparation of His eternal return so much so that the glory on Jesus's person began to show in an overpowering way they were unable to fully behold His presence.

The weight of God's glory during Jesus's transformation is the same weight of glory God allowed Moses to experience (see Exodus 33:19–23).

The power of God's glory is so heavy that no human can experience its magnitude and survive the encounter.

God said, "You cannot see My face, for no man can see Me and live" (Exodus 33:20). When the disciples came off the mountain, their minds had not caught up with the revelation their spirits had received; they were operating through their natural eyesight and natural mind-set. The flesh produces out of disorder, not out of divine order. Therefore, when the father asked the men to heal his son, they could do nothing because they had not adequately responded to the Word, who was with them. They had *not* tapped into the supernatural realm of faith they needed to respond to the power that *flowed* from *Jesus*. They thus lacked the supernatural power to discern what type of demon they were addressing.

Faith grants *access* to the realm of God to *identify* and *destroy* demons, but they were sightless and shell-shocked. They had not seen the triumphant end, so they responded to the beginning and not the end.

APPREHENDED IN TIME

In Mark 9:29, Jesus said to the three men about the demon, "This kind can come out by nothing but *prayer* and *fasting*." Prayer is the connection with the Father, which grants access to His power to destroy demonic forces. Prayer and Scripture are synonymous one with the other; Jesus said that was the key! Matthew 17:2

In verse 19, Jesus summoned the boy, and when Jesus saw the boy, the demon *immediately* recognized Jesus and responded. Satan and his forces recognized the power of the blood Christ through which Satan and his agents are destroyed. The demon in the boy tortured the boy because it needed a body. Before Jesus even spoke, the spirit recognized Him. Jesus, who is omniscient, knew how long the boy had been possessed, but He asked the father about that to inform the crowd that had gathered. They saw Jesus as they saw themselves, as flesh. However, when we see Christ as flesh, we fall! Jesus is and always will be the holiness of God in the Trinity, and if we discount His righteousness, Satan walks in. Jesus asked the question for those in the crowd who sought to challenge Him.

The father stood in disbelief of his son's healing until Jesus came on the scene. In his desperation, in his love, the father said, "If Jesus could anything, have compassion on us and help us" (Mark 9:22). The Word spoke directly to him in plain view, but he still asked Jesus if He could do anything. How many in the body of Christ ask Jesus the same thing as the father in the story? Why is this question still in our minds even after Christ has risen from the dead? Jesus the Christ swallowed up death and defeated the cross and many are still asking the King if He can do anything.

Many who attend church Sunday after Sunday have not grasped the fullness of Jesus the Christ through His Word. The church is confused, and the serpent had entered into the hearts of men to replace the truth of God's Word with his lies. We have the audacity to ask the King if He can do anything!

Many of us are blind to the authority Christ has given His church and are disoriented, crippled, and incapacitated because we are outside God's will for His people. Deliverance takes place when we pray, fast, and read and meditate on God's Word. We must do this to experience the fullness of Christ while we can. Many read about Jesus on the pages of what they believe is a "book"; this defames Scripture, which is so much more than a mere book. It is the unadulterated Word of God!

This is God's Word spoken and recorded for you and me to stand on and dispense in space and time for His glory. Nevertheless, many read it, but it is in the *study* portion *God releases revelation of whom He is*. The Bible is God-breathed, thus, when spoken, given a voice, His Word is released onto a situation to perform the thing it is supposed to perform.

Many read or hear His Word, but it is another thing in its entirety to experience His presence while reading. Reading His Word invites transformation to move and take root in the inner man. Because the men were not standing on the Word called Christ, they could do nothing, and the father of the boy asked Jesus the question "if."

I believe the father had heard of Jesus and His majesty yet had not *experienced* the supremacy of His hand for himself. The skepticism of the men stood resting on the heart and the mind-set of the father as well. The father's cloudy outlook of what did not happen when he asked the disciples to heal his son penetrated his old heart. The seed planted in the mind of the father was doubt.

As the father approached the disciples for the deliverance of his son, the three were restricted, unable to tap the realm of faith because they stood outside it. In other words, they were unable to **draw** *from* the person of *Jesus,* which would have provided for them the activation needed through demonstration to heal the boy.

I believe the father was desperate, so he used a conjunction before the question mark: "but if you can." Although the father was speaking to Jesus, he connected the words *but* and *if.* What proceeded from his mouth flowed from his heart, and I believe the two words were *connected* to an unresolved condition of his son not being healed by the men connected to the King. The father's discouragement was in response to what had happened instead of what or whom he stood in the presence of. This prohibited him from making a connection with the person he was addressing about the condition of him and his son.

Jesus Himself broke down the wall of separation of doubt and the twin conjunctions "but" and "if" in the father's mind by releasing **one** word: *Believe.* I believe Jesus could have spoken to the spirit at a distance and not called for the boy. I believe Jesus could have *loosed* the effects of the spirit from far off and the boy would have been free. However, in His compassion, the King chose to address and heal both the father and the son. I believe Jesus saw the sincerity in the father's heart that sought deliverance of his son although he did not know he needed to be delivered also. I believe Jesus understood the father's ear was unguarded because of his need, which became primary in the forefront of his "but" connected to his "if."

The desperation of the father outweighed the present, which blocked his ability to see the time of apprehension by eternity standing in front of him. The father's faith stood detached from his sight; therefore, he was unable to recognize that deliverance was there. He was unguarded, which permitted the spirit of doubt to take root, which attached itself to his sight, obstructing his vision of the King asking the question.

This rhetorical statement "if you can" in verse 23 became a time of clarity and no longer held power over the father or the boy. In Mark 9:24, the father's ear heard something his mind **could not** comprehend and his sight had never beheld. His spiritual ear made a connection to his spirit man, which came into alignment with Jesus when He said *"Believe."*

Immediately when his ear heard Jesus address his unbelief and his disconnect of sight, change took place. Jesus called this spirit by name (deaf and mute, v. 25) and commanded it to come out of the boy. Why did Jesus call this spirit by name? In His omniscient state, Jesus recognized there were spirits that manifest similarly yet differ in manifestation and degree, so He addressed this particular spirit dwelling in the boy. Jesus addressed the spirit by name and commanded it to leave the boy. Sure, Jesus could have just spoken to the spirit without addressing it by name. Jesus could have easily destroyed the spirit by uttering a simple decree, but He wanted to reveal to His disciples the protocols of heaven for destroying demons. He knew the demon in the boy would "come out by nothing but prayer and fasting."

Mark 9:26 says the spirit resisted by convulsing the boy, but in the end, it had to *submit* to the authority of Christ. The Bible says that when the spirit left him, the boy became as a dead person (v. 26). Still, the grave has no power over the boy because the Word, Jesus, pulled the spirit of death out of the boy, and Jesus grabbed the boy by his hand, indicating he was free. "Death is swallowed up in *victory*" (1 Corinthians 15:54). Death was unable to bind the boy; he was freed of the demon and the death he carried by the power of the Word—*Jesus*.

CHAPTER 4

Hitchhikers on Earth

Then Jesus asked him, "What is your name?" "My name is Legion,"
he replied, "For we are many." And he begged Jesus again and
again not to send them out of the area. The demons begged Jesus,
"Send us among the pigs. Allow us to go into them."
—Mark 5:9–13, KJV

Travelers and hitchhikers who walk along the road with their arms stretched out and their thumbs stuck out are immediately recognized for whom they are. Drivers mechanically recognize that they are in search of rides. Hitchhikers want transportation from one destination to the next free of charge and without care. They wait until someone stops and offers them a ride.

For years, there have always been thumb riders; from one generation to the next, from all lifestyles, hitchhikers have existed. Many drivers as well as passengers have seen persons thumbing, signaling motorists that they are seeking transportation to specific destinations.

Regardless of the possible dangers to either the hitchhikers or the drivers who pick them up, the information provided takes a backseat on their journey to somewhere. Climate is not a factor, nor is location during their quest to arrive at their destinations. What matters most to the person seeking to be transported is the arrival at his destination.

Well, I believe the same could be said of spiritual hitchhikers on earth. These demonic spirits are unwavering in their quest to dwell in physical bodies much like hitchhikers. Thus, from stranger to stranger or person to person, these demonic hitchhikers lurk for an open door, an open gateway into the lives of many seeking to destroy the individual. These demonic spirits are not walking with their thumbs obviously out in plain sight; they lay in wait for unprotected openings to transfer what they carry onto someone else and "steal, kill, and destroy" (John 10:10).

When people ignore the warnings and transport those they are not acquainted with, bad things can happen. Nor can hitchhikers always be sure of the characters and intentions of those who pick them up. Many in the church hitch rides with the powers of darkness—seducing spirits seeking to kill them.

Those who have not surrendered themselves to Christ can surrender their lives to evil, and according to Matthew 6:24, "No one can serve two masters." What you submit to becomes your Lord. They could pick up Satan unknowingly or be picked up by Satan unknowingly if they let him in or take a ride with him. Christ wants to rule over our thoughts and actions and close our doors.

"You are Peter, and upon this rock I will build my church, and the gates of Hades will not overcome it" (Matthew 16:18). This means Peter! I mean you, the reader of this book! Is Christ your King? He has established, certified, and built your person on the Rock, which is Christ Jesus. Because the body of Christ belongs to God, no demonic force will ever prevail against it (see Matthew 16:18). Dabbling in this or that outside of truth opens up our gates and grants the Enemy access.

In Mark 5:1, we read of a man held hostage at the tombs by a legion of demons. The man had been shackled; he was always shrieking and screaming, beating, and cutting himself. Hosts of demons were assigned to the border, the entryway to the waters of the country of Gadara, and according to Matthew, who described them as due to "exceeding fierce" demons. "When he saw Jesus afar, he ran and worshipped Him. And he cried out with a loud voice and said, what have I to do with You, Jesus, Son of the Most High God" (Mark 5:6–7). Matthew 8:29 says, "Suddenly they cried out." The demons respond to the presence of the King because they *recognized* His holiness and supremacy. They were aware of Jesus's authority and had to request His permission to stay in the region (see Mark 5:6) by hitchhiking into the swine. Once Jesus commanded them out, they had no legal right to stay in the body they had invaded.

Satan is just as manipulative today as he was then; he hitchhikes via drugs, music, entertainment, sex, and many other fleshly desires. He moves from one unguarded body to the next swiftly and destructively.

Before Jesus and the disciples entered the boat to journey to Gadara, Mark 4:36–37 says that they encountered a storm. I believe this storm's assignment was to stand as a point guard to interrupt change. Jesus was on His way to releasing the man tormented by the sea with Legion, an army of demons tormenting a man.

In basketball, the job of the point guard is to guard from a particular position on the perimeter of the plays and to observe all angles of the game. For the reason of their leadership role on the floor as point guards, they must be quick, skillful, and well equipped to attack plays at any given moment. Floor generals or coaches are the titles given to point guards. Point guards study the game and its films to recognize any weaknesses of the defense. As such, point guards must observe the strengths of their own offensive players as well in order to run the team's offensive position, thus the encountered storm at hand.

Mark 4 says that after Jesus fed the multitude, preached parables, and healed the blind man, He said, "Let us cross over to the other side." Mark 4:36–37 says Jesus and His disciples encountered a storm; this storm's assignment was to stand as the equivalent of a basketball point guard to stop Jesus from freeing the man tormented by the demons.

Their journey was interrupted by this storm. We have all experienced storms that have disrupted our travel from one place to another, whether on land or in our minds. Satan sends out strongmen to hinder us from reaching the spirit realm (see Daniel 10:12–13). He seeks to convince believers to abort the truth of God and the promise of His Word. When the things we seek from God do not become manifest when we want them to, our hearts grow tired and our ears become deaf, we become spiritually weary and given to doubt.

The Enemy sends storms to detach us from the King. Mark 4:37 indicates, "A great windstorm arose, and the waves beat into the boat, so that it was already filling." The disciples became frantic while Jesus was not distressed. I would venture to say Satan had sent the storm to divert Jesus from His mission.

CAPSIZED IN THE MIND

It is in the clutches of the storm that we see fear overtake the minds of the disciples even while Jesus was with them. The omnipotent King was at the stern of the boat, yet the disciples allowed the storm to paralyze them. Because the disciples gave their attention to the storm, their minds shifted and the spirit of panic and terror held on tightly to their minds. Truth and grace was at the stern of the boat on the cusp of the apprehension of a man tormented by a mob of demons inside him. Capsized in the mind by panic and fear, they ran for help (see Mark 4:38).

Capsize means to sink, to turn bottom up, to overturn. On the threshold of what they perceived as a terrifying ordeal, the mind-sets of the disciples began to capsize with the thoughts of premature death infused by the power of darkness. Their mind-sets began to overturn, crippling their thought capacity and yielding to the tumultuous storm that was spinning their emotions out of control. Had they forgotten the power of the King on the boat with them? I am certain the disciples had firsthand knowledge of Jesus performing miracle after miracle, but in their time of need, the disciples' faith in the King shrank as the angry storm arose.

Yes, the disciples experienced the power of Jesus speaking to a thing and the thing conforming to and producing that which He called forth. Yes, the men had an advantage firsthand hearing Jesus declare the power of resurrection through speech of something that was dead; nevertheless, with the wind and the waves beating the boat, fear governed their minds. Fear swallowed up truth, causing them to stand incapable to rule over that which sought to seize them.

Their unguarded gateways spoke defeat through the channel of panic, causing broken words to fall from their lips. In other words, their broken language of lies became their truth, causing their mind-sets to overturn through a capsizing process with the ship and themselves. Their position as those called of Jesus was to **develop** the *mind of Christ*, the **same** *language of truth*, and **stand** in the *full faith* of the King.

However, they allowed their mind-sets to tip over from the position of authority that Jesus had already given them. Instead, they stood powerless, incapacitated, and defenseless in the storm. Their hysteria overrode the fact that Jesus, the one who had the power over the storm, had given them that *same* authority, that *same* dominion to do what He did even in the clutches of the storm.

Fear had apprehended them and overturned their thinking; they feared death as the powers of darkness maneuvered through them. Why was the mentality of the disciples in a capsized state? They were operating on and in their natural state of being—the old man. In other words, the old mind-set connected to the world yielded to the storm at hand.

Yielding to defeat caused an unsettling disturbance between the legal dominion of heaven and the confusion of the flesh on earth. They stood in full authority in the earth through their connections to the King. Jesus had already sanctioned each person to walk spiritually by faith in Him in the second heaven, where thrones, dominions, principalities—the home of Satan and his powers of darkness as well as the earth—ruled. I believe the atmospheric realm, the central location of the storm, which was where the pressure was, was in operation by Satan and his powers of darkness.

The powers of darkness in the invisible realm of the air—the second domain—sent this disturbance, which threatened the boat. These powers of darkness struggled to stop the deliverance of the man tortured in the region of Gadara. This man was plagued with many demons that housed spirits of panic, premature death, doubt, fear, schizophrenia, and many more ills. Thus, the disturbance sent by Satan was no coincidence. The disciples did not know they were about to encounter a manic "mob" housing many demons in his person, but Jesus the Christ did.

Not one of them had any idea Jesus was about to set this man free. These men were in a broken, emotional state and had no idea the state in which they stood prohibited them from identifying the spirit at hand, so they called upon Jesus to do the work He had equipped them for.

It required Jesus to speak to their infirmity of brokenness on the inside. The Enemy over darkness touched something on the inside of them that had not *completely* **submitted** itself to the Father. The Enemy touched on something on the inside, which had not connected with heaven, which caused their flesh to panic in spite of the fact Jesus was on the boat with them.

Therefore, there was no need to panic as the omnipotence of the King was on the same boat as they were. However, when they began to *panic*, that produced *fear*, which *disengaged* them from the truth of what Jesus had *already* spoken. They were still operating through the lens of the natural wickedness of the immoral mind-set that had not completely accepted the kingdom reality Jesus had provided them.

Darkness connected them to the corridors of an unchanged mind-set, which located that place of unseen *fear* lodged within each of them to be drawn out by Satan. The disciples had the embodiment of the complete Godhead inside of the boat with them, but they still yielded to panic and fear.

In the midst of what appeared to be a sinking boat, the fullness of the Trinity wrapped in flesh was at the stern asleep (see Mark 4:38). Mark's account of the violence of the storm does not mention the deposited turmoil in those on the boat because of permeating thoughts of death. Mark 4:38 states the men thought they were heading to their deaths; nevertheless, there is no dialogue of what was happening on the inside of the men, the reality of their unknown truth on the inside. The deposit of death overturned truth, causing a capsized captivity inside each of the disciples.

The definition of *capsize* is to turn bottom up, to sink. The Bible does not convey that the boat capsized, but the writer does submit to the reader that the "great windstorm arose" and produced an enormous amount of waves that began to flood the boat. Matthew called the storm "furious," which means full of fury, violent, or full of rage. This is an indication of the violence the storm carried, the strength of it forces on its way to destroying whatever and whomever stood in its path in order to *prevent* this man with Legion becoming free.

That is until Jesus the Christ addressed it! According to Mark 4:37, the pressure of the storm caused waves at sea level to beat against the boat and fill it with water. I believe the storm had been summoned by darkness and had acted in accordance with its commander, Satan.

I believe agents of darkness controlled this disturbance to destroy not only the boat but also the mind-sets of the disciples. Understand that Satan is over the powers of the air (see Ephesians 2:2); he released the pressure from his chambers of darkness and headquarters to dispense and dispatch downward its effects.

Thus, the weight above the surface in the atmosphere of earth was in the air; nonetheless, the disturbance performed at sea level. Conversely, the disciples could **not** *see* the *weight* of the *pressure* of the *air* with their *natural* eyesight; however, they *experienced* firsthand the *effects* of the storm all while Jesus was asleep in the boat with them.

Their spiritual eyes had been blinded by the intensity of the storm. I believe they were unable to sense and discern the demonic darkness in the storm on the sea because of their lack of sight beyond what they stood present to see. Lack of sight in the supernatural realm caused the men to become frantic in the storm. For this reason, they were unable to see beyond sight the attack at hand while in the process of being transitioned themselves.

Although the boat appeared to be sinking, this was just the surface of what stood present before the fearful men that accompanied Jesus to the other side. Jesus the Christ was on His way to loose the man beset by demons, but the disciples' minds were also in need of being released of the shackles that bound them. Not one of the disciples rose up in authority to speak to the storm. It was as if the Word of God, which Jesus had previously deposited in them, had fallen on the ground but had failed to take root when they needed it the most (see Mark 4:15) because of their lack of faith (see Mark 4:38). They ran to the authority of the King instead of *responding* to the authority of the King in them to quash the storm at hand.

Made frantic and paranoid by the noise of the darkness ruling the storm, rather than stand, the disciples shrank. In the heat of battle, they struggled to find their own irrefutable Word of God that Jesus, the Word, had planted in them, certified, and sanctioned. They shrank into the lowest common denominator of defeat. *Fear* had **choked** their **authority** to *destroy* the power given the wind as well as its affects loosed by Satan. They responded to present fear instead of returning to the authoritative teachings of the King.

CEASE AND DESIST

Petrified with fear coated by the spirit of death that transferred its darkness onto the disciples, they ran to the stern in the middle of this disorder. The Bible declares in Mark 4:38 that Jesus was asleep on a pillow all nestled in comfortably in the midst of the uproar while His crew was on deck.

Jesus, the Theanthropos, the God-Man, was sound asleep belowdecks. The Bible says Jesus was fast asleep while the boat and His crew were under attack by the powers of the storm. The question is, did Jesus not hear the boisterous waves beating against the boat and the noise of the wind while He was asleep, all nestled snugly? Could the King not feel the sensation of rockiness of the sail or the noise of the men beneath the boat? Could the King not feel and hear the commotion all the way at the bottom of the boat?

I am sure the question on the minds of each of Jesus's disciples was *Where is Jesus?* In Hebrews 4:15, Paul said to the believer, "For we do not have a High Priest who cannot sympathize with our weaknesses, but was in all point tempted as we are, yet, without sin." This means that Jesus the Christ stands in touch with the weakness of the redeemed. Therefore, because He is Jesus, the all-knowing, supreme King, He could very well hear the hearts of the men speak and utter sounds beyond what any language on earth could communicate through sound.

The disciples did not have to say one word because Christ, the infinite King, already knew what had hoisted itself through unspoken language into the air. Be it life or death, the King already knew! Hence, while the boat was under fire, Jesus could have experienced the same disturbance of the waves as the men on the ship, but the King of Kings was asleep. Never mind the noise above His head; the King was asleep!

The fullness of divinity, Christ, stood complete in this dimension on earth, and what He carried on the inside of Him, He transferred to His disciples, and still they ran for the King. The totality of whom Jesus was as King stood beyond the five senses of the disciples.

Yet, in all the upheaval, Jesus was still asleep. In Hebrews 4:15, Paul said Jesus was in touch with our weakness, so Jesus was able to sense the heart of His disciples while he was belowdecks. Jesus could feel what they felt in the height of the storm that seemed to engulf them. All the same, Jesus was asleep!

The uproar caused by the storm had been summoned by darkness to move into action while Jesus was asleep. I believe Jesus heard the commotion and, in His all-knowing state of being, knew what was happening before it happened though He was asleep.

Jesus's posture of being asleep indicated He was in a state of tranquility. It also suggests the authority residing in His person as well as the rule of His tongue in heaven and on earth. That which passed through His lips was spoken from an eternal place. It was not from the realm in which he currently stood or positioned Himself while he was on the boat.

Understand that Jesus's language did not have to line up with the world. That which Jesus spoke had no choice but to conform and comply. Nonetheless, what Jesus had already deposited in the men had not fully developed, and that caused them to run, which specifies the urgency they were experiencing. Although the great windstorm was great, the disciples knew Jesus was greater. Nonetheless, they ran!

"'Teacher,' they said unto Him, 'Do you not care that we are perishing?'" (Mark 4:38). Unbeknownst to them, the language of defeat proceeded from their lips of clay when they sought the aid of the King rather than the language of the King. They would have condemned themselves to the place of death had the *Word* not been on the boat to *counteract* their language of defeat.

The Word—Jesus on the boat—*reversed* their language of defeat and death into the sphere of life. Jesus had already announced to the men of their going *over* to the **other** *side,* but when they ran toward truth, Jesus, the language that proceeded from their lips spoke of death, not life. Did they not know the power of their own tongues? Were they not familiar with Proverbs 18:21: "Death and life are in the power of the tongue, and those who live it will eat its fruit"? Why would the disciples speak a language that was indicative of the truth of what Jesus spoke?

Their language would have produced death had the eternal King of glory not been present on the boat to *dismantle* and *destroy* the power over the great storm to which they **gave** the **authority** to increase by their **own** language.

Jesus said to His disciples, "Let us **cross** *over*," which means that Jesus provided an all-inclusive declaration for each person on the boat (see Mark 4:35). Thus, the question at hand is, why were the disciples speaking the language of darkness instead of adhering to what the truth—Jesus—had already spoken. Why were they operating in their flesh? These men were called out, appointed, separated, and summoned by Jesus to function in and through Jesus's eternal position, while on earth. The question was asked of Jesus, "Do You care?" Though they were privileged to sit, walk, and just be in His presence, they asked Jesus if He cared. Although Jesus had previously given them glimpses of the realm of glory, they asked Him if He cared. Having shown them demonstration after demonstration of His authority to heal the sick, open blinded eyes, and cause the lame to walk, they asked Jesus if He cared.

They asked the One they *chose* to drop everything to follow, "Teacher, do you not care that we are perishing?" The disciples had not tapped into their individual kingdom authority on earth that had been distributed to each of them by Jesus Himself.

Although they walked under His Lordship, they were ignorant of His complete identity and even more ignorant of what He distributed to each of them through connection. Hence, the reason the question was asked of Jesus.

Is the twenty-first-century church standing any different from the disciples on the boat with Jesus? When going through a storm, many asked if Jesus cared. In Mark 11:23, Jesus said, "Truly I tell you, if anyone says to this mountain, 'Go, throw yourself into the sea,' and does not doubt in their heart but believes that what they say will happen, it will be done for them." However, the mountain—the situation—will not be moved when there is an *absence* of *faith* standing in opposition to the King. Mark was saying these things come by faith!

Equally, Jesus conveyed to the body in Luke 10:19, "Behold, I give you the authority to trample on serpents and scorpions and over all the powers of the enemy and nothing shall by any means hurt you." Yet many in the body of Christ are currently asking this same question of Jesus as the men in the boat did on the day of the great windstorm: "Master, do You care?"

I believe many in the church today are capsized in their mind-sets just as the men were in the storm. Is the church standing in the same mind-set of "perishing" when encountering great storms, or is it standing in the authority of the King? Many in the confines of the church are walking in defeat and in the "woe is me" mind-set because they are listing to the **wrong** voice.

Jesus had told the disciples where there were going, but they listened to the storm, which spoke something contrary to the King. Christ has given the body *keys* to **bind** and **loose** the strongman and its **effects** according the Matthew 16:19, and for this reason, God is positioning the church to rise up in dominion.

Matthew 16:19 says, "I will give you the keys of the kingdom of heaven; whatever you bind on earth will be bound in heaven, and whatever you loose on earth will be loosed in heaven." Why is the body of Christ not walking in the authority Christ has provided believers? Why? Why are we who stand under the umbrella of the King so passive toward the Enemy seeking to kill our souls? Why are we so passive when we encounter storms when Christ is our anchor? Does the body of Christ not understand the authority Christ has imbedded in His children over the storms and the effects of the storms? Are we unaware of the Word in our mouths that has the power to bind the strongman, or are we standing oblivious of the authority Christ imputed to the church?

According to the blueprint—God's Word—the body of Christ comprises ambassadors of the kingdom of God, which permits us full dominion on earth as it is in heaven. The Scriptures say, "We are in the world but not of the world" (2 Corinthians 10:3). This means we operate outside the earth's domain, and if we are called to function out of heaven, then why are we not *representing* the **kingdom of God** *authentically* while on earth?

Many maneuver through a spirit of passivity instead of confidently serving a **cease** and **desist** order to the Enemy over the storm instead of being despondent and incoherent in the midst of the storm's fury.

I am certain the disciples grumbled among themselves, asking the question in their minds or possibly even giving voice to that which was grumbled, "Why is Jesus still asleep?" If this concern did not arise within the mind-sets of the men during the time of the fight, I am certain it arose after the fight. Those chosen to walk hand in hand with the King undoubtedly asked themselves "Why?" as they were human. "Why, Jesus?" would have been their question. "Can you not feel the waves beat on the boat? Why, Jesus, are you asleep? Could You not feel the rockiness of the sail while we were in the heart of the storm? Why, Jesus? We needed you!"

All they needed was **faith** to *respond* to the *deposit* that flowed from the living water called Christ through the **transfer** of that which He had apportioned to each of them. The Bible says, "Whoever believes in me, as Scripture has said, rivers of living water will flow from within them" (John 7:38). Thus, the living water that flowed through Jesus was already accessible to them; they just needed to *respond* by *faith*. Nonetheless, the disciples stood frantic in view of the waves, which represented the world system of darkness that beat against the boat, and they responded to it with a defeatist attitude. The boisterous waves sent by Satan to beat against the kingdom assignment of the disciples caused the question to rise up in darkness instead of rising up in the position of light.

Instead of the church standing in the mandate of heaven—the stead of Christ and the call of God—many are still asking Jesus, "Why? Teacher, do you not care?" The powers of darkness—the hijacker—has hitchhiked himself into the church and has deceived believers into asking the question why instead of usurping the authority God has already given His body to walk in.

Is the church slipping back into the passivity of Eve from which Christ had delivered us? Many in the confines of the church are like the men on the boat—faithless. The question is, was their faith being tested? Were they being prepared and equipped beyond their situation? On the other hand, was the Enemy attempting to get the men to abort their kingdom assignment as he did with Adam?

I believe the storm's assignment was to divert the disciples from entering into a region where Legion was holding the man hostage. I believe Satan was attempting to prevent Jesus from entering the area to bind Legion. I believe the storm was orchestrated by Satan's rulers of darkness—*jurisdictional* powers, sent to apprehend the mind-sets of the men and their assignment on earth as well as to prevent the deliverance of this man.

Seizing the mentality of the mind-set of the men caused them to stand in doubt, which was in opposition to the authority Jesus had already lavished onto each of them. Because they did not retrieve this kingdom authority, their inner parts stood in opposition to truth. Therefore, the opposition, which rose up on the inside, confused their mind-sets, blocked their hearts, and obstructed their internal ability to rebuke the storm at hand.

In other words, what was previously transferred on the inside to each man had not caught up to their inner parts connected to the deposit of the transfer the King of Kings had put inside each of them. As a result, there was a lapse between the time of awareness and the place of responding to their position. None of the men stood in their positions to rebuke the storm and command it to cease.

THE POWER OF COMMAND

The command that they should have given was detached from their kingdom authority that Christ had given them. Their insight into the supernatural realm was Christ, who was at the stern of the boat. Had the disciples absorbed every word that fell from the Master's lips, their power of command through faith would have positioned them to dismantle and destroy the works of Satan in the storm.

However, their fear of death overrode what had been deposited in them right when they needed it the most. Jesus had previously equipped them to stand on the authority of His name on earth as it was in heaven. In Christ, they had everything they needed to interrupt demonic systems by the power of the eternal Word, the bread of heaven Himself, Jesus, the highest appearance of God's glory for humanity.

Nonetheless, they did not respond according to the teaching of the King, which provided them the power of command over the storm and the clutches of darkness over it. Luke 10:19 says, "Behold, I have given you authority to tread on serpents and scorpions, and over all the power of the enemy, and nothing will injure you." Each man stood complete in his position under the God-Man, Christ, who was completely armed with what was necessary in order to produce kingdom rule on earth as it is in heaven.

Jesus likewise declared in Matthew 18:18, "Truly I say to you, whatever you bind on earth shall have been bound in heaven; and whatever you loose on earth shall have been loosed in heaven." This means the men on the boat stood in Jesus's full authority over the storm as do all believers; those God has called out of darkness into the light of Christ (see 1 Peter 2:9). Instead, the storm conquered their mind-set, thereby causing a premature interruption in their eternal connection to the King even while Jesus was asleep.

Panic and fear from within began to bind, blind, and restrict them, and this ultimately *prevented* them from fully understanding and perceiving the heart and **love** of Jesus toward them in the clutches of the storm. It was *love* that came forth, *rebuked* the wind, and *spoke* to the storm that rendered the storm **powerless** in its effects.

The storm could **not** stand up to the **power of Jesus** or His power or position on earth because He, the King, had the full authority of heaven. In other words, the storm was no match for the Triune Godhead that stood present on earth! As a result, the storm was unable to harm, overtake, or swallow up the men on the boat. Why was this? The disciples of Jesus stood protected by *grace, protected* by the **blood** of **Jesus** that had not been shed on Calvary's cross as of yet. Nonetheless, they were protected!

The one who knew *no* sin was on the boat with them was protecting them under His sanctified Lordship. These men had no idea Jesus has already endorsed, sanctioned, and certified the disciples to take authority and had given them the power to change the purpose of the storm and command it to cease by arrest through the *power* of *command.*

The disciples did not understand that the endorsement Jesus had lavished on them *completely* fortified and sanctioned their persons to dominate on earth as it was in heaven. As such, they could have obstructed the movement of the demonic system, which had sent the storm to swallow them up. They stood in the rule of Jesus according to Luke 10:19: "I have given you authority to trample on snakes and scorpions and to overcome all the power of the enemy; nothing will harm you."

Their provision was in the stern of the boat, but they were operating under the curse of Adam **Jesus** had come to *destroy.* The power of the King was *on* them to trample on the snake—the serpent in the garden called Satan. In other words, they were operating out of an old system, the old rule, and not the complete reign of the King. What do I mean? The men had **head** *knowledge* of Jesus being the Son of God; nevertheless, they had not had a *revelation* of His divinity, His supremacy as *King.*

I believe the same head knowledge is running rampant in the twenty-first-century church. Many of God's people are operating with the same mind-set as the men on the boat who had not tapped into the supreme place of God's divine reign or His divine function to dominate the earth out of heaven's domain. I believe there are many in the body of Christ operating through or standing with *head knowledge* of the Father who are *still* **conforming** to *this world*, which Paul instructed believers not to do (see Romans 12:2).

Now the question may be how believers can be conformed to this world when they have been saved and are functioning in the church. Simple! Because there has not been a genuine transformation, a renewing of their mind-sets (see Romans 12:2). There has to be a change! There has to be **complete** inner *transformation* in them even when they have been saved. Yes, salvation does redeem a person and secures their eternal resting place with the Father; however, the individual must work diligently to live a *lifestyle* of **righteousness** in the now.

If those who are saved do not *relinquish* old habits, that will hinder their new persons from emerging in a fresh place with God. Many in the body function out of head knowledge and are thus *deficient* because they are not operating out of new hearts.

The Holy Spirit does **not** *reveal* the mystery of the kingdom of God to the old man, which operates out of the curse. Galatians 13:3 says Christ came to free believers from the curse. How do we obtain new hearts? We do so through adoption by Christ, according to Ephesians 1:5. We must ask Jesus the Christ to become Lord of our lives. He will connect us to God.

> The Spirit you received does not make you slaves, so that you live in fear again; rather, the Spirit you received brought about your adoption to sonship. And by him we cry, "Abba, Father." The Spirit Himself bears witness with our spirit that we are children of God, and if children, then heirs—heirs of God and joint heirs with Christ, if indeed we suffer with Him, that we may also be glorified together.
>
> —Romans 8:15–17, NKJV

Christ Himself **imputes** *righteousness* unto *us* by **His Spirit** through *adoption,* whereby we cry, "Abba! Father!" God gives us righteousness through adoption whereby believers become His heirs. Sonship comes through Christ, and as such, He *lavishes* it onto those His Son *certifies* as **His**. In order to obtain new hearts, we must ask Jesus to become our Lord. Jesus took on our wrongdoing on the cross. He carried our guilt, our shame, our sin, our punishment, our death that belongs to us. He chose to transfer all of these and more onto Himself. Jesus put on Himself something you and I deserve to have as our burden. What Jesus provides believers is something they cannot earn. Thus, His righteousness is obtained only through sonship. However, we *must* receive a new, changed heart! In other words, we must ask God for new hearts.

> I will sprinkle clean water on you and make you clean
> from all your idols and everything else that has defiled
> you. I will give you a new heart and a new mind. I will
> take away your stubborn heart of stone and give you an
> obedient heart. I will put My Spirit in you and I will see
> to it that you follow My laws and keep all the commands
> I have given you.
>
> —Ezekiel 36:25–27, GNB

Many in the body of Christ have not fully converted themselves to the truth of Jesus. Yes, there may be some submission, but there is no evidence of the full conversion God is seeking. As a result, our old hearts are tainted, corrupt; they may be redeemed, but they are not surrendered to God. We may have asked Jesus to become Lord of our lives through confession, but we may not have allowed the fullness of the *regeneration* of our spirits to be converted by God's Word. Why is this? Many in the body have not permitted the renewal of spirit to take place because their confessions were not whole and complete. What do I mean? To believe in—to have faith in Christ—is one thing; *however,* to walk out what one believes in actions through *submission—surrender—*is another.

We need to be reborn through confession and possession of Christ in order to walk in the **new** *heart* that Christ provides us through our surrender. Once we accept Christ as our Savior, we have access to the spiritual domain. Access to truth comes through God's Word and prayer, which is sweet communion with the King, a connection to His heart in the eternal realm.

Through this connection in prayer, the Father bypasses our minds, which are the seats that connect us to our minds, wills, and emotions. However, God bypasses these three in order to speak His heart of truth to His children. Thus, He bypasses the mind that He may speak to our spirit man connected to His Spirit in the fellowship of truth. This is only experienced in a new heart that reveals the revelation of who God is outside time. It is through revelation that God confirms who He is to His children. He unveils His righteousness, which releases heaven downward on us through the *regeneration* of our hearts. In other words, something has to die! The old heart must die for the new heart to become engrafted onto the Father's heart through the Son. The former heart of a man cannot access the truth of God because it is operating from a forfeited place in Adam.

Therefore, because many are still walking in their old hearts, they cannot fully understand how to *seize* the *authority* **Christ** *has* provided the church. Maneuvering within the parameters of the old man causes the head to be in control and function through the flesh rather than the Spirit connected to the King.

For this reason, many cannot discern *how* or *when* to release the power of command given by our Commander, Jesus the Christ. **Head** *knowledge* does *not* distribute nor does it release the truth of who God is. That comes *only* through *revelation* by the Holy Spirit.

Likewise, transformation opens up revelation, which is retrieved when the believer has a new heart. God does not call our heads; He calls our hearts. Consequently, many in the body of Christ are operating out of the old person connected to the fall although they are acknowledging to be born again. Thus, the flesh seeks to maneuver in the "I can do it myself" syndrome.

The old man draws from the old mind-set of experiences of the flesh. Consequently, this person *reverts* to the state of death in which he or she was drawn out of. This causes a gravitational **pull** *toward* his or her former state of being, former state of events, and former state of living in unrighteousness. Thus, experiences, past habits, and so forth **breed** and **intensify** because the old man is in control.

When a person is operating by conforming to the world, this signifies to God that the rebellious nature of our ancestors is more important than righteousness. Why is this? Because a *genuine* transformation has not taken root on the inside, and there is no evidence of an authentic connection to the Spirit of Christ as the spirit, man connects to the frequency of heaven although on earth.

Rebellion stands present and walks out of the wicked heart of old because it has lost its connection to the original state of connection to the King. The old heart functions out of the place of wickedness because its connection is not properly operating through the frequency of the Spirit of Christ, which brings all truth to life.

The old heart has **not** been changed, transformed, or connected to the heartbeat, the love of God. As a result, the heart's connection is operating on the world's frequency, the host of wickedness—Satan himself. Therefore, the ear connected to this frequency hears what is old, dead, and stinking.

Adhering and responding to what is rotten, dead, and stinking makes the ears walk toward lies. This ear is controlled by what it hears, so it is **unable** to *filter* out the tones of deceptions connected to the foreign sounds it hears. The heart of old functions through deception, and in like manner, it begins to operate from, through, and out of past habits, experiences, and old nature connected to this physical world.

As a result, the head gravitates toward that same place of old because it is familiar; it recognizes no other way except truth—Jesus. He shines His light, and believers must respond to the truth of His light. Likewise, in many cases today, there is a spirit of manipulation functioning as a spirit of darkness that hovers over many of our churches. This spirits is low key and is desperate for the applause of others although it operates out of darkness and moves from place to place, impersonating truth; however, it is a replication of darkness, a counterfeit of truth in its stance.

This spirit creeps in unnoticed, masking itself under a familiar sight and sound and causing the flesh to become easily aroused. The appetite of the flesh blinds the eyes of men and dulls the scenery through the illusionary mechanics of darkness's antics seen as an amazing church, while God is placed on the back pew or even pushed out of the church.

This spirit is rapidly manifesting itself in what is known as the new age movement, which does not include God. In other words, the study of self is first; many refer to the process as "getting in touch with our highest self" or "becoming one with the universe" and so much more in which the Father is given a backseat. This controlling spirit is sneaking in subtlety and undetected by many sitting in church.

Thus, those connecting to their "higher selves" are operating in and through the posture of Satan, which they begin to emulate unbeknownst to the unguarded ears of God's people right in the church. Much like God's children when they were in exile and under Babylonian rule in 597–586 BC, the church of today is mimicking the same posture as when the prophet Jeremiah and many other prophets were calling for God's people to live outside their surrounding pagan culture.

God's children gave themselves over to the foreign sounds instead of responding to the prophet called to plant the truth in their hearts. Thus, in the church today, many emulate what is seen as truth. When a person is operating with a perverted, rebellious, wicked heart, it is backward in operation and thus *reverts* to its fallen state, which is **opposite** to the redemptive work of Christ.

The Scriptures say, "As a dog returns to its vomit, so a fool repeats his foolishness. A pig that is washed goes back to wallow in the mud" (Proverbs 26:11and 2 Peter 2:22). Returning to his or her vomit—living in the old man state of being—causes a repeated cycle of brokenness. This old mind-set, which stood broken from the place of old, can be so seducing that if drawn backward, the former state may become worse than ever. It is called sin!

Backward is the opposite of forward, the motion by which Christ split the veil during the completion of the cross and provided believers with complete access to the holy God in their newness of life in Him. The veil was torn in two, and the curse was **destroyed**, which released the hearts of the believers to become *new* in the **King**.

However, in the church today, many are operating backward in hearing, backward in thinking, and backward in practices. In the twenty-first-century church, many are hearing opposing sounds with their outer ears influenced by the world's systematic thinking powered by darkness.

Therefore, this external sound wave of backward thinking penetrates the unfiltered ear canal, which transmits the world's methods through the developmental process of the brain that people move in out of habit. The problem with hearing with an ear not connected to the truth is that it hears things different from what the spiritual ear connected to the King hears. That which is caught outside of the spiritual realm of sounds is automatically received as normal. Thus, when a sound comes from heaven, it is dismissed and perceived as strange or foreign and dulls the senses from responding to the truth. Moreover, the strange sound that flows from heaven's domain is *rejected,* and what the Father desires to release does not penetrate, neither does it take root, because it was disallowed in its truth. What we must understand is that what travels through the ear attaches itself to the brain, which assigns the heart to respond in accordance with what the ear has gathered.

If God has not surgically repaired the heart through redemption, it will not function properly. What the physical ear latches onto can be confused with eternal truth because it functions out of the old man. It hears from an old place and maneuvers through an uncircumcised heart, one that has not allowed the hand of God to reconstruct it through His Son.

So now, how or what does the ear recognize as sound? The ear gathers sound, which translates information to the brain to process about what is being heard. It processes that sound to the brain through the understanding of the immoral, wicked heart of old; the *engrafted* Word of God *cannot stick* to an **uncircumcised** *heart.* The engrafted Word of God **cannot** *penetrate* a heart that has not been changed. Jeremiah 17:9 says, "The heart is deceitful above all things, and it is exceedingly perverse and corrupt and severely, mortally sick! Who can know it [perceive, understand, be acquainted with his own heart and mind]?" Thus, because the heart is mortally sick, there has to be a *rebirth,* there has to be a *renewal* through the Word of God. The **heart** has to become **new**. God has to make the individual hear *a new sound* through the **finished** work of Jesus. The old, sinful heart of transgression must **surrender** to God and be made *new* to experience the *truth* of who God is.

To *graft* means to perform surgery on living tissue and transplant it from one part of an individual to another or from one individual to another. Through the Son, the Father circumcises the heart; the corrupt, wicked heart, which is presented before a holy God. It must have a spiritual reconstruction in order to perform or function anew. Therefore, in order to operate within God's original plan, to *respond* to that place of *new*, the Father through the Son does surgery; He circumcises the old heart and *makes* it function according to His purpose. If not, it will cause the entire body to die because of its wickedness.

He surgically *removes* the dead tissue—the old heart—and *refashions* it unto His likeness: "Let us make man in our image" (Genesis 1:26). God surgically *infuses* the new tissue to produce His will through His seed on earth. The perfect will of the Father is obtained by a new heart of *submission* to Him through the regeneration produced by the Word. The blood of Christ will then cover the engrafted Word transferred, transported, and transplanted onto the seed of Abraham.

Reading the Word of God causes the new heart to emerge, and the daily application of the Word *engrafts* the Word onto the new heart. When the Word of God grips a new heart, He injects His truth into it, and it becomes in *harmony* with the Father.

It is only through Jesus, the main body, the "tender shoot" that positions the heart, that the heart functions completely normal in Him (see Isaiah 53:2). This signifies that the new, engrafted heart will begin to operate and function in its original state of being; the place God intended the heart of His seed to function before the fall of Adam in the Garden of Eden.

This new heart is **not** synchronized to its own pace, nor does it function out of its own rhythm. The new heart maintains the beat of the Father; it moves in **agreement** *with* Him and is **harmonious** with His; it does not operate disharmoniously, nor does it stand outside the synchronization of the Father. To remain in rhythm with the Father's heart is to be in His will, which demands *agreement* in the totality of whom He is.

Standing outside of God's will causes a separation, a detachment from Him. This place of being detached—walking outside His will—*invokes* the spirit of rebellion that summons the individual to set his or her face opposite that of the King. The old heart becomes master over the person instead of God.

There is an eternal rhythm of the heavens that draws the believer to the place where God is, not where Adam was. When the spiritual ear hears this rhythmic beat calling at a distance from realm of the eternal, the ear *positions itself* to **respond** to what it hears inside the beat.

As a result, the spiritual ear is now in pursuit of that which it has heard beforehand, during the time it was inside the Father before creation. The spiritual ear seeks to respond to the place that called it forth before birth. If the beat stands outside Christ, outside the Word, he or she will become seduced backward in movement to the familiar beat it *once* heard after the fall of Adam and not before. This beat is not harmonized with the King; it stands in opposition to Him. At that point, it becomes difficult to identify and distinguish the truth between the two beats heard.

However, when the ear is rooted in Christ, it responds to the heartbeat of God, which it realizes is not foreign at all. The spiritual ear **remembers** the *eternal beat* and **responds** to *it*. That which God created out of Himself is continually *pursuing* to *feed* that craving on the inside.

We cannot fill the emptiness of what belongs to God. Because the spirit man hears a separate beat from the flesh and the flesh does not recognize what it hears, the spirit recognizes the sound and knows what the flesh does not; it *remembers* God. The natural ear responds through the appetite of the flesh, which produces corruption and death. The sound the spiritual ears hears is the eternal sound of heaven.

When the rhythm of the heart is not synchronized to the Father's through the Spirit of the Son, chances are the old man is in operation. The old heart rejects the King and all He stands for because the flesh controls it. Only the new heart can be saturated in Christ. Jesus told Nicodemus in John 3:5–7, "Most assuredly, I say to you, unless one is born of water and the Spirit, he cannot enter the kingdom of God. That which is born of the flesh is flesh, and that which is born of the Spirit is spirit. Do not marvel that I said to you, 'You must be born again!'" God's Word cleanses the sinful heart. In the clutches of the storm in Mark 4, the disciples' old hearts blocked them from comprehending that Jesus had them covered!

Jesus could have appended the storm with one word at any time; life and death submit to the King. Philippians 2:10 says, "That at the name of Jesus every knee should bow, in heaven and on earth and under the earth." Still, they did not know!

CHAPTER 5

Hijackers of the Earth

Then He arose and rebuked the wind, and said to the sea, "Peach, be
still!" And the wind ceased and there was a great calm. But He said to
them, Why are you so fearful? How is it that you have no faith.
—Mark 4:39–40, KJV

These men had seen Jesus walk in levels of authority on earth
unlike no other, and although they were with the King,
each man stood deficient within himself. Thus, they ran to
the King for help. Mark 4:39 says, "Then He arose and rebuked the wind,
and said to the sea, 'Peace, be still!' And the wind ceased and there was a
great calm."

I believe the King never screamed at the wind or the sea, but both
submitted to His command. The men were impotent; they were blind in
the midst of the storm and oblivious to the power of Christ resting on
them. For this reason, Jesus stood in the fullness of His own authority
and rebuked the wind that was seeking to destroy His disciples as these
handpicked men remained unaware of the completeness of whom they
stood before on earth. Nonetheless, a feeling of lack arose where faith
should have helped the men. In their faith, they could have done what
Jesus did not by or in their own merit but by the power of the name of
Jesus the Christ.

If the men had stood on the authority of His name through faith, they would have rebuked the wind and spoken to the sea themselves by the authority of Christ as King. Jesus had equally distributed His power, rule, and posture to the disciples, but fear rose up and faith sat down in the *reverse* order of what Jesus has just come down from the mountain teaching.

In verse 35, Jesus said, "Let us go over to the other side." The disciples heard what He said through their natural rather than their spiritual ears. Jesus did not say what would happen during their passage. The King spoke of the place they were as opposed to the place they would be; however, the men heard only where they currently were. For that reason, they did not respond to the power of what Jesus had spoken. They did not internally respond to what Jesus had already revealed to each of them. Thus, because they were ineffective in their actions, the storm **hijacked** their newfound kingdom language on earth. This kingdom language gave them the ability to decree a thing, and the thing would conform to that order. Nevertheless, they stood defeated. The storm had hijacked their minds! Thus, through relinquishing their kingdom authority, their language became distorted and inhibited because they walked through the channel of fear.

The powers of darkness energized the wind, which blew over the sea. It was not only working on the mind-set of the men but also working over the wind, which came under the powers of darkness as well and churned the sea. Wind and sea were working together; evil does not work alone. Evil transmits its power into something or someone for its evil purposes. So when the sea responded to the command of the wind, which activated the spirit of panic and fear in the disciples. **Panic** and **fear** by design had hijacked their mind-sets and made them think they were going to die due to the storm. In church pews today are countless, *faceless* demons on assignments to activate the same twin spirits of darkness that the men encountered on the boat.

Demonic spirits stand outside the scope of our physical eyes; they are assigned by Satan to hijack God's people into mind-sets of uncontrollable terror to make mockeries of them and the church. They work to sway the thoughts and motives of those in the body of Christ to believe their lies. They latch onto unguarded ears and minds of those in congregational assemblies who are unaware of their presence. John 8:44 clearly identifies

Satan as the father of lies. Satan seeks to shake the foundation of believers. Many unguarded church pews have cracks wide enough to allow serpents through to bite. In other words, many people in the body of Christ have cracks, unguarded gateways in their lives providing the serpent of darkness an entrance to slither in and inject his poisonous venom.

Unseen by the natural eye, there are many copycat spirits in the church—the spirits of jealousy, domination, and manipulation are witchcraft spirits maneuvering inconspicuously in the body. The spirits of religion, pride, carnality, power, performance, and many more have crept in the church undetected because the doors are unprotected and the unseen deception of Satan is lurking within the church.

When the walls are down and the hedge is not protected, cracks are found in its foundation, and darkness finds a foothold. Therefore, the question is, why are the walls, doors, hedges, and gates unprotected in many churches? Many of its leaders have not sanctioned or positioned the office of the prophets called of God to stand on the wall as guards. When God has ordained and fortified the prophets to speak His heart to the body of Christ, carrying the full mantle of God's authority, many are shunned and reduced to people—*flesh*, not voices of God declaring His heart.

Yes, the prophets are humans; however, if God has called them to the position, they must seek God for an understanding of His will. Prophets are spirit beings transporting God's message on earth as it is in heaven. The language of the prophet is communicated through an eternal posture, directly from the heart of God, not their own. This gift is no different from any other gift God has legislated from heaven for His purpose. Every gift must *submit* to the Father's authority and be *given back* to Him for the purpose of His will being done on earth as it is in heaven.

God distributes and positions gifts in the body of Christ as He will (see 1 Corinthians 12:11–30). When a gift is given to the head of the church according to the Fathers will, the head must not stand apprehensive or intimidated, denying what God has already sanctioned to be. Many are not in their position because their leaders walk in this spirit of skepticism that Satan has instilled in them. They themselves may have unknowingly moved into the area of witchcraft—control and denounced the prophets, the guards sent by the Father to guard His sheep.

I've posted watchmen on your walls, Jerusalem. Day and night, they keep at it, praying, calling out, and reminding God to remember. They are to give him no peace until he does what he said, until he makes Jerusalem [the church] famous as the City of Praise.

—Isaiah 62:6–7, MSB

When the guards inform their leaders of the wolves at a distance, the leaders often ignore the sound of alarm although the warning has come from the Father, not the man. When the Enemy finds an unguarded door or cracks in the foundation of the soul, he enters because he has discovered there is minimal or no evidence of the King.

But if it's by God's power that I am sending the evil spirits packing, then God's kingdom is here for sure. How in the world do you think it is possible in broad daylight to enter the house of an awake, able-bodied man and walk off with his possessions unless you tie him up first? Tie him up, though, and you can clean him out.

—Matthew 12:29, MSB

Many sit bound and in a state of confusion in the house of God because there is no or minimal evidence of the King in their hearts. Who is in the house? The house is not abounded because God's instructions were to leave. Vacating the premises was the owner's choice, **not** *God's*. The choice is up to the owner to leave his or her house (person) vacant—*void* of the Word of God or stand on *His* truth and fight the Enemy. The Word *must* be applied; this renders Satan and his deeds powerless on earth as it is in heaven.

When operating with and in the old heart, the body is caught in the war between its soul and spirit. Although people may have invited Jesus into their hearts, if theirs are old hearts, such hearts act under old motives manufactured through sin. Thus, the two worlds clash; the kingdom of heaven, which brings light and life, and the kingdom of darkness, which brings darkness and death, fight each other. Why is the church today falling prey to this hijacking of spirits? Have we forgotten the sacredness of the cross? Has the heart of the body of Christ waxed cold? (See Matthew 24:12 and Matthew 5:15).

This wick, the Holy Spirit embedded in the candle, which is the church, provides light as well as heat. Christ is the body—the casing of wax. The wick is embedded in the wax to provide light to the area it is placed in. When the wick inside a candle is lit, it *ignites* the place in which it sits down. Because of what the wick carries when it is lit, heat is generated by the fire, which is produced once it is lit. This light—the fire of God—will burn away and consume impurities the natural eyes cannot see; however, they are there.

> No one, after lighting a lamp, puts it away in a cellar nor under a basket, but on the lampstand, so that those who enter may see the light. The eye is the lamp of your body; when your eye is clear; your whole body also is full of light; but when it is bad, your body also is full of darkness.

> —Luke 11:33, NASV

Has the light of God not grown in us? Do we worship not Him? Do we stand in the minds of the Israelites, who desired to return to bondage? (See Exodus 16:3.) Is the church much like the disciples who were paralyzed by the storm? The Israelites became idolaters to satisfy their fleshly desires; they forgot that the Shepherd had delivered them from bondage. Are we different? Our redeeming Jehovah God had led them into an unoccupied land He had set aside for His children, but they chose golden images over the truth.

God brought them through deserts, pits, and droughts, through the shadow of death, to a land where no evil had dwelt, a bountiful country, yet because of their wickedness, deceit, and old hearts, they defiled the land and their God (see Jeremiah 2). Today's church is in a state of confusion much like Israel was and much like the disciples were in the storm.

The children of Israel complained before a holy God; many acted as if they were still in bondage. It mattered not to them that God had delivered them from the Egyptians. They did not care that God was grieved by their blatant disrespect for Him.

Is the church of today any different from those who wandered in the wilderness for forty years? Are we different from them, who operated unguarded by choice? Are many not walking in rebellion in their actions and hardness of their heart, recycling the same erroneous mind-sets, as did God's chosen people? The select seed of God operated through immoral, tainted, unpurified hearts that were connected to the corrupt desires of the flesh. They were a faithless, sightless, and aimless generation *unresponsive* to the things of God. Many in the church today are the same; they do not recognize the hand of the almighty God. Their hearts are as barren as was the womb of Sarah; God had to unblock that which was blocking her womb.

Has the church of Christ lost sight of the King? Do we have the perverse hearts of the people of Sodom and Gomorrah? Has there been no real change in our hearts toward the truth? Where are the ambassadors who will order kingdom affairs on earth as they are in heaven? Professing believer of the Lord Jesus Christ, will you please stand?

This is the hour of repentance. We need to grab the horns of the altar, repent, and cry out to God for new hearts. God is speaking to His people to rise up and *align* themselves with heaven's protocols, not the works of darkness. His Spirit transfers the divine order of kingdom affairs for God's people onto those called by His name. However, when they are not kingdom representatives on earth, the Father removes His hand.

God wants to send His truth to the hearts of His people for His namesake. The question is where are those with clean hands and pure hearts? (See Psalm 24:4). The Spirit of Christ desires to transfer that which is from the Father to the church. However, He cannot transfer holiness to an unholy people. Where is the new heart? Furthermore, in order to receive the transfer of the download onto the servant of God, the old heart must be destroyed. The old heart—the old man—*cannot* handle or completely grasp what the new heart will receive. Nicodemus, you must be born again! (See John 3:1–16.)

DIPLOMATIC IMMUNITY

If the heart is not renewed by being washed in God's Word, it will not be able to contain the truth. Satan sends demonic spirits to interrupt that which the Holy Spirit desires to download from the heart of God through His Word into new hearts to make Himself understood.

The download from God must find new and submissive hearts in order to allow God Himself into them. When there is **proof** of *submissiveness*, God will download the mystery of Himself through revelation by His Spirit through the eternity, not through the earth. God downloads to the spirit what the mind cannot fathom or comprehend. In this hour, God desires to make Himself known to His children. The Holy Spirit looks for *evidence* of the Father in our hearts; to receive what God desires to release into our hearts, we must have a great thirst for it and offer a coveted spot in our hearts for it to reside. The Holy Spirit must find a hunger for righteousness within us *before* the release of God (see Matthew 5:6).

The Spirit of Christ must find a heart willing to receive the heart of God. It is only through the Father that the believer in Christ Jesus is able to access kingdom authority on earth as it is in heaven. When God finds the blood of Christ in our new hearts, He raises our spirits to sit in kingdom posture with Him, and we walk with the same authority Christ showed when He was on earth; we will have diplomatic immunity only His authority can grant us. This seat permits the children of God diplomatic immunity to walk in divine realms of kingdom authority that Satan and his powers of darkness are not permitted to operate.

> And [God] raised us up together, and made us sit together
> in the heavenly places in Christ Jesus, that in the ages to
> come He might show the exceeding riches of His grace in
> His kindness toward us in Christ Jesus.
>
> —Ephesians 2:6–7, NKJV

We, God's children, sit in the heavenly realm with Christ in spirit and have kingdom authority on earth. When we speak, we are the *voice* of

Christ, our Commander in Chief (see 2 Corinthians 5:20). Our bodies are present in this physical realm; however, our spirits are seated in heavenly places with the King.

We are ambassadors of Christ, and we have full diplomatic immunity. The definition of an ambassador is "a diplomatic official of the highest rank sent by the government to represent it." So now, what is the function of the diplomat in the earth? We are under the jurisdiction of heaven and under the banner of the King! How do ambassadors of God tap into the secrets of their kingdom position? How are the laws of heaven accessible beyond the natural ear? Through the reading of God's Word, prayer, and supplication, He speaks to our spirits through the Holy Spirit, who reveals God's heart to us.

Without such connection to the Father, we would have no idea how to destroy the workings of darkness. The *Word* unlocks heaven for us and provides profound, eternal insight that trains us to *war* in the *spirit* through **prayer**. Prayer grants the believer access into spheres, realms, domains, and regions other individuals are not permitted to visit.

The Holy Spirit guides believers through prayer into chambers not seen to *overthrow* the powers of Satan. These tools carry them **beyond** the natural into the supernatural, which is where God is.

Because Christ adopts us through redemption, we are strangers to the flesh, not the spirit. We are foreign representatives in a strange land representing the King. Our bodies are in the flesh, however, and in need of management through the Scriptures for living in righteousness.

In 1 Peter 2:10–12, we read,

> [We] who once were not a people ... are now the people of God, who had not obtained mercy, but now have obtained mercy. Beloved I beg you as sojourners [aliens] and pilgrims [strangers] abstain from fleshly lust which war against the soul.

Peter thus laid the foundation for the called out of God; he told us how we are to conduct ourselves as ambassadors of God to carry out kingdom duties on earth. Those covered by the salvation of Christ are embassy officials sanctioned by heaven. They operate *in* and *through* a heavenly dimension, the domain of Christ. John 18:36 says Jesus was in the world but operated with heaven's authority.

Once believers receive the Son, they receive life. This new life endorses and certifies the believers as joint heirs with Christ Jesus and are brought into *alignment* with **God** legally according to the promise (see Romans 8:17). They become heirs of Christ, which causes their ears to have access to a heavenly language not heard on earth.

The mind-set connected to the world **cannot** comprehend or discern the heart of God because the two are so different. What is revealed to the believer's spiritual ear is downloaded into his or her spirit *connected* to the King, not to the flesh.

What the Father *reveals* through **prayer**, the church is ordered to **legislate** out of another system, the domain of this world. Thus, the decree spoken out of the heart of God in prayer must stand in complete alignment with God's rule. In Matthew 18:18, Jesus said, "Whatever you bind on earth will be bound in heaven, and whatever you loose on earth will be loosed in heaven."

The believer stands as an ambassador under covenant with Christ. The believer thus gains the authority to legislate on earth and enforce heaven's rules according to that which the Spirit of Christ mandates according to His Word. It becomes the church's *responsibility* to **legislate**, **establish**, and **enforce** the kingdom rule of *heaven* on earth by the power of God. Through God's supremacy, the believer is to endorse and to legislate according to the posture of dominion set forth in the Garden of Eden. The believer's posture on earth is not lost as Christ came to make all things new (see 2 Corinthians 5:17).

Therefore, our dominion is still in effect. Matthew 16:19 says, "I will give you the keys of the kingdom of heaven; whatever you bind on earth will be bound in heaven, and whatever you loose on earth will be loosed in heaven." Understand that when you and I are sent by the Father to bind something on earth, the thing has already been bound in heaven through dominion.

In Christ, you and I enforce that which the Father has declared unlawful on earth by the authority of heavens rule. We have the power to untie things by the power of the Word of God and the posture of prayer. As believers in Christ, we have the authorization to loose the impact of the thing that has been restricting the believer in the earth through dominion. As kingdom representatives, we are to *bind any unlawful movement* by Satan and his minions through the power and dominion of Christ Jesus.

God have provided His seed the power to untie **all** visible manifestations seen on earth and their effects. In Christ, we have diplomatic reign; we can release the Word of God, which legislates the law of heaven on earth through believers to *overturn* and *overthrow* the powers of darkness and their source. Thus, whatever effects the thing once had over the person, place, or a thing stands *destroyed* by the **power of God**.

The assignment of the Enemy is to try to get believers to abort the decrees of heaven for our lives. John 10:10 says, "The thief does not come except to steal, and to kill, and to destroy." However, Jesus said, "I have come that they may have *life*, and that they may have *it* more abundantly." Therefore, the hitchhikers, hijackers, and faceless hackers of darkness are sent by Satan to steal, kill, and destroy.

DECEPTION IN THE PEWS

Jesus came to bring life more abundantly to those who believe in Him. Therefore, the "abundant life" John 10:10 conveys to the church of the Lord Jesus is *now*. However, many who sit in pews find it difficult to accept the abundance of *life* Jesus promised us. Many shout, speak in tongues, dance, and run in performance with no trace of eternal power within.

The powers of darkness have blinded our eyes, and we seek to fulfill our fleshly desires; some of us are having affairs with Satan and his minions, placing the truth of what John 10 professes on the back burner. Satan tells us, "It's all right. You can remain ignorant. Nobody cares. All you have to do is perform and shout," and all the while, he is measuring us for our coffins, fire, and brimstone (see Revelation 21:8). We have just one foot in the kingdom; Satan has divided our minds.

Nonetheless, believers in Christ Jesus have the authority to speak to thing, and it must conform to that which the Father commanded through His servant on earth as it is in heaven. Satan has slithered in and has deceived many of God's people because of ignorance, the absences of His truth.

Satan's strategic manipulations have not changed, so do not be fooled. He is still a deceiver; he is still a manipulator, and he is still a liar. Satan assigns demonic agents to regions, churches, homes, states, counties, and so on according to his pattern of destruction deemed necessary to achieve his plan. What is his plan? Simple: to steal, kill, and destroy the people of God on earth.

His systematic approach involves manipulation; thus, he rides in on the temptation he presents to the flesh. James 1:14 says that the temptations come in through the open door of our own desires. He manipulates through the desires of the flesh and walks through open doors. Desire is not always wrong, but misplaced desire is. The desires of the flesh can present themselves as good, although darkness many have sent them as evil. This is why there is a resistance between the spirit and the flesh as flesh seeks to override the Spirit of Christ in us that says no. James 1:15 says, "When desire conceives, it gives birth to sin and when it is full-grown, brings forth death." When fleshly cravings are conceived, the result is stillborn. That which we crave outside the Father's will can and will lead to mental, physical, and spiritual death.

Choice may lead a person toward God or from God. Therefore, when a person acts impulsively on the desires of the flesh, which will open chambers of darkness leading to destruction bit by bit. Once those doors are open and the individual travels through sin, this removes and detaches the person from the presence of the almighty God. Once this *sin* has given birth, once it has taken root and has imbedded itself deep enough in the mind-set and the unchanged heart, a person will ultimately do that which has been deeply rooted and is enclosed in death. Understand the Enemy feeds the flesh sin in *small intervals*, bit by bit, until the bits become massive, the size of a mountain, before believers are made aware of what has manifested mightily in their lives as a stronghold.

This is why James 1:15 says, "When it is full-grown, brings forth death." When we dabble in darkness, this simply leads to a full-blown sentence of death of the spirit and renders us subject to eternal damnation, but it is our choice.

God leaves the choice up to the individual! Satan has not changed his course of action of deceiving the world from Eve, to Saul, and to the men in the boat. From our yesterday to our now, Satan's methodology of deceit remains the same. The counterfeit king seeks to build a kingdom greater than the kingdom of God. Satan, the manipulator, summoned his demonic forces to terrify the disciples in the boat and to snatch away their faith. This is why we have to see beyond sight the King who is with us in the storm. I think, however, that one or all the disciples stood in a moment of clarity and began recalling the countless ways Jesus had healed the sick and had raised his friend Lazarus (see John 11) from the dead; that triggered them to run toward truth. Though the effects of darkness traumatized their core, something within them knew to call on Jesus in the midst of the storm.

The Enemy sent the storm to latch onto the men and swallowing up not only the boat but also its contents. That which latched from the sea onto the mind-set of the men was, I believe, an attempt to destroy their faith, thus positioning itself to disconnect their belief system in Christ. Satan cannot discredit Jesus Christ's name or authority, so he seeks to discredit those who follow Him. Many religious rulers were skeptical of Jesus's being the prophesied King, the Messiah, and sought to kill Him. The spirit of darkness had dropped nuggets of skepticism in them. Did Satan not think Jesus had authority over the sea, the wind, and the disciples? Did Satan not know that Jesus was the Messiah and held power over life and death? Did Satan not know, or was this more about the disciples' deliverance in the midst of the storm? Perhaps the storm was more about the disciples having to come out of their fear and impotence before they could move into the next dimension in Christ.

The men ran from the storm instead of speaking to it! The deep-rooted fear they stood in caused them to be incapable although Jesus had made them capable. The storm was powerless to do what Satan wanted it to; the prince of the air thought he could prevent the possessed man from having an encounter with the King (see Mark 5:3). Satan had a plan to swallow them up at sea, but he *underestimated* the King! The same way Satan tried to deceive the men on the boat is the same way he employs against the church. The serpent still tries to steer the world to receive him as the counterfeit king through the seven cultural mountains of the earth just as he did through Babylon during the exile.

The powers of darkness maneuver through business, government, arts, entertainment, education, family, and religion right before our eyes. Many of us see only the outer appearance, the flesh, but never discern the evil spirit operating below the surface. The impersonators of darkness mislead the systems of this world as well as many in the church. Satan presents his false doctrines as truth, and many fall victim to his deception because they have not made room for God's Word in their hearts.

Because the church has fallen prey to false doctrine, many are unconscious, and the head and the body are now on a slow fall to death. Satan sends his cohorts to prowl and lurk for that unguarded ear caught in between despondency and despair and on the verge of giving up on the truth of God. His attempt is to *catch* those who are straddling the fence to dominate and manipulate their mind-sets through his doctrine of evil. Moreover, because many walk blindly in the church, they gradually begin to respond to lies through the appetite of the flesh. The corruption of Satan is creeping into the church, and God is asking where the wall watchers are. This trickery of Satan makes it hard for those outside the church to distinguish between those belonging to God and those belonging to Satan. Many in the body are not certain of their own identities in the King because their hearts are still caught between the truth of the King and the manipulation of Satan.

Think of a double-minded individual club hopping on Saturday night, throwing back shots, and then being a worship leader on Sunday morning. That is confusion at its best, and Satan loves it! Many have front-row seats for this dysfunction in the church. The world knows no other way, as Satan has blinded the eyes of humanity (see 2 Corinthians 4:4).

What the world believes and receives as normal, the body of Christ must not. We are in the world but not of it (see 2 Corinthians 10:3); we operate through another system, by another standard, God's standard. Matthew 16:19 reads, "Whatsoever we [the church] bind on earth shall be bound in heaven."

When believers understand the place God has called them to rule in, they will rise up and take dominion over it. According to the authority of His Word, believers have the right to bind up unlawful activity produced by the powers of darkness.

BINDING ILLEGAL ENTRY

Jesus said in Matthew 16:18–19,

> I also say to you that you are Peter, and upon this rock
> I will build My church; and the gates of Hades will not
> overpower it. I will give you the keys of the kingdom of
> heaven; and whatever you bind on earth shall have been
> bound in heaven, and whatever you loose on earth shall
> have been loosed in heaven.

In this passage of Scripture, Jesus was shifting in assignment and position, and for this cause, Jesus *released* the keys of kingdom authority on His disciples. Jesus declared beforehand the shifting of one realm to the next, the authority they had in Him to accesses heaven's domain. Jesus revealed how the *keys* of the kingdom were deployed to the disciples for binding, loosing, and destroying the works of Satan. **Jesus** *is* the **door** that grants believers access to the arsenal of heaven through His Word and prayer. This access, which comes from the Father, was authorized through His Son and released through His Spirit into the lives of the children of God.

This *is* the hour for the members of the body of Christ to *elevate themselves* and *stand* in the *stead of Christ* and restrict, prohibit, bind, and tie up every demonic power of darkness on earth. The righteous mandate of heaven does not permit Satan to do anything without God's permission. Therefore, it is **unlawful** for Satan to pursue any blood-washed believer without God's permission.

What believers must understand is that when a thing is bound in its actions and activity, it **must** *cease* illegal movements according to the Word of God. How is demonic activity restricted? Once the believer binds the demonic strongman by the authority of God's Word through Jesus the Christ; that which is spoken out of the mouth by the power of God's Word must cease. Understand the tongue has the power to transport life, death, blessings, or even curses. Thus, what is *spoken* can either activate dark forces or command them to cease.

It is the Word of God accompanied by faith in what God has spoken that forcefully drives out demonic spirits from dwelling in that place. The mouth of the believer activates God's Word on earth. Thus, when God's Word is *spoken* on earth, it *responds* and *destroys* the action of the works of darkness over the air. As a result, the demons' illegal activities are restricted on earth as they are in heaven: "Thy will be done on earth as it is in heaven" (Matthew 6:10). The "as it is in heaven" is present tense, which means it is already complete. In other words, what you and I *release* from the **Father** according to His Word "as it is in heaven" is brought into *alignment*, full agreement, with the Father of heaven.

Once the believer binds a thing in its current state on earth, the actions of the thing that is bound becomes *restricted* in movement and *must cease*. The dark forces of hell have already been restricted in the third heaven, so the darkness of hell cannot overpower, overrule, or overthrow whatever has already been bound and restricted in the second heaven. Thus, the believer in Christ Jesus must bring into alignment that which the Father has restricted in movement in the third and second realm of heaven, to submit to the Father's rule on earth.

Neither Christ's language nor His dominion has changed. When a church is built *firmly* on the foundation of Christ, the gates of hell will not prevail against it (see Matthew 16:18). Please hear me; the church, the body of Christ **must** operate **under** the lordship of Jesus to active God's Word on earth. Thus, Satan seeks to make believers contradict the Word rather than give voice to the truth.

Jesus does not just hand over the keys of access to the kingdom of God to anyone; He restricts thieves and robbers, those who act in their own names. God's Word spoken by believers **halts** the powers of darkness on earth. That which carries life has authority over that which carries death. Therefore, when believers make arrests through the power of God, they bind demonic activity as well as the demons themselves. Understand, the body of Christ must *first* bind the demon, *secondly*, the effects of darkness left behind must be loosed also, and Christ as King must be *released* over the person's life to fill that space because they will attempt to revisit (see Matthew 12:44). Only the blood of Jesus the Christ, the *Word* can destroy darkness.

Whatever stands in opposition to God must *submit* to the rule of Christ, the authority of the Word, and the power of prayer. Believers must stand under the eternal weight of God's glory of divine protection; but Satan will wait for an opportunity when believers are outside the will of the Father to begin his deception. However, God has given believers the authority to bind him and his works.

Jesus the Christ has already triumphantly defeated death on Calvary. The Living Word, full of grace and truth, *satisfied* the requirements of the blood sacrifice by becoming the *complete atonement* for our sins far beyond what the blood of a bull or human could do. What do I mean? By His *own* blood, **Jesus** *bridged the gap* of separation, which came through Adam, back to the arms of a loving God. He took the keys of death and life and gave His bride His power and authority to seize that, which belongs to the Father on earth. The Word of God equips you and me to stand victorious over Satan and his powers of darkness.

Satan's name in Hebrew means obstruction, opposition, or adversary. Thus, the name set over him outside of the third realm of heaven because of his rebellion describes his functions in the atmosphere and toward God's people. Satan is persistently prowling about in search of unprotected avenues to infuse his schemes of wickedness, which yield death. He wanders about in search of gates and doors that are defenseless against his wiles.

Once darkness has found a target, Satan's agents move in to steal, kill, and destroy, and they do so through the corridors of lust, pride, pornography, abandonment, anger, abuse, sex, idolatry, brokenness, and much more. Satan and his demons instill a spirit of rebellion in their victims who operate with old hearts. Daily meditation on God's Word coupled with prayer will give believers new hearts. Both are essential!

Oftentimes, when you are in the posture of prayer, the Enemy will be in pursuit of your mind. The Enemy of your soul is in hot pursuit. That is why the body of Christ must be positioned and covered under the posture prayer and the Word of God. When they are in the posture of prayer, the Enemy will attempt to bombard their mind-sets with distractions to prevent them from dwelling in the posture of sweet communion and prayer with the Father.

There has to be a washing of our souls through **repentance**, which *releases* the hand of God and the oil of God's protection while Satan is pursuing us. Therefore, while the Enemy is pursuing us, God *hides* us under the shadow of His wings even while Satan tries to distract us in the midst of prayer. The Bible says in Psalm 91:1 says, "He who dwells in the secret place of the Most High Shall abide under the shadow of the Almighty." The Spirit of Christ hides us under the shadow of the Father, when our spirits have ascended before His throne in prayer. When He hides us, He protects our wandering minds and our hearts. The Holy Spirit *covers* our eyes and *hides* our faces; He **shields** us with His divine power when we press into Him in the posture of prayer. God wants to dig into our hearts to apply the bloodstained banner of the King on us and show us that through us, His glory can be revealed on earth.

An unprotected ear, eye, or mind-set is a gate or door of access through which the powers of darkness seek to detach and separate God's people. When our doors are left open, the Enemy steps in to hitchhike, hijack, and hack into us when we are separated from the Father. The corrupt mind-set of the world is creeping into the universal church today, and many of God's people have blinders on. Satan slithers in through our conversation, which opens doors to the mind and then to the heart.

Too many are unaware of how he operates. Some worship leaders stand outside God and walk with divided minds. They open themselves to the devices of Satan right in church. They may seem to be worshipping God, and many may hear familiar sounds of worship, but they do not hear the undertones—the manipulation of Satan, who is always on the prowl for souls.

He or she is "ministering" to God's people through a wicked, perverted heart, and this allows darkness to move over the entire atmosphere of the church. This individual has now summoned evil through sound waves that he or she has unconsciously spewed out *onto* listeners. The impregnable ear connected to heaven holds the ability to **detect** *corrupt* sounds through the power of the Holy Spirit because of their connection with the Father. The sound ejected by the powers of darkness through the flesh connected to its carnal state of the old man seeks to find a landing pad to settle into for its work.

It takes people of God to *detect* the darkness seeking to penetrate their hearts. It takes representatives of Christ to protect the hedge by their prayers and destroy the serpent and his false language in the atmosphere.

The church must stand under the blood of Christ. The **Holy Spirit** will tell us there is an *unidentifiable* language over the church, and thus, those connected to the King *must* stand *under* Christ to dismantle and destroy these seducing spirits and their sound.

Satan works to detach us from God and make us walk in darkness and feel powerless to discern what has been poured onto us through the sound of darkness released in the atmosphere. Therefore, he attempts produces a conflict, a war within the soul because the spirit is trying to resist the language released, but the carnal man desires to grab hold of it as truth, because there has been no real change on the inside.

The heart of the leader has not been completely transformed. We must understand that God is not glorified in the midst of this confusion. Many in this new, age church have been convinced by Satan that to be righteous and holy is for the old church and that righteousness is not a requirement for leading worship. These spirits try to make us double-minded and seek the things that satisfy the appetite of the flesh, things that draw us away from the presence of God, not toward Him. The wickedness of Satan tries to convince the double-minded person that, to "shake it fast," sip on XO Imperial Courvoisier, listen to deceptive music of pimps, prostitution, killing, and women being called out of their names, but nonetheless stand before the assembly of the upright on Sunday mornings to "lead" in "worship."

Satan has perverted the hearts of many through his deception in the house of God and through worship leaders, doorkeepers, and preachers who are not on guard. Many may in fact assume that worship is truly worship, but the question is worship of whom?

However, I say that those actions produced are in fact "worship"; however, the question is worship of whom? Many in the body of Christ stand in the posture of being lovers of themselves rather than lovers of God; thus, many worship *idols* and *objects* and call it genuine truth. The worship of truth is a *pure sacrificial offering unto the Father.* Those who drink too much, sleep with their boyfriends or girlfriends, batter their spouses, or do drugs and then stand before God's people to release worship are deceiving themselves and others. This does not please God. John 4:24 tells us believers that we must worship Him in spirit and in truth. However, when we serve two masters, the worship we offer flows *out* of the chambers of **hell** through the clutches of Satan (see Matthew 6:24).

This makes a mockery of God, and God is not to be mocked. Galatians 6:7 reads, "Do not be deceived, God is not mocked; for whatever a man sows, this he will also reap." For a short time, I grew up on a farm, and we fed our pigs slop. I can still remember the bucket in which Bootsie placed the slop for the pigs to eat. This was my worst task; slop stinks! The stench produced by old, rotten, stinking food was horrible, but the pigs ate it! They loved it! This is the same rotten, stinking form of "worship," released in many of our churches today. This form of ungodly "worship," is produced out of darkness through people leading worship while still serving under the clutches of Satan.

> But understand this, that in the last days will come (set in) perilous times of great stress *and* trouble [hard to deal with and hard to bear]. For people will be lovers of self *and* [utterly] self-centered, lovers of money *and* aroused by an inordinate [greedy] desire for wealth, proud *and* arrogant *and* contemptuous boasters. They will be abusive (blasphemous, scoffing), disobedient to parents, ungrateful, unholy *and* profane. [They will be] without natural [human] affection (callous and inhuman), relentless (admitting of no truce or appeasement); [they will be] slanderers (false accusers, troublemakers), intemperate *and* loose in morals *and* conduct, uncontrolled *and* fierce, haters of good. [They will be] treacherous [betrayers], rash, [and] inflated with self-conceit. [They will be] lovers of sensual pleasures *and* vain amusements more than *and* rather than lovers of God. For [although] they hold a form of piety (true religion), they deny *and* reject *and* are strangers to the power of it [their conduct belies the genuineness of their profession]. Avoid [all] such people [turn away from them]. For among them are those who worm their way into homes and captivate silly *and* weak-natured *and* spiritually dwarfed women, loaded down with [the burden of their] sins [and easily] swayed *and* led

away by various evil desires *and* seductive impulses. [These weak women will listen to anybody who will teach them]; they are forever inquiring *and* getting information, but are never able to arrive at a recognition *and* knowledge of the Truth.

—2 Timothy 3:1–7, MSB

Those with divided hearts can offer the Father only slop even though they call it worship. When they are divided in the heart, which is released in sound before the Father is indicative of the foul stench of slop the pigs eat. Not only are these persons seeking to offer it before the Father as pure worship; this is what darkness seek to infuse into other people's hearts. They offer God sloppy seconds and expect Him to provide them with His best. The divided mind produces a wicked heart that yields to Satan's seducing temptations. They do not understand the damage they commit by their false witness.

Repent and turn back to God! The subtle serpent is slithering into the church and masquerading as truth. Where are the wall watchers? Spirits in a bottle, pills in a jar, pornographic films, sex, envy, pride, addictions, and other evils have hijacked many of God's people. Right in the church, many need a *divine* touch from the King to be delivered. When the seat of emotions is deceived, the soul is in turmoil and is confused because it is **not** connected to Jesus the Christ, it is caught between the world of truth and the world of lies.

Jesus said in Matthew 7:21, "Not everyone who says to Me, 'Lord, Lord' shall enter the kingdom of heaven, but he who does the will of my Father." It is not the will of the Father for His children to walk in division of the soul and the spirit. He desires that His children *continually* "walk in the Spirit that you and I will not fulfill the lust of our flesh" (Galatians 5:16).

Many of today's leader of the church place unidentifiable ministers of music, worship leaders, doorkeepers, and leaders over the assembly of God's people without discovering by the Spirit if they are walking in and though Christ. Is there a match for the King found on the inside of them?

Satan tries to seduce the ear gate through sound by ushering demonic sounds into the atmosphere. The sounds heard by unguarded ears seem pleasing, but confusion enters, rests, and begins to erect walls of resistance and rebellion as it *responds* to what is hears.

Equally, many will attempt to reject the demonic sounds heard but can have difficulty doing so because there is the division within their souls that resists. Therefore, while the spirit in the divided heart resists and rejects truth, the divided soul begins to unintentionally **chase** after the sound or identity of that demon directed through worship, and an ear not connect to the King will not know it.

God is saying to the church that those called by His name cannot serve spirits in a bottle, strippers on a pole, pornography on the Internet, sexual addictions, and other cravings of the flesh over Him. **God is holy** and **must** be honored as such! God says you cannot love Satan and Him at the same time. Through deception, Satan calls the body of Christ to fall backward in posture from the place where the King **has** *redeemed* us. This is the hour of *urgency* for the body of Christ; is it serving the right master?

HEDGE KEEPERS, KEEP WATCH

The subtle spirit of carnality creeps into the church well dressed, polished, poised, popular, and disguised as truth. Many are sightless when it comes to spotting Satan's tactics. This spirit seeks to hijack the unguarded minds of believers in the church because the hedge has large openings and stands vulnerable to the attacks of Satan (see Ezekiel 22:30). The hedges around the church have been unprotected.

God spoke through the prophet Ezekiel of His chosen people, the Israelites, and God speaks to the church today. God selected not only Jews but also Gentiles through His Son, so we have been adopted and included under the umbrella of righteousness by the blood of Christ. God wants His people to stand on the wall to guard His sheep before breaches appear. Nevertheless, *where* are the guards of the church? Why haven't they risen to His call? Christ has already made the exchange of death for life so believers can keep watch.

Many believers charge their leaders with being intercessors, guards, counselors, and so on. I believe the Father has assigned a select people to stand guard over His sheep. The charge of the leaders set over the church is to keep watch over every soul under their care as the Father watches over His children (see Hebrews 13:17). Moreover, these leaders are not the only ambassadors sent by the Father to guard the hedge and govern earthly affairs according to the principles of the kingdom. For us to govern earthly affairs through a kingdom mind-set, we must undergo a spiritual awakening so the Word can do its work through us.

The Enemy attempts to transfer the world's system onto the church and brainwash its members with his counterfeit teachings and false doctrines. He seeks those with "itching ears" (2 Timothy 4:3) and draws them into his darkness through their lusts.

Many stand outside truth because they have been deceived; they will fall by the wayside because there has been no one to guard them against the wiles of Satan. Satan seeks to inject his doctrine into the church to make it appear as truth, yet it is false in its position and posture. He wants the church to appear shameful, disfigured, and worldly. Satan is watching for matches for himself in the pews; that is what we have to guard against.

Again, where are the watchmen? "Creation waits expectantly and yearns earnestly for God's sons to be made known" (Romans 8:19). The earth is waiting for the manifestation of the sons of God to stand in posture of their sonship, which will reveal the Father on earth. However, the sons of God **cannot** speak the heart of God if they walk with Satan and produce death and call it light.

Satan does not mind when your heart and mind are divided because he understands you will **not** be able to change a thing pertaining to the laws of God. Satan would prefer "Double minded man unstable in all [their] ways" (James 1:8).

You are either a servant of Satan or a servant of God; you cannot serve both! The world must be able to see Christ in you to distinguish between you and the world. However, many neglect the call to watch; they have dismissive attitudes and affirm with their mouths the deception deposited in their hearts that to watch is not their job but the pastor's.

This is a deception of the Enemy who hijacks the mind-sets of the hedge keepers called to keep watch over God's people. Rejecting this position *is* to *reject* the *Father*, thereby rejecting who He is.

Likewise, many will reject the vessel God has custom built the assignment for. *Woe* be to the person rejecting the King. We—Jews and Gentiles—belong to God. God chose the children of Israel as His people, but they rejected Him and sought after foreign gods instead of the true, living God. They began to worship idols and reject the Sabbath Day, which God set aside for His people as a holy day signifying that the believer belongs to Him. Is the church today any different?

Israel's hedge was unprotected, allowing the spirit of rebellion to slither in through the worship of falsehood rather than truth. Today in the church, the Enemy slides in through the sound of soothing music that in reality has darkness in the background. To the unguarded ear, this is soothing, but it is still poisonous venom. The mind, will, and emotions *revert* to the place of *old* and the flesh revels in its pleasures because the gates have become desensitized to the Spirit and the hedge keepers are too preoccupied to destroy the sounds of darkness.

Many are too preoccupied, too involved in ministry to keep watch. Because the hedges are not protected, perversion creeps in unnoticed. God sent Ezekiel to declare His Word over Jerusalem, a nation He found perverse, deceitful, wicked, and depraved. God told Ezekiel to prophesy to the children of Israel of forthcoming punishment because their actions were found unacceptable in His sight. God's children were rebellious in their hearts as if they were their own people and not a chosen generation belonging to God. God told Ezekiel (22:8–10) to tell the people,

> You show no respect for my sacred places and treat the Sabbath Just like any other day. Some of your own people tell lies, so that other will put to death. Therefore, of you eat meat sacrificed to idols at local shrines, and other never stops doing vulgar things. Men have sex with their father's wife or with women who are having their monthly [menstrual cycles], or with someone else's wife. Some men even sleep with their own daughter-in-law or half-sister.

Could God be saying the same about the body of Christ today? God told Ezekiel (22:3–4) to tell the people, "The city sheds blood in her own midst that her time may come and she makes idols within herself to defile herself." What God was saying to the people was that His people had murdered so many and had defiled themselves because they worshipped something or someone **over** Him. The Lord was saying, "I the Lord shall deal with you for your disrespect, unfaithful acts of disloyalty toward El Shaddai, The Lord God Almighty, I delivered you from your state of bondage, I delivered from where you were to where you are, nonetheless, you choose to remain in bondage." God said, "You are guilty of the murders and are defiled by idols you made, and so your day is coming, your time is up!"

Is this same mind-set slithering into the church of Christ today? God said to His people, "Can your heart endure, or can your hands remain strong, in the days when I shall deal with you? I the Lord, have spoken and will do it" (Ezekiel 22:14). Why was God going to deal harshly with His children? In Ezekiel 22:18, we read, "Son of man, the house of Israel has become to Me scum and wasted matter." God said (v. 19), "Therefore thus says the Lord God: Because you have all become scum and waste matter, Behold, therefore, I will gather you O Israel into the midst of Jerusalem."

God's own people "Her priest have done violence to My law and have profaned My holy things. They have made no distinction between the sacred and the secular, neither have they taught the people the difference between the unclean and the clean and have hid their eyes from My Sabbaths and I am profaned among them" (Ezekiel 22:26, NIV). God is prophesying the same to the doubled-minded state of the church today as He did yesterday. The powers of darkness have not changed their methodical attacks on God's people. Satan is still maneuvering through the corridors of his own deception in the same way today. He has positioned his dark forces to deliberately manipulate the saints of today, those called of God just as he did when the first Adam forfeited his position in the Garden of Eden. God said,

> The people of the land have used oppressions, committed robbery, mistreated the poor and needy, wrongfully oppress strangers. So I sought for a man among them

who would make a wall, and stand in the gap before Me
on behalf of the land, that I should not destroy it' but I
found no one.

—Ezekiel 22:29–31, NKJV

God seeks those after His own heart who will form a wall, stand in the gap, and set a perimeter around His church. The Holy Spirit is *looking* for *hearts* He can *trust* with the assignment of God on earth. The Father desires to download His revelation into the bellies of believers to command states, countries, regions, nations, and the church itself to walk in righteousness for His name's sake. God is calling for His body to stand on the wall for righteousness' sake, but He told Ezekiel He had found not one. God required (and **still** does require) those in His body to stand in the gap as intercessors for His people.

God desires those with changed hearts to seek Him through His Son and call down heaven's mandate on earth. Satan tries to make those who guard the hedge become preoccupied with earthly matters. Thus, he attempts to keep many working on being busy in any areas of ministry other than what the Father certified those persons to work in. Satan shifts the focus off the thing God has assigned them to do, and this lets the Enemy slither in undetected in the house of God.

ANOINTED TO DESTROY

God anointed His body on earth to "heal sickness and to cast out demons" (Mark 3:15). Someone connected to the King must stand on the wall and keep watch to destroy the powers of darkness. When the hedge is vulnerable, wolves creep in. Someone in the church has to *sense* the danger or the wolves will cause separation, division, and revolt against the leadership of the house.

The volatile presence of danger is **never** *revealed* to the five senses of men; however, the Holy Spirit does indeed reveal it. He is the one who will cause you to become sensitive to the Father and the darkness at hand.

It is only through the Spirit of Christ that we can become aware of the intruder at hand. This is why the watcher must **always** keep watch even when he or she is not in church. The sheep of God will scatter while the watcher is **asleep** or **busy doing** something different and leaving the sheep defenseless against Satan's wiles. God is still calling the intercessors to watch the wall. Ye chosen seed of Abraham *rise up* and take dominion *over* the earth. Rise up and make up the hedge, stand on the wall, stand in the realm of the spirit, and hear God because you are *anointed* to destroy evil!

It is through sweet communion with God and the Spirit of Christ that we believers gain access to the heart of God. When we are aligned with the Father in sweet communion, He downloads His plan to our new hearts that seek His face. It is when we are in *harmony* with the Spirit of Christ that the Father will unlock our spiritual eyes to recognize the workings of the Enemy. God will provide us with *strategic, precise* passageways through the spirit realm to dismantle and destroy the powers of darkness. God downloads strategies not to our flesh but to our spirits when they are connected to His. Understand that God does not download these strategies to the flesh because the flesh is carnal and manipulative at best and often, it is in a state of confusion. God downloads His plan to the spirit that is connected to His Spirit. Only the Spirit of Christ can *license* the *redeemed* to move into heavenly places and unlock the mystery of the gospel, which holds the *keys* to the kingdom and allows us to destroy the powers of darkness. We, the church, are anointed to destroy because we are God's ambassadors and have the ability to draw out the Enemy, expose his tactics and destroy them by the power of the Word.

Where are the wall watchers? Rise up! Wall watchers are elevated and carried away into heaven, where they are agents of God, who grants them the spiritual eyes they need to watch over His sheep. This realm of heaven is for the pure in heart, for those to whom God gives the keys to destroy the workings of Satan on earth. Psalm 24:3–4 says, "Who may go up on the mountain of the Lord? Who may stand in his holy Temple? Only those with clean hands and pure hearts, who have not worshiped idols, who have not made promises in the name of a false god."(NCV).

Wall watchers rise up! Stand! Take your post and watch! Wall watchers are to protect the gates of the city. Wall watchers are called to guard, having their radar elevated and connect to heaven's gates, where the heart of God is giving them profound instructions to destroy Satan's works. God amplifies believers' ears to hear *beyond* the physical. When the watchers' ears are *intensified*, the sound of wolves can be heard **prior** to any visible sightings of the predator. The Word of God is the *only* protection over every entryway of the city and keeps the Enemy from overthrowing it because someone left the gate open. In this hour, the body of Christ must stand under the authority of the Word of God, stand in holiness, and be set apart for the use of His kingdom.

We must observe the holiness of God if we want to destroy the witches and warlocks in the church. We must be in complete alignment with God and be a holy people belonging to God alone. Holiness is on the inside; it exudes *outward*. Holiness is not a matter of how we dress but of what *seeps* out of our pores—is it life or death? The body must renounce the flesh and forsake the lusts of the eyes and the pride of life in order to walk in the stead of Christ.

Where are the pure in heart of the church? Are we headed backward to the Babylonian system because we have forgotten God? The Israelites allowed sin into their hearts and minds when they began to follow dark spirits and listen to dark sounds. Their gates were unguarded, and they could not distinguish between God and foreign gods while they were in Babylon. Many gave into the cravings of the flesh and began to follow wickedness and perversion. Many chose to follow Satan and forsake the true God, who is a jealous God. Moses said in Deuteronomy 4:24, "For the Lord your God is a consuming fire, a jealous God." God will not take a backseat to anyone or anything, anywhere or anytime.

The new heart chases after the King. This is what the Father desires. Once we have surrendered our beings to the Father, His consuming fire will *purge* us of everything that does not reflect Him. God said in Deuteronomy 4:25,

> When you beget children and grandchildren and have grown old in the land, and act corruptly and make a carved image in the form of anything, and do evil in the sight of the Lord you God to provoke Him to anger.

A generation with wickedness in its heart has arisen. Many choose to rebel against the God who delivered them in favor of what makes them feel good now. Many decided to worship idols when Moses was the leader, and that *same* spirit of rebellion is in evidence in the church today. *Where is the reverence for God?* Many still walk in rebellion, disrespect, and wickedness as their ancestors did. In Ezekiel 20:12, God told Ezekiel to tell the people, "Moreover I [God] gave the children of Israel His Sabbath, to be a sign between them and Me that they might know that I am the Lord who sanctifies them." Nevertheless, God's own people rejected Him. The covenant of the Sabbath is not something observed only outwardly; it is an inward sign we are set apart from the world and belong to God.

The church is still called to sanctification, but has it lost sight of what the Father has called to be sacred? In Genesis 2:1–3, we read about the establishment of the Lord's Day. Contrary to the belief systems of the modern church, God still requires His people to rest in Him, in truth. God said in Isaiah 58:13–14 that when the church of Christ stood in observance of this holy day, the people have delighted themselves in Him.

Jesus said, "Do not think that I have come to do away with or undo the Law or the Prophets; I have come not to do away with or undo but to complete and fulfill them" (Matthew 5:17). Sanctification has not ceased, nor has the holiness of the Sabbath or of God's people. We are still God's chosen people called to honor the Lord's Day through the fulfillment of Christ. It is not just about attending church on Sunday; it is also about *consecration.* Jesus alone consecrates believers by washing their hearts through His Word. When His Word is planted in us, it *washes* our sin-sick souls, and prayer and fasting keep the flesh at bay and help believers to be embedded firmly under the banner of the King.

Jesus anoints us to destroy the powers of darkness. We **cannot** be divided within ourselves; that breeds only confusion and giving into lusts. When the devices of Satan go undetected, the church of Christ suffers storms just as the disciples did in the boat (see Mark 4:37–41). Satan still manipulates people by appealing to their flesh, their rebellious natures, their lusts, and their greed. The rebellion in the hearts of the children of Israel brought about their captivity by a government ruled by demonic systems for over seventy years. That mind-set of captivity through the spirit of Babylon is still lurking and plotting in the atmosphere today. The prince of the air governs the structural systems of this world and is the god of the depraved mind-set; 2 Corinthians 4:4 tells us, "The god of this age has blinded the minds of unbelievers, so that they cannot see the light of the gospel that displays the glory of Christ, who is the image of God."

Many in the body of Christ have accepted Jesus as Lord but are still operating in the old mind-set of bondage; they are slaves governed by the god of this age. Many are held captive by their own mental chains much as the disciples in the storm were. Their constricting, deaf, paralyzed spirits manipulate them today, even in the church. Many in the body are convinced that the diagnoses of doctors are true while Jesus, whom they confess, *is* completed. What do I mean? When the dark spirits over deaf hit the body, the crippled spirit, or the heart, many respond to the reports of the doctor rather than to the reports of the Lord. Many choose to walk in the diagnosis of darkness even after Jesus *completed* His work *on* the *cross* and gave us divine healing through His blood. Isaiah 53:5 says, "But He *was* wounded for our transgressions, *He was* bruised for our iniquities; the chastisement for our peace *was* upon Him, And by His stripes we are healed." Jesus took on every disease, every infirmity, and every demonic condition so that His body—you and me—would not have to endure it.

In faith, you and I must respond to the diagnoses by affirming the truth of the Scriptures in our now, "by His strips we are healed (see Isaiah 53:1). Whose message will you believe? The men believed the report of the sea, not of the Word that Jesus spoke to them, as they were crossing over to the other side. They stood in the presence of the Word made flesh and heard His teachings, but they did not draw from the well of recollection from within of this extraordinary Jesus and did not destroy the darkness on the sea.

However, Jesus remained panic free while His men stood in panic and fear, occupying a mind-set of death, opening an entryway, and allowing themselves to be held captive by darkness. On the cusp of their next transformation into another dimension in Jesus, the truth of their inward beings was exposed. This storm had hijacked their inner peace and had revealed what they were lacking on the inside. These men might have walked with Jesus, but they had not fully stepped into their next dimension on the inside. Right on the cusp of it, they were hijacked! Jesus could have spoken **one** *word* to the storm from the chambers where He lay at the lower level of the boat. However, King Jesus said not one word; He was fast asleep. Jesus released a door of *opportunity* to allow those on deck to *speak* to the storm for *themselves*. Nonetheless, each man stood incapacitated because of his inner inadequacies. The men were inadequate and ineffective; they were unable to respond to the truth. Instead, they answered the deposit of dysfunctional fear, unable to respond to the hijacking of the emotional turmoil *planted* from within by the effects of the storm. Their lack of faith kept them from responding to the kingdom posture of Jesus.

They were deficient because their mind-sets had been hijacked, which showed their inner incompleteness when the storm began to attack them. Their hijacked mental capacity choked in the heat of battle, which gave way to their inability to respond cognitively to chaos in the core of the storm, which had them bound.

The hijacking of the storm obstructed their mind-sets, blocking the cerebral cortex of its memory and the ability to decipher the intent of the storm at hand. Because the cerebral cortex "plays a key role in memory, attention, perceptual awareness, thought, language and consciousness," the hijacking tactics of darkness were being utilized here.

The frontal lobe involves consciousness as well as decision-making as it pertains to the function of the human brain. Therefore, when taking into account the functionality of the brain and the role of the Enemy over the storm, you can see the power Satan has over our minds if we let him deposit his darkness. The aggressiveness of the storm summoned the spirit of panic and of fear in the cerebral cortexes of the disciples, hijacking their memory, attention, perceptual awareness, thoughts, and language of consciousness at the precise time. The hostility of the storm confused the disciples. They had no idea that the spirit the storm had was in the wind and canopied onto the sea. It was causing such violence that the same spirit shifted their attention to death and snatched their faith. Jesus rebuked them and destroyed the storm, something they could have done if they had held onto their faith.

Mark 4:39 indicates they had to wake Jesus up: "'Rabbi—Teacher! Do you not care that we are perishing?' Jesus arose and rebuked the wind, and said to the sea, 'Peace, be still!'" The Bible says the wind *ceased* and there was a great calm. Jesus asked the disciples, "Why are you so fearful? How is it that you have no faith?" In other words, you are anointed to destroy!

CHAPTER 6

Faceless Hackers on Earth

Now before the Feast of the Passover, when Jesus knew that His hour had come
that He should depart from this world to the Father, having loved His own who
were in the word, He love them to the end. And supper being ended, the devil
having already put it into the heart of Judas Iscariot, Simon's son, to betray Him.
John 13:1–2, NKJV

*S*atan sends faceless hitchhikers, hijackers, and even hackers
to rattle the cages of shackled minds and tattered hearts and
devise "wicked schemes, feet that are quick to rush into evil"
(see Proverbs 6:16–18). These agents of Satan operate through demonic
channels to steal, kill, and destroy those called by His name.

The hackers of darkness try to break into our minds, wills, and
emotions. They try to breach our defenses to weaken, subvert, and destroy
our faith, position, and posture in the kingdom; they try to circumvent
our firewalls and gain access to us.

Thus, these hackers gain access when "firewalls"—entry points—have
not been well executed, implemented, and continually monitored on a
daily basis to prevent unauthorized users from obtaining information
illegally through what is commonly known as *hacking*.

An inspection of the systems is necessity and regularly advised in
order to prevent any intrusion of faceless hackers. Nevertheless, hackers are

experienced in their craft and highly motivated to breach even the highest level of security. They maliciously corrupt downloaded data and salvage any deleted information that would serve their evil purposes. Oftentimes, they are inconspicuous, invisible, not physically seen with the naked eye; however, you know they are there. Nevertheless, the indicators of their presence are not hidden, so in the realm of the spirit, the Father provides spiritual sight of their presence. These demonic, faceless hackers manifest in the outer appearance of a person, so the ability to perceive them is by revelation from the Father alone.

Much like this certified forensic examiner sent to detect any corruption or illegal activity within the system, the Father does the same within the walls church. He sends forth spiritual intelligence officers—*prayer* warriors who war in the spirit realm on the behalf of the kingdom of God. These spiritual intelligence officers are given spiritual eyes to see and hear in dominions that others may not have permission or authority to do so.

It is in the wickedness of sin found deep within the sinful heart of the old man; the double-minded man found straddling the fence, that you are likely find the surveillance of the demonic hacker. The place of double mindedness is what the Enemy seeks to draw out and use for his deception. The heart must be made anew, thereby forcing out the evil—the darkness of Satan and his cohorts.

By nature, seeds of darkness plant themselves in intervals according to the particular assignments they are governed by. Bit by bit, firm roots develop and establish themselves to *persistently* and *invasively* intertwine and latch onto that which is close to the path of darkness.

Hackers hack! They seek open gateways into the presence of others, invading their spaces in an attempt to completely annihilate them from the inside out. Immediately upon discovery that something has invaded your space or place in time, you must destroy it. If this darkness is not dismantled and destroyed by the power of God's Word, it will multiply, reproduce, and untimely consume that which it has attached itself to.

Matthew 5:24 tells us of how Satan manipulates the hearts of those caught between two realms and serving two masters. There are misleading, perverse, faceless hackers roaming about beyond what natural eyes can see. Nevertheless, the blood-washed children of the King have dominion over these foul spirits through the supremacy of Christ. King quickens our mortal bodies and commands that which is imputed to come *alive* and be *activated* to stand up in His stead (see Romans 8:11).

This alone gives believers access to the things of heaven and the authority heaven carries to rule on earth. The body of Christ thus has authority over demonic activity no matter weight of the storms we encounter. Through Christ's victory on the cross, we must understand it is illegal for the powers of darkness to have dominion over the earth or God's people. The light of Christ in us should never contend with any traces of the flesh, the nature we once lived in. "Old things pass away" (2 Corinthians 5:17). However, many in the body of Christ seek to hold on to the old man while operating within the new man. As a result, there is a friction, a power struggle going on between the two systems.

Light and darkness cannot cohabitate. The flesh desires total control over the spirit, while the new nature connected to the King is calling forth our imputed dominion to rise up and rule. In other words, the cravings of flesh are yearnings for the mind, will, and emotions to dominate the spirit. Why is it this way? The spirit of a new man is *connected* to the new creation *inside the King*. Thus, the struggle is in play!

When those in Christ Jesus are still dabbling in and with old patterns of behavior produced by the flesh, they become confused about lust and truth. The carnal flesh seeks to dominate the mind-set and commands the *will to yield* and the *emotions to be led* by base appetites. When we yield to the flesh and abandon our connections to the King, we yield to passions connected to rebellion. Light and dark are on opposite ends of the spectrum; we must draw a line in the sand between the flesh and the spirit because we cannot walk in both. The flesh must be crucified! "But I say, walk and live [habitually] in the [Holy] Spirit [responsive to and controlled and guided by the Spirit]; then you will certainly not gratify the cravings and desires of the flesh (of human nature without God)" (Galatians 5:16).

Understand that dark spirits cross our thresholds solely by permission. Recognize that we can allow darkness into our lives, and equally so, the Father may grant permission for a time such as He did with Job. God does not tempt us; however, He may allow a season of temptation to trim that which we are drawn to. There is always an expiration date attached to God's permission for the testing of our faith; this is the rule of heaven. Therefore, the powers of darkness cannot harm that which belongs to God (see Psalm 121:7). God will allow the friction to come in for purging and pruning of the diseased, dead, and useless waste that His light may shine on earth. James 1:2–3 says of the believer,

> Consider it all joy, my brethren, when you encounter various trials, knowing that the testing of your faith produces endurance. And let endurance have its perfect result, so that you may be perfect and complete, lacking in nothing.

In John 13:1, before Satan entered Judas to betray the Savior, we read, "Just before the Passover Feast, Jesus knew that the time had come to leave this world to go to the Father." Thus, before Passover and after the foot-washing ceremony, there was a shift in the Spirit realm taking place beyond sight. Because Jesus was the God-Man on earth, His eternal omnipotence outweighed His human side sent to redeem us.

Jesus was connected to eternity though He stood on earth! So the Bible says just before the Feast of Passover, Jesus said that His hour had come (see John 13:1). In other words, just before Passover, heaven touched down and met up with the God-Man, the Theanthropos who had come from eternity yet stood on earth. The Bible says that just before the feast, Jesus knew within Himself that His hour had come and His completion of His earthly assignment for which He was custom-built for was imminent. Jesus was not referring to a literal moment in time; He was referring to a shift, a transition, an appointed space in time set by the chambers of eternality with His name on it.

No one else could stand in this change; no one else could stand in this hour, no one could stand in His stead. No one else could do this except the King. Therefore, Jesus sensed His hour had come. The hour in which He stood on the cusp of was a set season in which the human mind-set could not comprehend beyond sight that which Jesus was about to step into.

While on the cusp of the Feast of Unleavened Bread, the Passover, Luke 22:2–3 says the "chief priest and the teacher of the law were looking for some way to get rid of Jesus, for they were afraid of the people. Then Satan entered Judas, called Iscariot, one of the Twelve. And Judas went to the chief priests and the officers of the temple guard and discussed with them how he might betray Jesus." John 13:2 says, "And supper being ended, the devil having already put into the heart of Judas Iscariot, Simon's son, to betray Him." Luke says that Satan *plotted* against Jesus, while John's version speaks of Satan's influencing Judas. John explained the nature of Satan's name and his character and thus provided the believer insight into the powers of darkness that entered Judas and shifted his posture as a slanderer, a liar, which is the meaning of the word *devil*. According to Wikipedia, the word *devil* means slander or accuser. Devil is from the Greek word *diábolos* (pronounced dee-ab'-al-os) which means slanderer or false accuser. The word *diábolos* also means the liar or the one who commits perjury; it comes from the verb *diabálló*, pronounced dee-ab-al'-lo, which means to bring charge, to throw in, to generate confusion, to divide, or to make someone fall.

Later Christian writers used the word *diábolos* as "the liar who speaks against God." Although John conveyed the character of Satan as the Devil, they were the same but operating differently. Nonetheless, there was a time when the Devil could not move onto the person of Judas. When Jesus said His hour was at hand, the transition began.

None of the disciples knew that shortly, they would no longer need to apply the blood of a sacrificial offering between the two cherubs on the altar for the sins of many. The disciples did not fully understand Jesus was to be the ultimate sacrifice, beyond what any of them could have imagined. The fullness of the Lamb stood in their sight, but they could not see beyond their sight.

The word *Pesach* means "passover," which refers to Biblical facts of "G-d" (God) to pass over the houses of the Jews when the death angle was passing over. Exodus 12:7 says, "And they shall take of the blood, and strike it on the two side posts and on the upper door post of the houses, wherein they shall eat it." What I found interesting is that when the Jewish nation referred to the Father in writing, it was as "G-d" or "L-rd." The reason was that there was a cultural, reverential fear of misrepresenting His name on earth. Thus, "G-d" was written with respect, not in a derogatory or defamatory manner. To diminish His holiness carried a penalty of its own. Therefore, in Jewish custom, it was customary not to fully write out His name the way you and I would write it. Thus, the name *pesach* (*pay*-sahch, with a "ch"), which comes from the Hebrew root word *Pei-Samekh-Cheit*, means to pass through, to pass over, to exempt, or to spare. This word refers to the time God passed over the houses of the Jews during the time when the firstborn of Egypt were smitten (see Exodus 11, 12).

Pesach also denotes the deliverance of the children of Israel from Egyptian bondage. John 13 provides insight to the beginning stages of Jesus drawing near for the preparation of Him becoming the Passover Lamb in His announcement that His hour had come. God was setting the stage. Understand that the Father had not changed the necessity of blood sacrifice for the atonement of sin. Instead, God allowed a greater sacrifice to "pass over" from one place to the next beyond the grave.

The blood of Christ was applied once and is *perpetual*. His blood is an *everlasting*, continuing, complete sacrifice and does not need to be reapplied. His blood does not have to be smeared or poured out on the altar yearly for forgiveness of sin. God provided an ultimate settlement in the heavens, which was *executed*—**made** *complete*—before time, outside of time. What God did was change—reverse the order—as it is in heaven. God did not abolish it altogether; He just *shifted* it. He just **settled** its yearly assignment *permanently*. The word *dispensation* means a divine ordering of the affairs of the world; a dispensing with, doing away with, or doing without something; a certain order, system, arrangement, or management.

God did not change His mind about the sacrificial offering to be given to Him; He just changed the order of the transfer in which it was to be fulfilled. The consecrated offering provided unto God by Aaron as priest and his sons was not perpetual.

The sacrifice had to be of a *greater worth* and of far *more value* to provide something permanent with everlasting results for the sins of humanity. There had to be a greater sacrifice provided by the grace of a loving God. Something *greater* was coming!

What am I saying? The sacrifice Aaron and his son were to offer to God for sins were many, continual sacrifices made yearly. However, this was not everlasting. What the blood of Jesus did was enter for the last time with His own blood an *uninterrupted flow* of love for the sins of humanity. The blood of Christ is continual in what it did and is doing—providing a way back to God.

The all-knowing God wrapped inside the Godhead called the Trinity provided an everlasting atonement to bridge the gap back between Himself and His creation called man. God bridged the gap of reconciliation from that fallen place of Adam when the serpent beguiled Eve, which detached humanity from God's original place for His children and removed our hearts far off. The enticement of the serpent partially interrupted the divine, vertical alignment between God and man, and as a result, God provided a way back to His loving arm, which was snatched away with one bite.

Thus, you and I were in times past a far-removed people now brought back into alignment with and relationship with God through the blood of Jesus. What His blood did was provide an excellent place of redemption beyond what any other sacrifice has made in times past.

Aaron and his sons could be ushered to the door only because they were the only ones qualified by God to enter on behalf of the people. Only the high priest could enter the Holy of Holies (see Leviticus 16:3–11), but Jesus qualified His children to be in His presence and bring their sacrificial offering of themselves in truth to a holy God.

Psalm 24:4 says, "He who has clean hands and hearts are pure, who do not worship idols and never tell lies." Although they had permission to enter into the place where God was hovering in a cloud, they could not proceed without having clean hands and pure hearts. Moreover, the Bible says, "Who has not lifted up his soul to an idol." They had to come in clean before a holy God. Where are the clean hands? Where is the church? Understand that when the priest went in to sacrifice unto God, it was for himself as well as for the people. Their hearts had to be clean that God might accept the sacrifice.

Thus, Aaron and his sons were ushered to the door of the tabernacle, but those who ushered them there could not go in. No one could enter except the sacred men called by God to stand before His presence. The greatness of God changed the order. In Christ's hour that was to come, His blood would supersede any other sacrifice ever offered before the mercy seat.

Exodus 30:10 says, "And Aaron shall make atonement upon it horns once a year with the blood of the sin offering of atonement; once a year he shall make atonement for it throughout your generations it is most holy to the Lord." However, God made a shift in the order of atonement for the sins of his children; **Jesus** *covered* the mercy seat.

The God of Abraham, Isaac, and Jacob was *predestined* to cover the mercy seat as an unblemished lamb *qualified* to preserve life in the blood. Jesus is the perpetual, sweet-smelling sacrifice smeared on the mercy seat for redemption's sake. His blood was smeared between the two cherubs with their wings covering the offering as the two cherubs turned toward the seat where God's Son, Jesus the Christ blood would *permanently cover.* He was and is the living sacrifice made for you and me, and I believe many in the church today have **forgotten** about the *mercy seat* in its **position of power.** We see Jesus, but we do not see what He has done for the sins of humanity. Jesus did something **not one** of us **deserved.** However, the King did it anyway!

THE MERCY SEAT

The aroma of the King of Kings went back to God and sat beside the Father, *elevating* the seed of Abraham to sit beside Him in His reign as Commander in Chief of the armies of God (see Ephesians 2:6). Christ sat on the seat for the last time. That's grace! God switched the order! There was and is no longer a need to spread the sacrificial blood on the doorpost. Jesus the Christ is the divine exchange for the mercy of God.

In Leviticus 16, the priest who went in to make a sacrifice on the Day of Atonement for the sins of the people, went in and came back out. In other words, the priest went in solely to offer something *temporary* for something that would be permanent after the fulfillment of Christ.

What the priest went into the holiest place to offer was not everlasting nor was it perpetual. This means the effects of the sacrifice did not last a lifetime; it was not perpetually moving on our behalf. "The bodies of those animals whose blood is brought into the sanctuary [holy place] by the high priest for sin, are burned outside the camp" (Hebrews 13:11–12). The high priest of the Old Testament brought the blood into the holy place with him, and he went back out. He and the blood he brought in with him had to go through a qualifying process to be acceptable before entering. Hebrews 9:7 says, "But only the high priest entered the inner room, and that only once a year, and never without blood, which he offered for himself and for the sins the people had committed in ignorance." Thus, when the priest went in, he had something to offer God. Has this changed when you and I make an offering? Are we void of sacrifice, worship, praise, prayer, and thanksgiving? Are we entering empty handed? Are our hearts filled with so much junk that there is **no room for God** to *enter* us?

The purification process requires purified blood, but the blood of the believer is contaminated without Christ. Not one of us could have done what Christ did. Jesus the King reversed the order! *Jesus* became the **atonement**—the *bridge* between God and humanity. Christ came to remove and redeem the effects of the Garden of Eden. When Christ defeated death, the grave, and the cross, that which was put in place of the old stood null and void while Jesus was on the cusp of His hour. In other words, the cross was set before Him (see Philippians 2:8). He won absolute victory over death. After He finished the work of the cross, He ascended and sat down in completion (see Hebrews 10:12). Confucius could not do that. Buddha could not do that. Brahma could not do that. **Only Jesus** could. Acts 2:34 says of the prophetic fulfillment through the line of David, "For David did not ascend into the heaven, but he says himself; the Lord said to my Lord [Jesus], 'Sit at My right hand, till I make Your enemies Your footstool.'" The Bible says God said to Jesus, "Sit!" signifying the completion of His work. No one and nothing can reverse, reject, or remove His victory through His shed blood.

Philippians 2:10 says, "That at the name of Jesus every knee should bow, of those in heaven, and of those on earth, and of those under the earth," which denotes His omnipotence as King. Jesus Himself is God's mercy seat; He is the propitiation, the atoning sacrifice for our sin. *Mercy*— Jesus sat down in **completion**, in the fullness of the Godhead and became God's mercy on the seat in exchange for us. That's grace! We are seated with Him in a heavenly place because His blood afforded us something our flesh could not!

Thus, His blood **escorts** the spirit of the believer into a heavenly place where the Father is, which provides us access to God. Grace called Jesus did that! The divine protocol of heaven *exchanged* the order of sacrificial offering to supersede—go beyond—time to complete the work He was sent to do. Exodus 24:8 says, "Moses then took the blood, sprinkled it on the people and said, 'This is the blood of the covenant that the LORD has made with you in accordance with all these words.'" However, Jesus told His disciples during the Last Supper that His hour was at hand: "In the same way, after the supper He took the cup, saying, 'This cup is the new covenant in my blood, which is poured out for you'" (Luke 22:20, NIV). Jesus was saying His covenant was everlasting.

Isaiah 53:7 foretold of Jesus the Christ: "He was oppressed and He was afflicted, Yet He opened not His mouth; He was led as a lamb to the slaughter, and as a sheep before its shearers is silent, so He opened not His mouth." Isaiah's declaration foretold of a mightier One than the one of whom he as the prophet was speaking. He was and is the chosen One of the Father. He is the Theanthropos, the God-Man who stood on earth sent to redeem humanity. This Jesus is the one of whom the prophet Isaiah was speaking—the eternal King, the Savior of the world.

Again, Isaiah announced Jesus as "a *tender* plant and as a shoot out of dry ground" (Isaiah 53:2). This revealed His rejection, majesty, and unattractive appearance through the eyes of society; this Jesus could not have been the *One.* Nevertheless, Isaiah announced the awesomeness of the King who manifested as a seed in the womb of Mary. His blood became for us the mercy of God on the seat. Isaiah 53:11 says of Jesus, "He shall see the labor of His soul, and be satisfied. By His knowledge My righteous Servant shall justify many, For He shall bear their iniquities" thus Jesus was and is still God's complete, best *new order,* His never-ending atonement.

Many saw only Jesus's physical body; they did not see His supremacy, His spiritual nature that draws us to Him. The disciples did not completely understand that He was the fullness of the Godhead in the flesh. Equally so, how would they have known He would be the Passover Lamb as the mercy of God on the seat? They did not know that the blood of the King would *communicate* an *eternal language* beyond that of an unblemished goat or any other sacrificial offering the priest was positioned to offer for the sins of many.

They did not know that the blood of our Savior endlessly communicates a language on our behalf that you and I cannot. They did not know the Father of our Lord had *already* provided *in* Himself an exceedingly **greater** *sacrifice* before the host of heaven. Did not the disciples hear of John's testimony in John 1:29, "The next day John saw Jesus coming toward him, and said, "Behold! The Lamb of God who takes away the sin of the world", would ultimately be for us what we could not be for ourselves. They did not know!

Jesus the Christ, an *uninterrupted*, continuing flow of sweet communion, sweet-smelling aroma, took our place of death to bring life. When the Father sees us, He sees His Son, and for this reason, we have *complete* access to God through a sacrifice that went beyond any sacrifice we could have ever made. The disciples, the naysayers, the religious leaders, and the government officials did not know Jesus was the Christ. Many stood nearby; others stood far off, and still others sat at His feet and still did not know Jesus the Christ was God's *mercy* on the seat. They could not see Jesus being prophetically positioned in His divine assignment. Many could not ascertain the supremacy of Christ or the totality of His person as the Son of God except His Spirit *unlock* the *revelation* of who His is.

God revealed His fullness to us through His Son. God is a mystery, and the only way to unlock the fullness of who He is, is through Jesus. Jesus alone sends His Sprit that carries to the believer the revelation of the *Trinity*. There must be a divine connection beyond the soul before the reveal of God is released. Many could not fully understand the announcement of God, our Creator when He released the reveal of heaven through Isaiah the prophet. Because of Adam's sin, Jesus had to come and grab hold of deaths grip, and its sting of separation between God and His children on earth. Adams sin brought with it the consequences of death which Jesus the Christ came to nullify its sting through the cross. The sting of death lost its grip when Christ *sat* down in completion at the right hand of the Father (see Hebrews 10:12). Many could not see that Jesus was the all-encompassing, complete fullness of the Godhead in front of their physical eyes. I believe no one could have known completely that Jesus was fully God and fully Man who had been *chosen* to "give His life as a ransom for many" (Matthew 20:28).

Not recognizing the exchange Christ made to refute sin will cause hearts to be disconnected from the Father. The governmental and religious leaders seeking to kill Jesus did not know the truth of the King because they were spiritually void of the truth (see 1 Corinthians 2:14). They did not know or care who Jesus was; they considered Him a disruption who had caused a social and political uproar; *He shook up time* and caused the eyes of many to see a disturbance, an imbalance, a demonic rule being *overturned.*

Even those in the crowd who had called Him Messiah turned on Him! None of them could have foreseen that their plot to crucify Jesus was part of the Father's plan. Jesus disrupted earthly patterns by calling heaven down to earth with His presence. Even Jews did not recognize Him. His own people followed the darkness within the hearts of the rulers demanding that the King be crucified.

Jesus did not justify His supremacy to Pilate, but Pilate, standing in his own idiotic thinking, thought that because he was a Roman official, he had the final rule over Jesus's life. In John 19:11, Jesus said to Pilate, "You would have no authority over Me, unless it had been given you from above; for this reason he who delivered Me to you has the greater sin." Pilate became afraid and wanted to release Jesus, but the Jews, the leaders, and the naysayers wanted Him killed. Nonetheless, Jesus stood for His supremacy!

What Jesus was saying to the Roman officials, the Jews, and those standing around was that God had the final say. The thing they sought to do could never be done except by the fulfillment of Scripture. In this twofold ruling, Jesus pointed out the greater sin was done through the betrayal of Him being delivered to be crucified, and their unbelief in Him, and still, they did not know! When Jesus rose in His righteousness, the leaders became confused, as His appearance did not match the title that had been given Him from the Father. In their eyes, the legitimacy of the claim of the disciples did not line up with the King that stood before them.

They believed that Jesus was nothing compared to those holding important and distinguished titles and offices. In the eyes of the Roman government, which governed the land and the province, Jesus was nothing. They did not pay Jesus much attention until He began to shake up things. When the rumbling of what Jesus had done on earth began to be felt beyond words, they took notice. In other words, when Jesus began to shake up and challenge the systems of this world, I believe they started fearing Jesus, who stood before them.

Because Jesus began to stir up imbalance in the system, the leaders of Rome could not ignore Him or His followers. They could not physically see or sense His divinity, but Jesus was challenging the systems of this world, and because of the accuracy of what proceeded out of His mouth, they accused him of blasphemy.

Since Satan had influenced their hearts and confused their minds, they could not comprehend Jesus's eternal language or His eternal posture, which caused the rulers to become uneasy. Satan had blinded their eyes, blocked their ears, and constricted their thoughts from recognizing and hearing the truth of who He was. Thus, what Jesus spoke went immediately to hardened hearts. Truth had no place to stick! Jesus spoke from an everlasting posture while being physically present on earth, and because the leaders were not functioning through heaven, the dialect of Jesus was muffled and *unable* to penetrate their hardened hearts.

YEAST RISES FROM THE INSIDE

Inner signals of darkness caused a thick wall of separation that hardened their inner parts. Thus, what Jesus spoke in John 6:35–51, settling Himself as the *Word*—bread of life—King Jesus, landed on uncultivated soil in their hearts. As a result, that which He spoke produced barrenness in their convictions that truth could not penetrate. Thus, the eternal language of Jesus had nothing to stick to in them. Darkness kept those signals of truth from entering. Rejection of the truth caused the darkness of their hearts to increase just as dough does when yeast is added to it during the bread-making process. The process of making bread requires many ingredients, especially yeast. In the beginning phase of the bread-creation process, ingredients are gathered, mixed, and kneaded. What does yeast do?

> Yeast develops and reproduce by producing buds on mother cells that subsequently enlarge and produce more buds. During growth, carbohydrates in the dough are metabolized to carbon dioxide that is trapped in the dough in the form of bubbles.

Now the kneading process is an essential component; it mixes the ingredients adding, strength to the final product, and its importance becomes apparent in the mixing of flour with water. During the kneading process, the dough itself must be pulled, pressed, stretched, and beaten for its optimal use. After this process of kneading, the dough is formed, covered, and set aside in order to rise.

Satan, the prince of the power of the air, methodically operates in a manner as yeast does. *Rebellion* is the ingredient Satan searches for in the heart that is not connected to the King. Once the rebellion is located, Satan tugs on the other parts of sin deposited that are fashioned inconspicuously in the old heart. Hence, Satan draws on these hidden sin deposits, which are needed to make the final product come to life in the end. It is within this base component of hate found within the hearts of the scribes, Pharisees, and the Roman officials that the process of deception began.

Satan knows he cannot obtain the final product by skipping ingredients or dismissing any steps. Satan understands the entire process is needed to become the final product of ruin. Once all the ingredients are gathered, darkness activates the kneading process of controlling the heart. Once the base ingredient is found—rebellion—other traces of sin are pulled on, tugged at, pressed on, and stretched out of the individual and placed aside to rise and to increase to maximize the effects for his plan of darkness. This is how methodical Satan and his powers of darkness are.

Once Satan observes those acts of rebellion in a heart that has not been created anew and following the King, Satan *pulls* on that **old man** for his own dark purpose. Just as dough must be set aside for rising, Satan does the same. He calls his dark host to wait for the appointed time of approval—the process of kneading and rising—for his plan to become activated. It is here that we see the ingredients kneaded together in the hearts of the religious leaders.

Jesus told His disciples in Matthew 16:6, "Take heed and beware of the leaven of the Pharisees and the Sadducees." However, the disciples did not understand the metaphor. The Pharisees and Sadducees were always testing and resisting Jesus because of the level of authority with which He spoke. Many sought for a sign from heaven of evidence that He was in fact the Messiah (see Matthew 16:1–4). However, Jesus considered them members of a wicked, adulterous generation seeking signs and wonders of who He was instead of believing by faith that He had been, and was, and was to come. Jesus told His disciples to beware of yeast—sin—swelling and consuming the insides of those needing a sign of who He was.

As their doctrine is of Satan, which produces death mentally, physically, and spiritually and separation between God and men, it is death nonetheless. Leaven is the equivalent of sin, and for this reason, during the Feast of Unleavened Bread; Israel was to leave out yeast. Nevertheless, yeast spread on the inside of government and religious officials, infecting their hearts not submitted to Christ. They were spiritually impure for resisting God's kingdom through Jesus. Denying Christ was denying the Father (see 1 John 2:23). Sin, like yeast, took over their insides and began spreading and increasing.

There are about 80,000 species of organisms in the kingdom Fungi, and these include yeasts. The religious leaders who resisted Christ as King were operating under demonic influences—a *fungus* swelling in their hearts and consuming it. If the Enemy can keep people in a crippled state, which will damage their minds and make them resist change. As 1 Corinthians 15:33 tells us, "Do not be deceived; Evil company corrupts good habits." These men of stature depicted here in the text fed off one another through the influences of the demonic powers of the air that caused evil to swell internally. Jesus's words fell to the ground because the power of darkness had such a strong hold on their minds that truth could not enter. When Satan shut down their circuits on the inside, their flesh could respond only to the lies they lived in; the truth had no way to enter their minds. They could not comprehend the truth; the Word of God was perceived as encrypted, hidden, and therefore was rejected.

The definition of encryption is "to change (information) from one form to another to hide it meaning." This is the mechanism of Satan and his powers of darkness. He is manipulating, calculating, and precise in his mission to meticulously influence ear gates, eye gates, and he seeks to control the senses of the flesh so that the truth finds no landing place in an individual. Satan disguises his lies by swaying thoughts of influencing darkness and scheming through encryption to hide the truth of his darkness.

Thus, the sound coming into the ears of the hearer is interrupted—disturbed—by Satan, the master deceiver himself. Equally, through his patters of disruption, Satan, the hitchhiker, hijacker, and hacker, began dulling the hearts and ears of the government. He sought to turn their hearts against Jesus, but he did not know that God had switched the order! The judgment passed against Jesus was an act of treason that condemned Him to death through crucifixion, and still they did not know.

The truth of the King's reigning authority of His eternal person began to speak for itself a language never heard before. Jesus's authority began to supersede the power of the government, the posture of lies, and the opposition of Satan all at once. In their foolishness, they assumed this crucifixion would be the end of Jesus. The Roman Empire plotted the "death" of Jesus, but it was actually Satan plotting against them to kill man's dominion on earth and the plan of redemption. In 1 Corinthians 2:8, we read, "None of the rulers of this age knew; for had they known, they would not have crucified the Lord of glory." None of them saw God's Son about to be offered for humanity's offenses.

Jesus told Lazarus to come forth from his grave, according to (see John 11:43), which showed them that Jesus has power *over* sickness and death. Jesus, the **new** sacrificial order and His atoning blood was complete before and after His crucifixion. **Jesus** *covered* the old sacrifice, which was set over our ancestors that God might dwell in the midst of His people. The mercy seat was a foreshadowing of what was to come through Christ's shed blood. Still, they did not know!

That which the priest offered on the altar to God for the sins of the people was the blood of goats, bullocks et cetera, as the permanent sacrifice was on its way. This offering of old stood as the foreshadowing of Christ offering His blood as a *perpetual* sacrificial atonement that carried redemption. Jesus the Christ did this for the sins of humanity.

> Then the cloud covered the tabernacle of meeting, and the glory of the Lord filled the tabernacle. And Moses was not able to enter the tabernacle of meeting, because the cloud rested above it, and the glory of the Lord filled the tabernacle. Whenever the cloud was taken up from above the tabernacle, the children of Israel would go onward in all their journeys. But if the cloud was not taken up, then they did not journey till the day that it was taken up. For

the cloud of the Lord was above the tabernacle by day,
and fire was over it by night, in the sight of all the house
of Israel, throughout all their journeys.

—Exodus 40:34–38, NKJV

God's presence is no longer filling the tent of the tabernacle; however, through the atoning death, burial, and resurrection of His Son, it now is the *indwelling* presence of the Holy Spirit for God's people. The blood, the power, and the presence of the King is now *smeared* on the hearts of God's children instead of the doorposts.

God Himself *switched* the *order* from the place where He *was* to the place where He *is* through Christ. The old mercy seat released that which was temporary, a place where God was. Jesus, God's mercy on the seat *shifted* the believer to the place where He is. Christ became the Passover Lamb, which made atonement through His own blood, which eternally speaks on our behalf before the Father. Jesus is the complete endorsement of heaven in the Old Testament and is the same promise John announced on His "Preparation Day" in John 19:14.

EXCHANGING THE OLD

Thus, it is here we see the old order of sacrifice transitioning from promise to promise of the majesty of the King. The brilliance of His glory seen in heaven and witnessed out of three persons was making His brilliant appearance on earth to restore the fallen position of man. Jesus the Christ was the *final* Passover Lamb, *full* of *grace* and *truth*, and He *completed* the work of the cross for us. The new order of the Passover Lamb, Jesus the Christ, is the blood on the doorpost of the hearts of men who believe. Thus, our only way to the Father is through the Son. John 14:6 says, "Jesus said to him, I am the way, the truth, and the life: no man cometh unto the Father, but by me." So now, in between time and the cusp of eternity, Jesus began demonstrating His ability to clean a person from the inside out, causing a disturbance on earth.

Nonetheless, Jesus stayed the course, and when His hour came, Jesus imparted more of Himself into His disciples. In John 13:5, Jesus washed the feet of the disciples. I believe Jesus was *consecrating* each of them with the washing of the complete manifestation of the Word of God, Himself. Jesus was transmitting light into His disciples when He washed their feet. I believe that Jesus was pouring Himself into the disciples as He washed their feet. Though Jesus knew darkness was nearby in Judas Iscariot, He remained faithful to His eternal position. In John 13:10, Jesus said, "He who is bathed needs only to wash *his* feet, but is completely clean; and you are clean, but not all of you." In John 13:18, Jesus said, "I do not speak concerning all of you. I know whom I have chosen, but who eat bread with Me has lifted up his heel against Me." Jesus began to set the stage for His dimensional shift: "Now I tell you before it comes, that when it does come to pass, you may believe that I am He. Most assuredly, I say to you, he who receives whomever I send receives Me; and he who receives Me receives Him who sent Me" (John 13:19–20). Jesus began to download the new order of heaven into those in the room and declared their privilege of receiving the message of the gospel. Thus, He foretold of His ascension back to heaven to His eternal position beside His Father.

Equally, Jesus forewarned about, dismantled, and destroyed the belief systems of this world, thereby interrupting the patterns of the Roman government, which suggested He was not the Christ. He disrupted the processes of thinking outside the systems of the earth and overthrew the foundation of Satan and his demonic systems, which had no idea He was and is God's mercy on the seat.

Jesus said to His disciples, "very truly I tell you, whoever accepts anyone I send accepts me; and whoever accepts me accepts the one who sent me" (John 13:20). John 10:30 says, "'I and the Father are one.'" Wrapped inside the Trinity rests the Triune Godhead—the Father, the Son, and the Holy Spirit. You cannot receive the Father and not receive the Son or His Spirit, as they are three in one.

By receiving Him, you recognize the *truth* that He and His Father are one. At the very moment Jesus revealed the kingdom order to His disciples, John 13:21 says, "He was troubled in spirit, and testified and said, 'Most assuredly, I say to you, one of you will betray Me.'" At that moment, Jesus bore witness with His own eternal order of heaven and testified with the Godhead—the Father, Himself, and His Spirit.

Jesus testified about the rumblings He was experiencing within. Something was supernaturally about to happen! When He testified about the rumblings of His own body, He was revealing that He was experiencing on the inside that His time of shifting was drawing near. The all-knowing King announced, "One of you will betray me" (John 13:21). Jesus shared heaven among those in the room with Him, and the men became perplexed and confused; they wondered which one would betray Jesus (see John 13:21).

John 13:22 says, "The disciples looked at on another" and I believe each man began inspecting the heart of the other wondering which one among them would betray the King. Who would do such a thing to Jesus? Jesus the King, who healed the sick and the blind and raised the dead—who would betray the Messiah sent to earth to redeem humanity. Who would betray our Lord? That was the thought running through the minds of each man at Jesus's announcement.

Perhaps they were perplexed and confused because they could not comprehend what Jesus had said. Alternatively, perhaps they concluded within themselves that surely no one in their circle could do such a thing to our Lord. They thought Jesus called us, the elite, to Himself. Thus, none of us could possibly commit such an act. Or could we? I believe this would be the echoing thought in the room. All the while, the powers of darkness were awaiting divine approval to set in motion that which was *already* the order of the heavens. I believe Satan thought his manipulation of Judas would be beneficial and serve his purpose rather than that of the Father. Satan knew Jesus was the Son of the Living God.

Matthew 4:1–11 says that when "Jesus had been in the wilderness for forty days," Satan came to tempt Him, already knowing who He was. "Then Jesus was led up by the Spirit into the wilderness to be tempted by the devil. And when He had fasted forty days and forty nights, afterward He was hungry." Understand that the Spirit *led* Jesus. Matthew 4:2–3 says, "After fasting forty days and forty nights, He was hungry. The tempter came to him and said, 'If you are the Son of God, tell these stones to become bread.'" Even then, Satan tried to get Jesus to forfeit His assignment just as he had tried to do with Adam. Thus, Satan knew the authority of the King; nevertheless, he attempted to overthrow Jesus right in the midst of Him being released from His earthly assignment for the church. Satan attempted to distract Jesus in the midst of His release in an attempt to have Jesus abort His position as King. I believe he also tried to have Jesus step outside of the will of His Father to make a mockery of Him, the Father, and the church.

Nevertheless, Satan could not see the fullness of the Godhead being released in the wilderness. Because Jesus fasted and positioned Himself in the Spirit, He was able to stand in His earthly posture and see Satan's manipulations. Jesus was open, which allowed His next dimensional shift and authority to flow through Him, which caused His pure robe of flesh to sit down and eternity to take a seat next to the King because of His obedience to His Father in the wilderness.

Thus, darkness could not touch Him except by permission of Jesus's deciding to abort and forsake the purpose for which He came. Hence, Satan told Jesus in Matthew 4:3, "If You are the Son of God, command that theses stones become bread." Do you not know that Jesus was *led* to be tempted?

There was a *purpose* for His temptation. Satan could not tempt Jesus without having the permission of the Father during His time on the mountain. Jesus was fully equipped with the power to withstand the serpent. Satan did not realize this was the eternal plan of God for the fulfillment of Scriptures. Isaiah 55:11 tells us, "So will My Word be which goes forth from My mouth; It will not return to Me empty, Without accomplishing what I desire, And without succeeding in the matter for which I sent it." The fulfillment of Scriptures is in John 1:14: "And the Word became flesh and dwelt among us, and we beheld His glory, the glory as of the only begotten of the Father, full of grace and truth." This means Jesus preexisted and became to us that which He already *was* in heaven. God spoke Jesus out of Himself into time.

A word spoken out of eternity shifted Jesus to stand inside what God has already spoken into existence. There is a law on earth for flesh to dwell by design, and God will not refute His law. In other words, God will not change the rule of His own decree. What God decreed out of Himself, He will remain faithful to. Thus, when He said, "Let there be …" whatever the "be" was came into existence. The Trinity was wrapped up in a robe of flesh, which gave Him permission to dwell where only flesh and blood were permitted to dwell according to heaven's law. Jesus the Christ, being qualified of the Godhead, solidified Himself through the completion of the cross eternally as God's mercy on the seat. Even the counterfeit king could never duplicate what Christ did through the shedding of His blood on the cross. Christ exchanged His life for you and me. The redemptive power of the blood of Christ solidified the seed of Abram whereby you and I have access to the throne of grace (see Hebrews 4:16). To solidify a thing means to make secure or firmly fixed, or to unite it firmly.

The redemptive power of the sacrificial, atoning blood of Christ firmly fixed our redemption as God's people. His blood unites us *firmly* in Him, thereby binding us through a covenant in His position as King. He secures, surrounds, and firmly positions us under His glorious weight of excellence for His name's sake. Christ, the chief cornerstone, secured our adoption as children of God Most High through His blood at Calvary. He exchanged out the old order of redemption by preparing Himself to be the new order of redemption. The power of His blood *permanently* broke the barriers, the walls of separation that stood between God and us erected during the fall in the garden.

Eternity came into alignment through Christ and stood harmoniously in the Godhead, thereby reversing the curse of Adam when He exchanged His life for ours. Christ did that! What the Father spoke from heaven stood present on earth unblemished and full of grace, mercy, and truth. The Word—*Christ* was declared by the Father to be on earth, and that which He was sent to do could not return to God empty, null, and void because He was *beforehand* certified as King.

Thus, according to God's own principle, whatever He has spoken was already complete in heaven (see Isaiah 55:11). *In other words, time in the earth must catch up with eternity, where it is complete first.* Not one of God's words can fall to the ground and die if He sends them out! When God speaks, His Word is final.

As a child of God in Christ, **you** *activate His Word* on earth through dominion, which allows you to execute His Word effectively through convent. His children must activate his Word on earth. *His Word will not morph into something that it has not been assigned to do or become.* For instance, to use God's Word in speaking death over a person is not of God but of Satan; it is witchcraft, manipulation. When God calls a person, place, or thing what it is, it is what He says it is! To take the Word of God and manipulate it to say what we choose for it to say or mean is the manipulation of a witch. Therefore, God spoke forth Jesus as a seed on earth, and as such, Jesus could not remain a seed, nor could He remain on earth forever.

There is always a seedtime and a harvest time. Ecclesiastes 3 tells us, "To everything there is a season." This was always a set time for the complete manifestation of Christ's assignment as the Passover Lamb. What the prince of the powers of the air did not know is that the Passover Lamb was moving into *divine alignment* according to that which was spoken out of the Godhead. According to Isaiah 55:11, the will of God had to be accomplished.

For that to happen, Christ had to dwell among us in flesh and blood. Satan did not know Jesus's earthly body was not the end of His rule on earth; he did not see that the Theanthropos exceeded time. Did he not know Jesus was complete in the fullness of the Godhead even while on earth? Did Satan not understand that according to Luke 9:22, "The Son of Man must suffer many things and be rejected by the elders, the chief priests and the teachers of the law, and he must be killed and on the third day be raised to life"?

Nevertheless, as His time neared to experience the cross, Jesus remained faithful to His assignment. Because Jesus stood in His humanity, the cross that was set before Him in joy through His supremacy, He endured the cross (see Hebrews 12:2).

What was that joy? The complete work of bridging the gap—bringing God's people back into alignment through His atoning blood. Although the divine part of Jesus remained faithful, His soul connected to His humanity became sorrowful, and while He was praying, He asked the Father, "Let this cup pass from Me" (Matthew 26:39).

Jesus, baring our heavy, *stinking, retched, filthy* cup—*sin*, began to experience the cost of taking on the filthiness of humanity, but because of love, He stayed the course. And even though Jesus was about to experience suffering for the sake of humanity, the eternity in Him said in the same breath, "*Nevertheless*, not as I will, but as You will." Although the agony of the cross was set before Him and was discomforting to His robe of flesh,

He understood the *importance* of *remaining* steadfast in completing *His divine assignment* on earth.

Jesus understood that the fulfillment of Scripture was at hand. "Do you think that I cannot now pray to My father, and He will provide Me with more than twelve legions of angels? How then could the Scriptures be fulfilled, that it must happen thus?" (Matthew 26:53–54). He understood the cost of reconciliation. *Grace* did that!

John 13:22 says the men were perplexed by the revelation of heaven spoken through the eternal realm, proceeding out of the belly of the eternal One called the Christ. The disciples did not completely understand that Jesus had come to *exchange* the old order for the new. Zechariah spoke of Jesus being betrayed for thirty pieces of silver; the exchange for the life of the King was valued at a low cost because the rulers chose not accept that Jesus was the Christ (see Zechariah 11:13). Christ has this foreknowledge when He and His disciples were with the thief of darkness, Satan, awaiting his appointed time to enter Judas.

WITH THE THIEF OF DARKNESS

The men themselves did not fully understand His hour was at hand even at His announcement of His betrayal. The disciples did not fully understand what was about to happen to Jesus on earth, and they equally lacked full understanding of Jesus's authority over time and seasons in heaven and on earth, but Jesus knew His hour had come.

The fullness of the Trinity stood complete on the inside of Christ; thus, Jesus was not ever divided, not ever separated or detached from His Father, His eternal position, or His High Priest posture. In other words, *Jesus was concealed to be revealed.* Moreover, in time, the revelation of the fullness of the Godhead stood present before every eye.

There is always a seedtime and a harvest time in all things. There was always a Kairos—*right* time for the revealing of the King. Jesus often announced, "For I have come down from heaven not to do my will but to do the will of him who sent me," demonstrating that Jesus and the Father are One (see John 6:38 and many other Scriptures).

In other words, although Jesus was wrapped in the fullness of the Godhead, He still submitted to His Father's will. So Jesus said in John 13:1 that His hour, His time to become the final sin offering for humanity, had come. The King acknowledged His time of transition before those He loved because of love. Thus, He indicated His willingness to *yield* to the timing of His Father on earth as it is in heaven.

Jesus did not allow time or people to interrupt the plan of God or the mission for which He had come to earth. Therefore, Jesus said His hour had come. When He said that, He was referring to the climatic events in the days to come that led to His death on earth.

When He announced His hour, he was not speaking of time as in a twenty-four-hour day; He was speaking of an eternal, appointed time spoken out of His eternal posture. He was speaking of an eternal place *prepared* for within the time slot designated on earth for His death, burial, and the completion of His eternal resurrection on earth. His hour would begin His glorification process according to John 12:23.

By definition, *to glorify* is to elevate to celestial glory or to cause to be better than the actual condition. Thus, the announcement of Jesus stood in the place of overturning death in the flesh, the stench of the grave, and victory over death. Jesus stood in His appointed time so He could return to His eternal state of glory in heaven and be seated on His throne at the right hand of His Father. The order of heaven was about to be fulfilled on earth in the midst of a perplexed, uncertain people. Jesus was about to shake off His sinless robe of flesh and disarm Satan and his forces; 2 Corinthians 5:21 tells us, "God made him who had no sin to be sin for us, so that in him we might become the righteousness of God."

Jesus the Christ, who knew no sin, became sin for humanity to reconcile an underserved people back with a loving God. The time for the new order of heaven had arrived to bring the alignment of heaven as the fulfillment of truth in the earth through the King. Thus, I believe it is here in John 13 that Jesus began to experience the atmospheric shift of heaven's order on the inside—in other words, eternity.

Jesus was being prepared to move out of one realm back to the next. I believe the stars and clouds were being prepared to fold back and prepare for the return of the King. I believe the angelic hosts of heaven in their celestial posture began to prepare to receive the only begotten Son of God, King Jesus.

I believe the shifting had already begun when Jesus made His announcement in John 13:1, and if I could visualize the transition of the King, I would envision it would be as lightning is observed during a thunderstorm. Oftentimes, before the lightning is accurately seen through the natural lens of the eyes, there is always rumbling in the atmosphere. Thus, the sound of lightning is always heard from a distance. Moreover, when the sound is heard, it is heard at a distance, thus, what you and I hear is the aftereffect of that which has already happened.

There is a *time delay* from the place of *release* to the point of *manifestation*. Thus, the individual may atmospherically sense a thing in the spirit before the proof of the thing is actually seen. Hence, I believe Jesus heard the rumbling in His Spirit from a realm outside earth before the disciples could hear, see, or sense the *new order* of *heaven* that was about to be released through the person of Christ. Jesus, in all His compassion, communicated His eternal rumblings felt internally to the men before the actual hour. Therefore, Jesus told His disciples His time was at hand. They could not spiritually or physically see at a distance what Jesus could see, nor could they hear the rumblings of what Jesus heard. I would venture to say that what Jesus communicated to them came through as a strange sound to their natural ears because they themselves did not experience the rumblings to the magnitude that Jesus did. I believe the sound was foreign to their ears. I believe these completed Words that Christ spoke in the midst of His disciples fell from the eternal place of the Master but were spoken with His earthly lips.

As a result, the dialect heard through the King caused the men to become perplexed and confused at the sound they heard coming from Jesus's mouth and not from His eternal position. They did not know the eternal King, who sat in their midst, was speaking from His eternal place, so it became difficult for them to interpret what His actual hour meant. Though Jesus's posture was present in their now, His posture and position are eternal. They did not know! Nevertheless, out of love, the compassionate King *prepared* them for His and their next shift.

They did not know that before the heavens were split in two, Christ the King would bridge the gap between them. Thus, *Jesus acknowledged the shift and transition into it,* and at the time of His release, *the heavens began preparing for His infinite return.* Jesus was speaking through prophetic place, a prophetic time, and a prophetic position outside the earth's twenty-four-hour constraints.

His hour, a moment through eternity, had arrived, and Satan thought he could change heaven's rule by devising a plan to prevent the earth from producing its eternal effects concerning the death of Jesus. Satan, the counterfeit king, must have known that the fullness of Christ would cause death to be of no effect, rendering its sting powerless over the King.

Did Satan not know the shedding of Christ's blood would cause even Satan himself to become subject to Christ's authority? The *complete rule of heaven's assignment* placed a *demand on Jesus to stand as the firstfruits* of those who have fallen asleep before Him on the day of His resurrection (see 1 Corinthians 15:20).

Satan thought he had the upper hand in victory. He did not see the finality of victory coming through in completion in the conquering King. However the Bible says everything shall be brought unto the subjection of Christ in *final victory,* "when He put an end to all rule and all authority and powers" (1 Corinthians 15:24–28).

John 13:2 says, "And supper being ended, the devil having *already* put it into the heart of Judas Iscariot, Simon's son, to betray Him." Judas's heart was *already entertaining* darkness, and this gave an *opening* to Satan operating as the devil maneuvering over Judas to begin to slander Jesus's name and authority.

How is this? John 13:2 says, "The devil [had] already put it into the heart of Judas to betray" Jesus. What is this saying? Judas's doors, gates, walls, mind-set, and heart were *beforehand* diseased by the powers of darkness. Thus, because Judas had left his gates open, darkness began to overtake his being, thereby *depositing seeds of Satan himself on the inside* of Judas before supper had ended (see John 13:2). The one Jesus called Judas Iscariot was no longer operating in a place he was called to walk in, in connection with the King. Because Judas was *divided* in his own heart, he moved away from the place Jesus had appointed for him and carried him to be part of something *greater* than himself.

As a result, Judas no longer had the mind or heart of Christ when Satan began operating through his body, infusing his own spirit of confusion, division, and accusation. Through Judas, Satan began plotting against Jesus before the government officials of Rome, who were already under the authority of Satan.

How did the devil, the accuser called Satan, use the heart of Judas? He did so by appealing to his flesh, his greed, and his lust, which is the same tactic he uses today. Satan uses the desire of the flesh for power and authority *under* the *umbrella* of titles, positions, jealousy, and other cravings of the flesh to control people. Here in the text, Jesus acknowledged the presence of the devil in John 13:18, and He did so "that the Scripture may be fulfilled."

Nonetheless, at the declaration of Jesus, the men sitting together were confused and were wondering which one of them was going to betray Jesus. The men did not know the betrayer had already betrayed Jesus in his heart. They were confused as to which one it was, but Jesus knew. In John 13:18, we read, "I do not speak concerning all of you. I know whom I have chosen, but that the Scriptures may be fulfilled, 'He who eats bread with Me has lifted up his heel against Me.'"

Jesus announced the fulfillment of Scriptures; however, the men did not spiritually hear the prophetic fulfillment of what Jesus had spoken, as what they heard fell on their natural ears only. Jesus, the embodiment of the Godhead sent to redeem humanity, spoke a Word that bypassed what their natural minds could comprehend. Jesus said, "Now I tell you *before* it comes that when it does come to pass, you may believe that I am He" (v. 19). Jesus loved them enough to *prepare* them, so He said, "He who eats bread with Me has lifted up his heel against Me" (John 13:18). What Jesus was saying was that one of them had turned against Him; someone who He had called "friend" had left the gate open.

Judas's doorpost, the walls of his being, had an opening that gave access to the wiles of Satan to enter. An opening, a foothold granted the accuser of the brethren permission to enter into his being because he has chosen to entertain darkness all while sitting in the midst of Light. All the time within the view of the presence of the King, Judas plotted to plant his kiss of death on the King. John 13:21 says, "When Jesus had said these things, He was troubled in spirit, and testified and said, 'Most assuredly, I say to you, one of you will betray Me.'"

This shows the separation of time and eternity altogether. After Jesus released the mandate of heaven through what He spoke, He gave time *permission* to align itself and to become activated on earth. The rumblings Jesus experienced were a *prerequisite* to what heaven was about to release before the manifestation arrived.

Thus, what was to be seen on earth needed the *permission* of God in order for it to move and be experienced on earth. There is a **requirement** for **any** movement in the land to comply with what is allowed or disallowed in heaven according to His Word. The earth **cannot move** unless God grants permission for it to do so. In other words, nothing in heaven or on earth can do, become, or operate in any fashion unless God grants permission for it to do so.

Jesus was saying to His disciples that which stood far off was in the present. That which Jesus spoke became activated upon His releasing heaven's language out of His eternal position on earth. Although what proceeded from His mouth stood far above the intellectual capacity of His disciples, the Roman government, and every demonic power, it had to be released. Jesus said, "My hour is at hand."

CHAPTER 7

Influenced by Darkness

Then after [he had taken] the bit of food, Satan entered into and took possession of [Judas]. Jesus said to him [Satan], "what you are going to do, do more swiftly than you seem to intend and make quick work of it." As soon as Judas took the bread, Satan entered into him. So Jesus told him, "What you are about to do, do quickly."
—John 13:27, AMB/NIV

The disciples were perplexed and confused as they tried to figure out who was about to betray Jesus. Not one of them knew the adversary, Satan, was lurking in the atmosphere awaiting Jesus's permission to enter Judas Iscariot and set in motion the appointed time of His hour.

Unbeknownst to the men, the powers of darkness Judas the betrayer had been entertaining were lurking in the atmosphere. The adversary was waiting to move forward by permission in a plot to kill King Jesus to destroy the rule of heaven. Nonetheless, Satan did not see the final victory, or the power of the cross, or the complete victory of Christ and His resurrection. All Satan saw was Christ being crucified. He could not hear beyond his domain, his posture, after Jesus said, "It is finished."

Satan did not know the all-inclusive victory *tied* to *Jesus's words* **"It is finished"** (John 19:30). Satan did not know, and neither did the rulers! The conspiracy of Judas Iscariot and the darkness he was entertaining did not understand the *full* impact of the kiss Jesus would receive from Judas (see Luke 22:47). Judas left the door of his heart open and accessible to the wiles of Satan.

Judas allowed Satan to become active in motion through his **lust**, **greed**, and **rebellion**, which *unlocked hidden channels* of darkness in the chambers of Judas Iscariot's heart. In other words, there was a match! Satan found a match of darkness, a match of himself within Judas to draw from and out of. Satan tempted Judas through the channel of lust and won him over. Satan maneuvered through Judas and the rulers to conspire against Jesus with unfounded accusations. Dark powers of influences began to set the stage. If Judas had not been engaging with darkness in his heart, he would not have been available for Satan. The Bible does not say when Judas became available for the powers of darkness to enter. However, the prophetic alignment of Zechariah 11:12 and Matthew 26:14 declared by heavens rule the cost of the King's life was thirty pieces of sliver. Matthew 26:14 says Judas met with the high priest Caiaphas to plot against Jesus as Judas's fleshly cravings came into compliance with Satan and his plan. In other words, the lust of Judas's flesh made contact with Satan.

Had there not been any deceit in the heart of Judas, Satan could not have embedded himself in Judas and convinced Judas to betray the Lord. Nevertheless, the spirit of wickedness was found in Judas Iscariot, waiting to manifest and be employed and deployed by the wiles of Satan himself for the betrayal of the King.

Therefore, because wickedness ruled the heart of Judas, Satan used that seed of lust inside him, drew it out, and manipulated his heart to lust after greed. As a result, darkness began to infuse and influence the mind-set of Judas because his heart was contaminated and polluted with the likeness of rebellion found in Eve in the garden.

Although Judas stood in the presence of Jesus, we know that Judas acknowledged Jesus with his head, not completely with his heart. *The head* can *acknowledge* a thing and *still not believe* it is real. The heart has to be made anew! Judas in his person responded to the corruptible traces of Satan, which crept into his being through his own greed. Satan sought after a match for himself on the inside to move his plan in action once the King gave permission to proceed. Through Judas's responding to Satan, deception and darkness found a matching seat inside Judas's unchanged, tattered heart. In other words, Satan found a match for himself on the inside of Judas and therefore lodged himself and *sat down* in that *identifiable* space that *duplicated himself.*

Influence by definition is the power to cause changes without directly forcing them to happen or the corrupt interference with authority for personal gain. Satan uses his dark powers of corruption and infuses his agenda into the hearts of a divided people who have not fully given themselves to Christ Jesus as Lord. Satan maneuvers through the enticement of the flesh, the lust of the eyes, and the pride of life in deception. It is in these things in the divided heart Satan tugs on, thereby utilizing its cravings to influence individuals through the powers of wickedness to bring to ruin that which they encounter. This counterfeit king presents himself as something he is not to the cravings of the flesh of men in an attempt to steal, kill, and destroy the members of the church though they are called as disciples of the King. Through the wickedness found in Judas's heart, Satan maneuvered around him for his own dark purpose.

The pathology Satan used in John 13:27 convinced Caiaphas, Judas, and the Roman government to murder the King. They did not know the cross would *transport* Jesus to His final victory. Death in its position could not hold what it has no power over. They did not know! Did Satan not see the completion and final victory of Jesus's death over hell and the grave when He sat on the mercy seat? Many stood on the crossover of the prophetic fulfillment and did not know it. God set a watch over His Word of the prophesied King for over forty-two generations, and still, they did not know. Nonetheless, the King affectionately explained to his disciples the next phase of His ministry. He told them that He was standing in the *final hours* of His humanity and that His divinity would be challenged.

Those who hated Jesus because He had challenged their flesh and "religious" laws wanted Him dead. They awaited word from Judas, but they did not understand they were not on their timeline but on that of the King's. Therefore, Jesus sat with them at Passover and saw the wickedness in the heart of Judas Iscariot and the infestation of darkness there. Jesus knew darkness had mounted Judas's heart, so the control of Satan was at the forefront of his divided heart.

Jesus knew darkness had *already* penetrated Judas's heart and had prepared him for the exchange of the dipped bread of approval. Therefore,

Jesus knew, but the others had no clue about the wickedness hovering overhead and awaiting permission to move quickly into action.

Judas's heart was divided; his mind-set was cloudy because he had yielded to the powers of darkness while in the midst of the One he had been called by. He betrayed Him anyway. Judas was still emotionally straddling the fence and stood heavily entangled in his lust, which caused his mind-set to become cooperative with the plan of Satan.

I believe Judas could have dismissed the urgent cravings of his flesh and resisted the tugging of darkness. Instead, he chose to yield to the devices of Satan through the wicked seeds he had ingested and that had taken root. Satan used the desires of the old man in Judas and drew out that cord of wickedness that matched Satan's pivot point in his plan to kill Jesus.

Judas was essential to the plan of Satan; *nevertheless,* God *was* and *is* always *in control.* In essence, Judas was the "center point" used in the rotation of Satan to control the mind-set of the people as well as the government seeking the death of Jesus. Thus, the adversary used an open door of Judas's heart that Satan stepped in this accessible door to activate his own deceit in the presence of the King. Judas had a choice!

Sowing corruption reaps the same in value! Galatians 6:8 declares, "For the one who sows to his own flesh will from the flesh reap corruption." Judas's heart became divided within itself, which in turn gave him over to rebellion, which produced sin and corruption through his own flesh. Galatians 5:17 says, "For the flesh lusts against the Spirit, and the Spirit against the flesh; and theses are contrary to one another." Therefore, because Judas began to function through the wickedness in his heart, darkness identified a match and began digging up deep-seated roots out of his old man. Satan in turn interwove his plan through what had begun manifesting itself in the heart of Judas, thereby igniting that place of memory of old, which became fuel for the devices of Satan.

The rebellion found within Judas was produced from his original state of being; it produced corruption beyond what I believe even Judas himself could understand or even handle. Rebellion by definition is open opposition to person or group in authority or the refusal to obey rules or accept reasonable standards of behavior.

That is what happened to Judas! He began to rebel and resist the authority of Jesus while in the presence of the fullness of the Trinity. Satan used the rebellion kindling within Judas to entice through channels of lust from within Judas's own heart. I believe Judas himself had no foreknowledge of the magnitude of what his own betrayal would bring about.

Nevertheless, God had a plan! The everlasting domain of heaven began a new divine order beyond what the church had ever seen before. The divine providence of God planted the seed of grace on earth for the redemption of humanity, and still they did not know. Hence, when Jesus released heaven's language, I do not believe those present with the King fully internalized the importance of the statement released from the belly of eternity. Christ understood His hour had come. None of them could have fathomed the magnitude of heaven's work to overthrow darkness that would come about through Judas's betrayal of the King. They could not see beyond sight the Messiah standing on the cusp of being flogged by the hands of the accuser. With one swipe over the body, Jesus would take on Himself what you and I *deserve* for our sins. Jesus took it!

I do not believe they had any idea that Jesus would incur wounds He had not earned but *still* suffered on our behalf. I do not think they could thoroughly understand the next turn of events about to transpire for the sake of love. They did not know!

Comprehension stood at a distance in their persons; they did not realize how each open wound on Jesus's flesh would cover *every* sickness on earth. They could not perceive that Jesus would take on Himself *every* disease and willingly receive each one for His divine purpose of redemption. I do not believe they could have comprehended what the ripping of His flesh would entail beyond natural sight. They had no idea of the ripping of Jesus's flesh down to the bone was in fact the fulfillment of the prophetic call spoken of by the prophet Isaiah concerning the Christ. The prophet declared that the King of Kings would be "wounded for our transgression, He was bruised for our iniquities" (Isaiah 53:5). Thus, Jesus released heaven's rule through these words: *"My hour has come."* Did they understand the promise that God previously declared in which the prophesied King would come through? In 2 Samuel 7:12–13, we read,

When your days are fulfilled and you rest with your fathers, I will set up your seed after you, who will come from your body, and I will establish His kingdom. He shall build a house for My name, and I will establish the throne of His Kingdom forever.

The prophet Nathan delivered an oracle from of God to King David, who had been set over Israel, concerning God's promised seed through the linage of King David. This is the fulfillment of Jesus being divinely set up as an everlasting covenant on earth. God told Nathan to tell David of His promise to him that God's seed would *spring forth* through his lineage. According to this Davidic covenant, God declared that Jesus would build a house, a people for His namesake alone, and would establish His throne *forever*. This means that **nothing** and **no one** could *interrupt* that which God spoke and made manifest through a *perpetual decree* from His eternal throne. As a result, the manifestation of that which God spoke had to manifest itself on earth according to the Davidic promise that God established in Himself first. The prophetic timing of God revealed the King long before He appeared on earth in seed form through a virgin named Mary.

SEEING BEYOND SIGHT

God announced through Nathan the prophet that **Jesus the Christ**, *the Lion of the tribe of Judah, the Root of David, would come forth triumphantly as King* (see Revelation 5:5). Jesus is the Messiah—*Christ*. The King has released His reign on earth. Before the manifestation of His promise, He was. Before the crucifixion, He was. When He rose on the third day, He was. **Jesus** *always was*, but no one could see that the prophesied King was there!

Satan and his demonic powers were plotting to kill Jesus, but the disciples could not see beyond sight what the promised seed of David would have to endure to achieve ultimate victory. They did not fully discern the anguish that Christ our King would bear in His body.

Jesus carried our violations and in so doing broke the curse! Isaiah, the eagle-eyed prophet, said Jesus the Christ was wounded for our transgressions (see Isaiah 53). Isaiah spoke in past tense, not in the present tense in which Jesus stood with the disciples in John 13. Isaiah spoke from a space, place, and time in which the King called the Christ had not manifested in seed form on earth, but on the other hand, He always was. What the prophet spoke did not come through his own belly; it was spoken out of *revelation*, which came through the heart of God and connected to the spirit of the prophet. Isaiah spoke the heart of God into space and time, **beyond** *time,* **through** eternity. This eagle-eyed prophet spoke of a Triune God and the completed course of events though they were *already* complete.

The full manifestation of Jesus being the redemption of God was positioned on earth for the purpose of love; Jesus was the fullness of what Isaiah and his eagle eyes saw in a domain before He was seen as a seed on earth. Isaiah said that Jesus, the Messiah, already was. In other words, Isaiah saw *before* seeing the seen. *Before* the disciples *saw,* Isaiah had **already** *seen.* Therefore, the prophet of old announced Jesus the Christ being wounded before current events began to happen.

Isaiah had been given revelation of the complete fullness of the person of Christ. He saw the *finished* beforehand of "a man of sorrows and acquainted with grief." Isaiah's eagle eyes saw through revelation Jesus being violently beaten and brutally suffering in His body for the sins of humanity.

For our sins, Jesus suffered in His body; His flesh was stripped away by the whips. Jesus, violently beaten for our sins, took on Himself our *broken* moral code of conduct before God and seized on our infractions we had committed in our rebellion. Jesus did that. "He was bruised for our iniquities," our wickedness, and our deceit (see Isaiah 53:5). Jesus did that! Jesus put on our wicked, filthy, immoral acts of sin with every blow that ripped the very essence of the King. Not one of them could have fully identified with the agony of the cross Jesus was about to endure. No! I do not think so. They could not perceive that Jesus had been sent to be God's mercy on the seat.

Understand the sacrifice presented before the Lord had specific requirements that had to be met before an offering of any kind was brought before God our Father. Giving an unacceptable offering as a sacrifice could mean the death of the one having access to enter the most holy place where God was hovering. Only the qualifying of God had access to meet with God face to face to hear the ordinance of God for God's people.

The priest could not enter inside filthy and stinking of sin, as this was detrimental for himself and for the people in whose name he went into the temple. Still, the high priest went in to ask for forgiveness of God for the sins of the entire camp of God's people. However, the Messiah went *beyond* where the high priests of old could go as He submitted to the cross on behalf of humanity and out of obedience to His Father. He gave of Himself freely for an undeserving people, an ungrateful people so His blood would perfect that that stood imperfect due to sin.

In Him, the believer became acceptable because He stood in complete perfection—unblemished, completely pure, and without sin. The cross came through the rebellion of Adam, but Jesus finished it! Satan used governments and political channels to influence them and engage in a fight they could not win. Satan himself did not see the order of the new covenant come down from heaven *already complete*. Matthew 6:10 says, "Thy Kingdom come," which means that heaven—Jesus's presence—is present. "Thy will be done," which means that Christ was calling for an alignment of the two to be made manifest on earth. The complete manifest glory of the supremacy of God stood present in the earth, stepped out of eternity **prepared**. *Prepare* means to put in proper condition or readiness, to arrange, to order.

The magnificent majesty of His splendor stepped out of heaven already prepared to prepare! Therefore, Jesus the Christ could not have been in a position to rule, reign, or call a thing a thing *unless* He *was* who He was—**already** *prepared as King.*

The eternal Trinity wrapped in power and authority was already inclusive in His name, His person, and His being. He was and is Jesus. He came to put all things in proper order, to make ready, to arrange matters on earth. The Godhead Himself came down *already* **prepared** and **equipped** to earth. Jesus came in the form of a seed in the virgin womb of a woman named Mary already prepared! Beyond eagles' wings, Jesus the Christ, the soon and coming King, came down prepared to win!

They did not know Jesus came down from heaven as a spoken Word while being made manifest in the flesh already prepared. Shine on, Jesus!

Jesus the Christ came prepared to *apprehend* doctrines of devils, prepared to overthrow dominions, prepared to cast out demons, and prepared to heal the sick and raise the dead. Jesus the Christ came down from heaven already prepared! He was and is the prepared King poured out in completion of His assignment on earth for the forgiveness of sin (see Matthew 26:28).

People did not know Jesus had come down from heaven already prepared for His hour, which He stood on the cusp of. Heaven came down prepared. The seed of Christ had to catch up in time with what was already prepared in eternity and made manifest on earth. They did not know! The Roman government, the political movers and shakers coaxed by Satan, saw His death and burial as the end. They did not see what was done beyond that. Jesus came down from heaven already prepared from start to finish. He came ready to grab hold of death, hell, and the grave, shake off the sting of death, and destroy Satan and his principalities, powers, and rulers of darkness of this age, and his spiritual hosts of wickedness. Jesus came to restore that which was lost! They thought the book of Christ was permanently shut. Spiritual wickedness—the domain of Satan and all his evil powers—thought this was the end of all ends.

Others did not see the fullness of God's kingdom in Jesus the Christ. They saw what they thought was the end, but it was just the beginning. They could not see beyond sight the truth that stood before them. They did not understand Jesus was the perfect, blemish-free Passover Lamb sent by the Father to atone for our sins, far superior to any past blood sacrifices.

The Ark of the Covenant was temporary; it was a foreshadowing of our prophesied Messiah. The ark was erected so God could dwell with His people. However, due to Adam's fall, our connection to heaven was broken. Though our rebellion cut off direct communication with God, He provided another way—the sacrifice of His Son. An undeserving people were forgiven, and Jesus's blood made us clean in the sight of God. Jesus's blood carries us in, beyond the outer court, which in the past only the high priest had access to. He is the eternal and sinless offering.

Moses's sacrificial offerings prefigured Christ's. The stench of the old sacrificial offerings I believe would draw the people into subjection to God. The stench served as a reminder of just how filthy they were. They stood outside the tent waiting to see if God would accept their sacrifice for their sins. The disciples could not see beyond sight the foreshadowing of the Savior and His atoning that surpassed the sacrifices of old. Jesus's blood did what we could not do.

BEYOND THE BLOOD OF BULLS AND GOATS

None of them fully made the connection. Instead of the bulls or goats being brought inside the door to be slain at the altar, the sacrifice would be the King. The offering shifted into the prophetic superiority of the King. The eternal King is our atonement beyond what any other sacrifice could do. I believe that the high priest, who went in for the people, had an unbelievable, supernatural experience that God had specifically chosen for him in this sacramental process. Was it messy? Yes, I believe it was. However, to be selected to meet God is *inexpressible.* This is what Jesus has called the believer to through His sacrifice on the cross. You and I are now able to have the supernatural experience, one on one with the Father.

In times past, the high priest was specially chosen to smear blood on the four horns of the Brazen Altar. After the blood was smeared, the priest continue to the Bronze Laver to washed his hands and feet and asked for cleansing for himself and the people behind the curtain of separation (see Exodus 30:18). Understand that the high priest had to leave sin outside the curtain before he could go behind it. It was strategically placed by God because there had to be a separation between sin and God. Those standing outside of the tent could not see what was waiting behind the curtain as the high priest went in. The people of God could not see beyond sight the menorah and the golden altar of incense in the holy place before the high priest could go beyond the veil to the ark. The curtain isolated them from the presence of God.

I do not believe they saw the exchange Christ would bring to completion on the cross. They did not fully comprehend the symbolism of Christ in each step in the tent of the tabernacle. Matthew 27:50–51 declares the completion of the cross: "And Jesus cried out again with a loud voice, and yielded up His spirit. And behold, the veil of the temple was torn in two from top to bottom; and the earth shook and the rocks were split."

Through His death on the cross, Jesus broke the power of the old order of animals sacrificed to God by becoming our permanent sin offering. God demonstrated His grace and love by providing His *best* atonement, His *highest* expression of mercy on the seat. Jesus split the veil and shook the earth; nothing will ever destroy or even diminish who Christ is, our redeeming King.

> Knowing that you were not redeemed with corruptible things, *like* silver or gold, from your aimless conduct *received* by tradition from your fathers, but with the precious blood of Christ, as of a lamb without blemish and without spot. He indeed was foreordained before the foundation of the world, but was manifest in these last times for you.
>
> —1 Peter 1:18–20, NKJV

Peter was speaking to the church, and I believe he was reminding those of us called by His name how we ourselves came to obtain redemption on earth in spite of our fallen, sinful nature. Peter says this redemption came through the person of Christ the King. Peter was speaking to an ear; no flesh, no deity established or erected has or ever had anything to do with this thing called redemption.

Sliver or gold have no redemptive power to bring us back into alignment with the Father. Peter is saying that if we want to be brought back to the Father, we must be born again. We need a divine bridge to restore a right-standing connection and to bridge the gap of separation between God and us *before* we can be redeemed. Buddha could not do that; only Christ could reconcile His people with God, reconcile us back to having an eternal ear attuned to God, and reconcile us back to the heart of God.

It is only complete by the blood of Christ shed on the *altar* for our sin-sick souls. **Jesus** *is* **God's** *mercy* **on** the *seat* for *our* **sins**. It is not through tangible things but through the mercy of God that we have access to Him. Peter conveys to the hearts of men that it is through the perfection of Christ, who purchased us and brought us back *through* the *cross* at Calvary. The purchased came through the King!

Person, places, or things could have been in a position to bring us into the arms of a loving God. Redemption came through the sacrificial place of Christ Jesus. Only His blood *cancels* our sickness, death, and disease. His blood *remains* smeared; *perpetually* **echoing** *our names* on the mercy seat, and replaces the blood of bulls and goats. Christ *yielded* His Spirit for the sake of reconciliation to all who believe in His name!

No other deity possesses the power or the authority to split the veil of separation from the top to bottom, destroy the power of sin and death and realign God and His sheep causing realms to transition to receive the King. The earth shook in *response* to the Kings posture on the cross being fulfilled. Only the blood of Christ could have done that. Christ yielded His Spirit and caused bodies of them that were asleep to shake off the sting of death because He won the victory over death. Jesus became the permanent sacrifice for humanity before Judas had even begun the betraying process.

The assignment of Christ Jesus to cover the incomplete on the mercy seat was not an accident. His blood did not just happen to be spotless. He did not just happen to stumble upon the cross. Nor did He just happen to complete it. The betrayal did not just accidently happen. No! Jesus's assignment of redemption was *preordained.* The ridiculers, the mockers, and those plotting to kill the King did not know Jesus was the *absolute* supremacy from eternity. Jesus positioned Himself in the midst of the disciples as Satan was in the atmosphere awaiting permission to enter Judas; nonetheless, Jesus stayed the course.

Christ's obedience to the Father surpassed the limits of the grave; death no longer has power over those in Christ Jesus. Numbers 9:12 says that according to Moses, the decree for the sacrificial Passover offering required that *none* of its bones be broken. During the feast, there were certain restrictions for God's people (see Exodus 12:43–51). This Scripture parallels with the new order of the Passover, Christ Jesus and His crucifixion.

The gospel of John twins the declaration of Moses in John 19:33–36, declaring that *not one* of Jesus's bones was to be broken, which was prophetic fulfillment. John 19:33 says, "But when they came to Jesus and saw that He was already dead, they did not break His legs" that the Scriptures be fulfilled. Death on the cross could take two or three days; it could be a slow death with no food or water, resulting in starvation and dehydration. When the soldiers came to conclude the crucifixion, *Jesus the*

Christ was already dead. What God spoke concerning Christ on earth came to pass. To have broken any of Christ's bones would have gone against the oracles of God spoken through forty-two generation of His fulfillment. Still, they had no idea!

I believe they could not have completely foreseen or perceived within themselves the severity of the beating that revealed vital organs; some laughed at Jesus as blood gushed out of His body. They could not have foreseen the wickedness of the rulers shoving a crown of twisted thrones upon His head as blood began gushing down His face (see Matthew 27). In order to do what He did, He had to take on Himself our transgressions, our iniquities. Our sin could not go where He was!

I am blown away by what happened to my Lord for my sake. I love Him. Many believers cannot grasp what Christ endured for our sins, for our sake. Selah! The full manifestation of the Father's glory stood full of compassion; love made provisions because of love. Jesus was about to finish His work. God chose to provide His Son as His mercy on the seat.

Jesus the Christ was flogged with cat-o'-nine-tails; each tear ripped through flesh and muscle as He carried His heavy cross. He hung on the cross pierced by nine-inch nails through His hands and feet to redeem those standing at His feet and mocking Him. No sacrifice of goats or bulls **could have released us** from the *penalty we deserved.*

Jesus shifted the order. That which was created for our deliverance is Christ Jesus our King. He is the Passover Lamb! Still, Jesus said His hour had come, and as He became troubled in His spirit, Satan was waiting. At His statement, the men were perplexed and asked themselves to whom Jesus was referring. However, the omniscience of Jesus knew Judas Iscariot had left the gate open to his mind. The God-Man called Christ knew that Satan, the faceless hacker, was awaiting permission to enter Judas. The disciples had no idea that the disloyalty in Judas's heart would be the catalyst the redemption of humanity. In Matthew 26:2, Jesus said to His disciples, "You know that after two days is the Passover and the Son of Man will be delivered up to be crucified."

The cunning Enemy still did not recognize the authority of the cross and the power of His resurrection. Caiaphas, the chief priests, the scribes, the elders, and Judas collectively plotted to kill Jesus after the feast; they thought they had the upper hand. None of them could have Christ seated at the right hand of God the Father in the end.

FLASK FIT FOR THE KING

Influenced by the powers of darkness, they thought this would be the end of Jesus's reign on earth; they were not privy to the realm of heaven. They did not see that Jesus's death would benefit those who love Him! They did not have spiritual eyes to see this would serve as an "as it is in heaven." Satan's plot would *backfire*. They did not understand that Jesus *was* and *is* the Bread of Life that all may receive (see John 6:51). Christ is the door to eternal life (see John 10:9). He is the *only* way to the Father. Nevertheless, the skeptics were blind. Matthew 15:14 says, "Let them alone; they are blind guides of the blind. And if a blind man guides a blind man, both will fall into a pit." They were blind in their minds, eyes, and souls. The blind were leading the blind.

All the naysayers fell into the ditch when Jesus split the veil when He uttered, "It is finished" (see John 19:30). Satan had blinded their minds and corrupted their hearts. Time, on earth, continued to move, but they were at a standstill. The rulers stood contrary to the new order Jesus had introduced, a new order of heaven personified as the living truth on earth; Satan was manipulating their thoughts and preventing the truth from penetrating. Demonic systems had so infiltrated the mentality of the government and many of the people that the truth Jesus spoke fell on deaf ears. There was no way that the truth could penetrate the hardness of their heats. Each complete word spoken by the King fell on barren ground, so the word of truth could not take root and reproduce after its own kind.

The cross was a means to an end for them in the distorted, Communist thinking according to the laws that governed the earth. They could not see beyond sight that this King was the Christ.

> Then, behold, the veil of the temple was torn in two from
> top to bottom; and the earth quaked, and the rocks were
> split, and the graves were opened; and many bodies of the

saints who had fallen asleep were raised; and coming out
of the graves after His resurrection, they went into the
holy city and appeared to many

—Matthew 27:51–53, NKJV

When the veil of the temple tore at the completion of the cross, the power of the King and the transition in which He stepped into caused the earth to *respond* to what was tied to "It is finished." Why was there shaking in the power of the cross? The shaking of the earth I believe was a sign of Christ's dimensional shift taking place on earth, beneath the earth, and above the earth, because eternity itself was in transition. Christ was shifting, and the effects of His change caused the earth to respond to that, which was taking place. The shaking woke up everything that was *connected* to the King! It was not just the trees, it was not just the mountains, and it was not just the hillside of the cross. Matthew 27:51 says the earth shook! Rocks split and graves opened as Christ became a God's mercy on the seat. Matthew 27:51 says the veil in the temple was torn. Jesus in His fullness ripped the curtain in two; the old order was no more. The earth shaking I believe was signifying that Christ reversed the place and ordered of worship unto God.

Wikipedia describes earthquakes as "the result of a sudden release of energy in the Earth's crust that creates seismic waves. The shallower an earthquake, the **more** *damage* to structures it causes, all else being equal. At the Earth's surface, earthquakes manifest themselves by shaking and sometimes displacement of the ground."

Therefore, when Christ yielded Himself before the Father and completed His assignment, the earth **responded** by *shaking* things loose according to the position of heaven. Jesus the Christ revered the place in which the ark sat in times past as commanded by Moses and those thereafter called of God for assignments. Until then, the Ark of the Covenant was restricted to a particular location, person, and time in order to meet with God. However, the redemptive power of Christ calls for His bride to no longer pitch a tent (Numbers 1:52) in a place, location, or through a particular person to meet with God through His blood.

There no longer had to be a tent erected outside in a specific location for the children of Israel to put up or take down if they wanted to seek the face of God. **Jesus** *shifted* God's children to another domain outside of the earth's realm, outside of a tangible tent that needed to be erected in order to meet with God.

Through Christ Jesus, our *tents* should rest *within us* with **reverential fear** before a holy God. The completion of the cross and the effects of death remove the church from being restricted to standing outside of the camp to having full access to stand in the presence of the King. Christ has brought us back in.

Jesus exchanged Himself as the new order of God's mercy on the seat that every believer in His Son could have rest rather than a wall of separation. His blood gave believers access to God through Christ (see Hebrews 10:19–22). Little did those who killed Christ know that this was just the beginning. Eternity was in their midst, but they could not see it; they were blind to the magnitude of His supremacy.

Moreover, for this reason, many fell into the ditch. This was the beginning of the prophetic fulfillment of heaven being made manifest in completion when the woman poured oil on the Savior to prepare Him for burial. They did not know the flask fit for the King was on its way to fulfilling the burial process of the King's transition for His body to switch the order (see Matthew 26:7).

This flask was merely a container, but the *oil* had *purpose*, and assignment, a mandate on the arrival time for its destination precisely set apart for our Lord. Therefore, this oil was a *vital* component of the transitional process of our Lord. Matthew 2:11 identifies the gifts that were brought to celebrate the birth of King Jesus: gold, frankincense, and myrrh, which this flask fit for the King contained.

Myrrh stood as an essential oil this woman lavishly poured onto the King as if preparing His body for burial (see Matthew 26:12). This unveiled the greed in the heart of Judas and his craving for something he thought he needed; he did not comprehend the richness of the grace in Christ he stood in the face of. Christ was all he needed, yet his appetite called him more than did his love for the One he sat with.

Judas must have had some wrestling going in within himself due to this act of treason that he willingly walked into. The bowels of hell stood up on the inside of Judas, and still, he decided to accept the flesh rather than the truth. Lust began to eat away the insides of Judas; he yielded to the darkness he was entertaining. Unaware of the purpose of the oil, the disciples were indignant of this woman as they thought she was wasting costly oil although pouring it on the King (see Matthew 26:8).

They could not see that time on earth had already begun the process of preparing the transition to redemption through the rumblings Jesus was experiencing unbeknownst to those who sought to kill the King. God *preordained* the *assignment* of the *oil* long before the disciples met the woman pouring the oil on the Master.

Matthew 26:6–7 says, "When Jesus was in Bethany at the house of Simon the leper, a woman come to Him having an alabaster flask of very costly fragrant oil, and she poured it on His head as He sat at the table." Here we see Jesus's body being physically prepared for His supernatural transition beyond what any natural eyes could have seen. Why oil? Matthew says this oil poured onto Jesus's head was costly. The oil was not only expensive in part because of the process involved in producing it. The crushing process of the oil as well as the crucifixion of Jesus were *necessary* to produce the Father's assignment for them both. The olive had to be broken in order to *produce* what Jesus needed in His hour, which had come.

The first step in producing the oil confined in the olive is the *extraction* of the olive itself from the tree. Second, all impurities must be separated, removed from the olive before the progression of extracting oils from the cells beneath the skin of the olive can begin. Thus, the next step in the process is *crushing*—the grinding of the olive into a paste for the removal of its skin or covering surrounding the oil. The removal of the skin encasing the olive exposes the membrane housing the oil. The crushing process is necessary for the olive to produce oil just as Christ's suffering beatings and crucifixion was necessary to produce our salvation.

By the same token, the symbolism of the crushing process of the outer casing of the olive—the flesh, if you will—as well as the grinding process of extracting the oil is synonymous with the course of the cross and the process Jesus went through. The crushing process of the olive is synonymous with the beatings with the cat-o'-nine-tails, the tearing of His flesh, the nails in His hands, and the crown of thorns placed on His head for you and me.

The crushing (crucifixion) process of the cross *released* the oil—the power of Jesus—on earth and onto those who believe in Him. The cross and the releasing of the oil Jesus dispensed upon completion of His sacrifice on the cross did not die with His flesh but was *released* through His Spirit onto the children of God.

Leviticus 8:12 says, "And he [Moses] poured some of the anointing oil on Aaron's head and anointed him to consecrate him." Before Aaron went into the most holy place as a priest to offer a sacrifice, he had to be consecrated. The oil represents the anointing power of God (see Leviticus 8:10). Their hands had to be holy, their hearts had to be holy, and their minds had to be detached from their flesh to hear anything holy from a Holy God. Aaron had to empty himself of himself before he could enter the most holy place to meet with God. To consecrate is to dedicate something to a sacred purpose, but the disciples did not realize that Christ was being consecrated with the oil!

Matthew 26:7 says she poured the oil on Jesus's head. He sat while the indignant Judas was entertaining the Devil; the accuser stood in total ignorance of the assignment of the woman and her oil "fit for the King."

> And when Jesus was in Bethany at the house of Simon the leper, a woman came to Him having an alabaster flask of very costly fragrant oil, and she poured *it* on His head as He sat *at the table*. But when His disciples saw *it*, they were indignant, saying, "Why this waste? For this fragrant oil might have been sold for much and given to *the* poor." But when Jesus was aware of *it*, He said to them, "Why do you trouble the woman? For she has done a good work for Me. For you have the poor with you always, but Me you do not have always. For in pouring this fragrant oil on My body, she did *it* for My burial. Assuredly, I say to you, wherever this gospel is preached in the whole world, what this woman has done will also be told as a memorial to her."
>
> —Matthew 26:6–13, NKJV

Matthew says Jesus sat! A woman weeping, sorrowfully over the transition that Jesus was about to experience anointed the King. In her weeping, I believe she did not completely understand the reason she became sorrowful in the presence of the King. I believe her spirit began to intercede on the behalf of the King in "His hour" which caused her spirit to *respond* in action by *weeping*. I believe she began to demonstrate in deed, what the Father had revealed to her spirit of what Jesus was about to endure. The spirit of intercession began to move in a profound and unspeakable way in this woman as tears poured down her face; preparing the Lord's body before every eye in the room. As her spirit began grieving in the presence of the King, she unfastened her hair and washed His feet with her tears, and dried them with her hair as Jesus was on His way to the most holy place as God's mercy on the seat (see Luke 7:36–50).

The place in which Jesus sat in the natural expressed His position in the Spirit realm. This woman's oil prepared Jesus for His burial. The inexpressible oil poured on Jesus prepared the King's body to enter the inner court and split the veil of the temple as His blood poured out. Aaron and His sons had access to God's dwelling, but Christ went beyond the most holy place as our final holy sacrifice.

The woman was *obedient* to her assignment; the oil *aided* in the transport of the King. The magnitude of the assignment she undertook with the oil as well as what the oil did for the preparation of our Savior and His transition back to His Father are more important matters than her name. Her obedience to her assignment supernaturally prepared the body of Jesus for His burial on earth, transitioning to heaven's domain. Thus, although many were baffled by her actions, Jesus was not. In His loving stead, Jesus's words weren't meant for His disciples' natural ears. He spoke to the heart. Thus, Jesus *bypassed* their *natural mind-set;* He spoke beyond their ear gates concerning the cost in value of the oil used for the preparation of His body.

Jesus informed His disciples that the woman had *obeyed* the assignment she and the *oil* were *sent* to do. Jesus said, "Assuredly, I say to you, wherever this gospel is preached in the whole world, what this woman has done will also be told as a memorial to her" (Matthew 26:13). This act in the natural *shifted* the prophetic *alignment* of the *cross* with the *supernatural* shift that was taking place in the realm of the Spirit. Thus, the *oil's assignment* and the woman *sent* to anoint Jesus's head were not coincidental; the assignment for the woman and her oil had been *predestined in heaven*.

Timing on earth is always subject to God's plan. When she arrived at Simon's house, she did not ask for oil; she had come **prepared** to **move** into **action** according to what had been spoken to her spirit of her assignment; she already had the oil in hand. Thus, before she moved into action, she had to have *already responded* to the call of *God* beyond her natural ears. A *rumbling* from *within* her spirit told her Jesus the Christ was at Simon the leper's house, and something in her told her to go with the oil.

ACCESS GRANTED

The timing this woman showed is evidence of her connection to the King. Something inside her called her out of her usual position to another level of grace. She moved toward the King as heaven moved toward Him; these were different levels and dimensions of the shift, but they were in the shift! Understand the rumblings did not occur until Jesus connected the disciples thoughts to heaven (v. 19); outside of the place they stood on earth. Once their thoughts *shifted* to Him, He said, "He who receives whomever I send receives Me; and he who receives Me receives Him who sent Me" (John 13:20).

Jesus was speaking beyond their flesh and minds and directly to their spirits, but they still did not recognize the fullness of His supremacy standing in front of them. Jesus informed them that to inherit eternal life, all must come through the Son.

John 13:21 says, "When He said these things, He was troubled in spirit." This means the rumblings passed from one place to the next. Christ experienced in His Spirit what flowed from heaven to earth, from one chamber to the next. In other words, the rumbling on earth was the landing pad for the effects originating in heaven. The Word of God was released from the mouth of the King for divine purposes. Jesus activated the Word! Heaven's process had *already* begun aligning with the realm of the spirit as she poured the oil on Jesus's head.

Jesus responded to the troubling of His Spirit when He said, "One of you will betray Me" (John 13:21) but not before He prepared them for the shift in (v. 19), "Now I tell you before it come, that when it does come to pass, you may believe that I am He." It is here that Jesus lovingly communicated heaven's will to His disciples. What Jesus was saying was that His body was being prepared to release His oil onto them, that he was being prepared to return to His Father as His mercy on the seat to cover the sins of the world. Through Jesus's mouth, the earth had to make its transition to match what heaven was doing, thus He began to dispense eternity onto their hearts to prepare them for His being crucified and rising from the dead.

Nonetheless, though Jesus prepared them for what the betrayal would bring, they could not comprehend or recognize heaven's truth; it was plainly beyond their scope of natural thinking. Even after Jesus poured truth into His disciples, they could not understand His language. He spoke eternal, but they heard earth. Their faith needed stirring. The heart of Judas was already prepared to betray Jesus, and Satan stood in the wings, awaiting the King's approval to enter Judas. Thus, Jesus declared with certainty of the things He spoke about concerning the religious people's plot to kill Him.

Nonetheless, Judas's heart was the place of conspiracy of Satan against Christ. Thus, Judas had already linked himself with the adversary, but he did not fully perceive within himself that the end of his own story could mean destruction because he had linked himself with death while he was living. Judas was living, breathing, and moving, but he was still completely blind in the presence of the King. In other words, Judas was completely functional, but death—Satan already had a grip on him, constricting his mind from perceiving truth.

Many in the body of Christ are as Judas was. Because Judas chose the darkness of Satan, he experienced the effects of death before dying. The anguish he would experience for betraying the King would be too much for him to withstand. Satan moved methodically and found a likeness of himself in Judas—traces of rebellion, pride, greed, and betrayal. Greed had caused the same spirit of rebellion that had gotten Satan thrown out of heaven; it was actively present in Judas; it served as a vehicle of destruction in the plan of Satan. Judas was still operating through the carnal channel of his flesh, which Satan the deceiver sought after and drew from as he wandered about in the systems of this world plotting to kill the King.

It was the plight of greed that was knocking at the front door of Judas's old heart that cause him to be divided from within. The entanglement of Judas's natural man was functioning *through* the darkness of Satan's influence, which stimulated the flesh, and Judas began responding to its cravings.

Satan wanders about in the earth today, "seeking whom he may devour" (1 Peter 5:8) by looking for any trace of evil to match his precise plan of destruction. The match is the thing Satan employed yesterday, and he is still seeking identifiable pieces of darkness in the individuals who have not submitted themselves to the almighty God through Christ. This is the match Satan ambled through in the Roman government, conspiring against Jesus.

Judas did not see he stood as a conduit for the prophetic fulfillment of Christ the Messiah as God's mercy on the seat for you and me. Judas did not know Satan was manipulating his strings. Again, when Jesus told His disciples in John 13:18, "One of you will betray me," the announcement was foreign to their ears; they heard and earthly language, not the eternal, so they could not fully comprehend Jesus's upcoming anguishing travail on the cross.

Not one of our finite mind-set has the ability to understand that Jesus the Christ overlaid—*covered*—the mercy seat with His blood for you and me. Christ, the consecrated King, took on our violations and captured death with His blood. For this cause, unbeknownst to Judas, the thing he was about to do had *already* been planned. Satan did not orchestrate this event, nor did the Roman officials or those having political influence. God had approved this thing done, thus Jesus surrendered to His Father's plan.

Agape love took our place on the cross. Darkness plotted, but it was nevertheless restricted in plan and posture, as Satan knew he could not move outside the authority of God no matter what. For this reason, Satan could not move in his plot against Jesus *until* he had been authorized to do so. Therefore, in order for Satan to move into the heart of Judas to convince him to betray King Jesus (see John 13:26), he had to wait for the permission of the King to do so.

Although Judas had already been entertaining Satan, he could not move until Christ gave permission to proceed. What am I saying? Satan still had to wait for his "access granted" from the Lord Jesus to move into action to crucify Jesus. Why was this? Satan is a created being under the supreme authority of God the Father, and created beings are *always* subject to their Creator. Satan can *never* move outside of the perimeters of God's authority. Therefore, his permission *had* to come *through* the reign of *Christ* on earth as it is in heaven. Jesus said, "One of you will betray me." I believe at His announcement, not one of them could begin to fathom the magnitude of these six words; they had no idea. Satan, the prince of the powers of the air, had positioned himself and was waiting. This is one of the strongest methodical characteristics of Satan—his ability to *wait*. He waits to see which of us will *respond* to our pride, lust, or greed in the old man.

Unbeknownst to the divided heart, Satan waits for an open door to enter and dominate. Judas had an open door. In John 13:24, Simon Peter asked Jesus whom it was He spoke of. Peter wanted the inside scoop. I believe Jesus spoke for two reasons. What seems a reply was not solely an answer to Peter's question. I believe Jesus responded to Peter as well as the presence of Satan lurking beyond sight and awaiting permission of the King to begin the process on earth as it is in heaven.

What you and I must recognize is the bread in its position had a place in time, which signified on earth that the *shifting* of God's rule was *active* in heaven. For this reason, the earth could not move into place until *Jesus lifted the restrictions* of its posture and position. Therefore, Jesus, in His posture of release, came through Him. Extending his hand gave earth permission to comply with what heaven had already activated. In John 13:26, Jesus answered, "It is he to whom I shall give a piece of bread when I have dipped it." Satan could not move until Jesus dipped the bread.

The dipping of the bread was the second sign of a visible manifestation of the events on earth before Jesus's ruling verdict *moved* into *action* and *released* the result of heaven on earth. Therefore, what Jesus released through His mouth from His eternal position **permitted** God's divine will to move on earth. In verse 26, Satan was given a starting point to move. As with any professional race, there are always rules of etiquette and protocol that every participant must adhere to before, during, and after the race. Equally, before the participant proceeds to move within the parameter of the race, he or she must go to the starting line. Once an individual is placed in the right space, he or she must wait for the signal that will start the race. Likewise, there is always a divine protocol sanctioned by heaven in accordance with God's will. God's protocol reverberates through heaven and *overshadows* every sphere, person, place, and thing.

God's commands the sun to set, the moon to rise, the firmaments to be still, and the oceans to remain at His majesty. All things are subject to God; nothing moves outside the instructions of the Godhead. Thus, the divine protocol of heaven has placed *everything under* **Christ**, and it is through Him that the believer has dominion over the earth according to God's will in heaven.

Thus, Jesus explicitly replied with a twofold answer to Peter's question of who would betray Him. Jesus said in John 13:26, "It is he to whom I shall give a piece of bread when I have dipped *it*." And having dipped the bread, He gave *it* to Judas Iscariot, *the son* of Simon." Henceforth, "When I have dipped it" fell not only on the ears of the disciples; I believe Jesus was also giving Satan permission to position himself according to verse 27; He was authorizing Satan to move.

Judas did not know his greed would cause the next shift on earth as it was in heaven. It is vital that we understand Jesus Himself initiated the shift, not Satan. The exchange of bread was the *preparation* for the release. The Bible says Jesus *gave* the bread to Judas and **then** Satan entered Judas (see John 13:26–27).

Understand that had Judas not already feasted on the nuggets of darkness Satan had fed him, he may have been able to resist Satan. The ruling power of the Godhead that had called Lazarus out of the grave (see John 11:43) *was* and *is* the **same** ruling power Judas sat in the midst of but did not completely respond to. He chose lust over the King. Judas had reunited with his old heart and had aligned himself with Satan. I believe Jesus afforded Judas the opportunity to *repent* and be made entirely new just as Jesus did with the thief on the cross beside Him when he asked Jesus to "Remember me" (see Luke 23:42–43). This man identified Jesus's divinity, His supreme being; all he asked of Jesus was "Remember me."

Jesus had not shaken off the effects of the cross, or ever gathered the keys to death and Hades (Revelaton1:18); nevertheless, before He took His last breath, Jesus the Christ told the one who had humbly *submitted* himself to the King, "Today you shall be with me in paradise" (Luke 23:43). Recognizing who Jesus was even before the resurrection, something beyond his sight shifted from within him and informed him that Jesus was in fact the Christ.

Jesus and this man were nailed to crosses, and yet his heart had been made *anew*. How was this? This man **responded** to the **truth**. How could Jesus make this kind of promise before His resurrection? Although Jesus's earthly assignment had not ended, Jesus consistently conveyed to all with **certainty** that He held power over life and death.

In John 11:25, Jesus said to the woman, "I am the resurrection," which was eternity announcing to the earth that Jesus was the prophesied Messiah. Nevertheless, even with all this head knowledge, Judas did not have enough heart knowledge, so he responded to evil. In other words, Judas did not submit to God as James 4:7 says: "Submit therefore to God. Resist the devil and he will flee from you. Submit therefore to God. Resist the devil and he will flee from you."

Judas and his divided heart, was right in the midst of the King, thus all he had to do was turn, submit, and soak up Jesus in his own body beyond his flesh. If he had, darkness would have had no choice but to bow down in submission and become subject to the King. However, Satan had found a match. Judas was seeing through old eyes, listening with old ears, thinking with and through an old mind-set from the place in which Adam fell but Jesus the Christ came to restore.

The man Jesus called friend positioned himself in the midst of eternity, within earshot of the Triune God, and footsteps away from Christ, and still he did not know. This Jesus, this God-Man, was eternally seated far above principalities, above every ruler of darkness, above dominions and thrones, but still, Judas chose death. Judas was still walking in and through the channels of his unchanged, uncommitted, and unfaithful old state of being, which opened up the way for Satan to enter his person. Judas did not completely draw near to Jesus, which would have drawn him to the Father.

Drawing near to God *prohibits* anyone or anything from entering a space, place, and time in which God resides. Instead of Judas standing complete in Christ, his heart became wicked, and evil flowed through him, and out came the spirit of rebellion that unlocked greed and opened the door for Satan.

God did not strip away the rebellion in the hearts of Judas, the religious leaders, or the Roman government, nor did He force them to comply and conspire with the powers of darkness in an attempt to kill the King. Still, God did not spare His own Son but delivered Him up for us all (see Romans 8:32).

The Bible says that Jesus "was delivered up because of our offenses, and was raised because of our justification" (Romans 4:25). Love stood on the exchange of bread for our sake. Satan was waiting for Jesus to execute His place of exchange so he could move into Judas's heart because it was God's timing to release the plot to conspire against Jesus on earth, no Satan's.

Leading up to the exchange of bread and the agony of Golgotha's Hill, love would release what no man could. Thus, the woman, the dipped bread, Jesus's extension of His hand clutching the bread, and the exchange of bread remained *connected* to the costly oil poured on Jesus's body, and still they did not know. Jesus said to His disciples that His hour had come. All the while, Satan was waiting for the go-ahead from Jesus to enter Judas Iscariot. Not one of them could see beyond sight the unfolding of the plan of redemption in which they stood.

Therefore, Jesus informed His perplexed disciples who was to betray Him. Jesus replied, "It is he to whom I shall give a piece of bread." Thus, Jesus extended His hand, dipped the bread, and Satan entered the person of Judas. Influenced by darkness, Judas Iscariot *responded* to the place where Jesus extended His hand and took the piece of bread from the loving hand of the King. Can you imagine the heart of Jesus connected to His humanity in His God-Man state when He gave the bread to someone He loved? Can you imagine how hurtful it was for Jesus to give permission to the one who He already knew had betrayed Him? Can you imagine His heart?

I guarantee you Jesus loved Judas anyway. The redeeming King dipped the bread and gave it to His betrayer, and Judas grabbed what eternity held, granting permission for the *shifting* of time to begin on earth as it is in heaven. It was not until the exchange of bread that Satan entered Judas; Satan still could not move until he received Jesus's permission to do so! He still had to **wait** for **Jesus** to give him *permission* to move. Thus, he waited! This is the manipulation of the powers of darkness—they wait. These spirits wait for an opening to come into a person's life through hatred, envy, oppression, depression, pride, drugs, and other open door ways to disrupt things and wreak havoc.

Satan can enter unguarded hearts that have not submitted and connected to the King. Satan will then manipulate circumstances, mind-sets, emotions and more to detached individuals from the King. Many in the body of Christ are not guarded, and the Father is saying to His children, "Wake up!" Many in the church invoke powers of darkness through horoscopes, bitterness, anger, idolatry, rebellion, lust, arrogance, witchcraft, and so much more. Thus, Satan has seduced many of God's children into thinking that the Father approves of this kind of behavior.

Do you not understand that this is the same divided heart the children of Israel walked in and became a rebellious nation? God gave the Israelites over to the lust of their own flesh and its cravings, and Judas was no different. Jesus gave the bread to Judas, and this was the fulfillment of Scripture. Jesus said to Satan, "What you do, do quickly." I believe many thought Jesus was speaking to Judas, and He was; however, they did not know that Jesus was *releasing* the darkness planted on the inside of Judas to move into fulfillment of timing as well. Jesus ordered Satan to move quickly into his assignment.

In John 13:30, we read that Judas went out *immediately.* Jesus was washing the feet of Judas in John 13:5, and in the blink of an eye, Judas shifted. In the presence of the King, the heart of Judas began operating from that place of old Jesus already delivered Judas from. Nonetheless, darkness infiltrated Judas's heart. The fickleness of his flesh craved lust over truth even though he sat at the feet of the King. Still, Judas did not know the truth. His flesh craved that which it was not in need of. The greed of Judas's flesh stepped into a place his spirit could not identify, which caused his feet to stumble into a *strange* land that was foreign to his spirit. However, his flesh was familiar—well *acquainted* with the place he entered.

Judas stood in a position of lust, pleasure, and desire on earth through the darkness of the god of this age—Satan. Thus, the surpassing thirst for the carnality of Judas's flesh superseded the thirsting of his soul to reconnect to its place of origin that he was about to betray. Judas allowed what his flesh craved in his *now* through lust, which overshadowed, overrode, and overruled the restorative point Jesus brought to each of them. Many in the church are in the same posture as Judas because they give heed to seducing spirits. In 1 Timothy 4:1, we read, "Now the Spirit speaks expressly, that in the latter times some shall depart from the faith, giving heed to seducing spirits, and doctrines of devils." Satan drew from the well of Judas's old man and paraded the desires of his flesh to conspire against the King. Little did Judas know the assignment of the King was being fulfilled on earth, as it was already complete in heaven.

In John 13:31 we read, "So, when he had gone out, Jesus said, now the Son of Man is glorified, and God is glorified in Him." This sound released the earth to move into position when Jesus said "Now." It was the time for the Son of Man to be glorified. The *highest expression* of His glory on earth was being made fully known; He was in fact God's Son. Although many still saw Jesus as Joseph's son, the fullness of the Godhead was about to *shine* like never before through the unveiling of the redemption of the King's resurrection. Thus, no false prophet, no demonic systems, no religious régime ruled by the clutches of Satan could have stopped or interrupted this process of release when Jesus said, "Now the Son of Man is gloried and God is glorified in Him"(John 13:31). Earth was standing in agreement with heaven. Jesus said to Judas to *move quickly*, and at the command of the King, Judas moved into action. I wonder if Judas saw his own action beyond the effects of Satan. I wonder if Judas had a battle going on inside.

Jesus told Judas to act expeditiously to complete the act of betrayal. The prophetic destiny of Jesus did not rest on the betrayal of Judas alone, although God allowed him to become a part of the plan; God used them *all.* Nevertheless, the prophetic destiny of King Jesus was by *God's design* from the beginning of the fall in the garden up to today. The animal skin Adam and Eve covered themselves with in the garden represented the saving power of Jesus and His covering for humanity before He was even planted on the inside of Mary, His mother.

Adam and Eve wore the covering of the Passover Lamb—King Jesus— on their bodies before He stood on earth as the Theanthropos, long before the oil, long before the bread, and long before the exchange. Thus, the divine significance of the covering they wore may not have been apparent to them at the time, but Jesus stood as the only way for them and us to return to God.

The animal that provided Adam and Eve's skins stood as the essence of Christ, the final Passover Lamb. This was the invisible covering in time that stood in the appearance of God's mercy on the seat even in the garden. The representation of Christ covered the sins of humanity long before His completion on the cross two thousand years ago. God made sure that His children were covered; not out of obligation, but out of love. Thus, when God saw Adam and Eve in their covering, He saw His Son. God had a plan. When Adam and Eve saw they were guilty of something, they covered themselves instinctually before the presence of God because of the connection they once had had with Him.

My question is, could Judas have known deep within himself that His betrayal of the King would cost something? The cost for Adam and Eve's betrayal of God was their removal from the garden. Did Judas know what his betrayal would cost him? Though Satan was manipulating Judas, he must have known he would have to pay the consequences; he must have known there would be a cost attached to the kiss. He must have recognized there had to be a cost. Nevertheless, his greed, his appetite for more overrode his conscious state of being although he was seated at the table with the King. The greed in his belly was associated with the betrayal of a kiss powered by the temptation of his own flesh, which he became a slave to instead of yielding to the King.

Judas soon walked through the door of fire that would ultimately consume him (see Matthew 27:5), so I believe he did not entirely count the cost of betraying the King or the guilt and shame that would follow his actions as a result. Thus, Jesus said to Judas—Satan—"What you do, do quickly" and "He then went out immediately" after the release of the King (see John 13:30).

Even in the end, I still believe Jesus loved Judas. You never read where Jesus reprimanded Judas for betraying Him, as He *already* knew Judas was entertaining the powers of darkness long before the exchange of bread and Satan entering his person. Jesus knew Judas would become sorrowful for betraying the King. Nevertheless, I believe that Jesus love him beyond the betrayal. Jesus knew what His hour entailed, but He stayed the course.

> When Judas, the traitor, learned that Jesus had been condemned, he repented and took back the thirty silver

coins to the chief priests and the elders. "I have sinned by betraying an innocent man to death!" he said.

—Matthew 3:4, GNT

Judas returned the money and repented for the wickedness of his heart, I believe the bread that Judas ate represented the body of Christ, covered him, and his transgressions of sin (see Matthew 27:3).

Jesus released Satan to move in time through the exchange of the bread. The authorization that allowed Satan to move was not by accident but by divine providence, though Satan thought he was influencing the situation in its entirety.

Darkness has not changed, and in this hour, I believe the body of Christ must understand that Satan's manipulations have not changed. Just as Jesus extended His hand to Judas during the feast, which subsequently gave Satan permission to move after Judas had received the bread, he is actively seeking any invitation to enter us.

Satan gains access to us through our words, thoughts, and actions. When the body of Christ speaks contrary to God's Word, it grants the powers of darkness access to move into it. Thus, I believe that Satan could not have moved into the heart of Judas unless something within him had been accessible to the powers of darkness. Jesus could have spoken a word of release for Satan to move into the plot to have Jesus crucified, but He chose to release the hand of Satan another way. Jesus had already addressed the presence of Satan looming in the atmosphere in John 13:2. The bread Jesus gave Judas signified what Jesus had said in John 6:35: "I *am* the bread of life. Whoever comes to me will *never* go hungry, and whoever believes in me will never be thirsty." The full embodiment of the Scripture stood with the eyes of love and a heart of compassion for God's people and gave Satan *permission* to instigate *heaven's shift* on earth. For this cause, I heard the Holy Spirit saying, "Judas, my friend, I am the manna that fell from heaven for My children, the Israelites when they were in the wilderness. I am that same bread, Judas that you received from me. I am the grace your ancestors received. Satan, I give you permission to move into Judas. You could not stop the plan of God in the garden, and you cannot stop it now. Thus, I give you permission to move. Now, what you will do, do it quickly, and do *My* will."

The exchange of bread had nothing to do with Satan and everything to do with love. That same grace found on Noah is the *same grace* that reached out His hand, dipped the bread, and offered Himself up as the *final sacrifice* for the sins of many.

> And as they were eating, Jesus took bread, blessed *it*, and broke *it*, and gave it to the disciples and said, "Take, eat; this is My body." Then He took the cup, and gave thanks, and gave *it* to them, saying "Drink from it, all of you, For this is My blood of the new covenant, which is shed for many for the remission of sins."
>
> —Matthew 26:26–28, NKJV

Now, "Take, eat; this is *My* body which is broken for you."

DOXOLOGY

Now to Him who is able to keep you from stumbling, and to make you stand in the presence of His glory blameless with great joy, to the only God our Savior, through Jesus Christ our Lord, be glory, majesty, dominion and authority, before all time, now and forever. Amen.

Lovingly submitted,
De'Ron Hopkins

ACKNOWLEDGMENTS

To my father and mother, words cannot express the countless words of encouragement and endless prayers during my fight to birth this book. Thank you for believing in the God in me during labor and delivery of this treasure God has entrusted unto my hands. To all of my family and friends who covered me in prayer, endless words of wisdom, and encouragement into me, I thank you.

The editorial insight of Martin McHugh is phenomenal. Thank you. To the staff at Westbow Press I appreciate your help throughout this entire process.

ABOUT THE AUTHOR

*D*ERON HOPKINS has dedicated her life to serving God. She is a multidimensional business woman, a wife, motivational speaker, prophet, preacher, and a prayer warrior, called of God to active and stirrup God's people to respond to the eternal voice of the Father calling forth repentance in the land. Armed and appointed by the Father, her assignment is to sound the alarm of an intruder breaching the perimeters of church. Her kingdom posture fortifies her to stand as an ambassador for Christ and to summons God's people to rise up in kingdom dominion and take authority over the counterfeit impostor at hand—Satan and his powers of darkness. In this hour, the Father has positioned her prophetic voice on earth to uproot the atmospheric imbalances, systematic methodologies of darkness, and every conflicting sound standing in opposition of God's truth. With a mandate of intercession, her assignment is to transport God's supreme order from heaven to earth, call disorder to order, shakeup, and shift God's people to respond to the voice of the King. Learn more about De'Ron and her ministry at deronhopkins.org

SOCIAL MEDIA

Find De'Ron online at:
www.deronhopkins.org
https://www.facebook.com/DeRon-Hopkins-
www.twitter.com/deronhopkins

Printed in the United States
by BookMasters

Printed in the United States
By Bookmasters